Red Star Sister

Red Star Sister

Leslie Brody

HUNGRY MIND PRESS

ST. PAUL · MINNESOTA

Published by Hungry Mind Press
1648 Grand Avenue
Saint Paul, MN 55105

The author is indebted to the following for the
permission to reprint excerpts from the following:

"I-Feel-Like-I'm-Fixin'-to-Die Rag," words and music by Joe McDonald.
Copyright 1965, renewed 1993 Alkatraz Corner Music Co. Used by permission.

Murray Bookchin's "Between the 30s and the 60s," in *The 60s without Apology,*
edited by Sohnya Sayres, Anders Stephanson, Stanley Aronowitz, and
Fredric Jameson. University of Minnesota Press, in cooperation with *Social Text.*
Copyright 1984 by *Social Text.* Used by permission.

Samuel Beckett's *Waiting for Godot,* copyright 1954, Grove Press.
Used with the permission of Grove/Atlantic, Inc.

Sylvia Plath's "Lady Lazarus," from *Ariel.* Copyright 1963 by Ted Hughes,
copyright renewed. Used with the permission of HarperCollins Publishers, Inc.

"Pencilled Notes" in *The Oblivion Seekers and Other Writings* by
Isabelle Eberhardt. Copyright © 1972, 1975 by Paul Bowles.
Reprinted by permission of City Lights Books.

"The Media Freaks Meet the Movement" by Black Shadow
from *Rolling Stone* July 23, 1970, by Straight Arrow Publishers, Inc.
All rights reserved. Reprinted by permission.

Howl from *Selected Poems 1947–1995* by Allen Ginsberg. Copyright 1996.
Reprinted with permission from HarperCollins Publishers, Inc.

Excerpt from "I ask for silence" from *Extravagaria* by Pablo Neruda,
translated by Alastair Reid. Translation copyright © by Alastair Reid.
Reprinted by permission of Farrar, Straus & Giroux, Inc.

First Hungry Mind Press printing 1998
Printed in the United States of America

10 9 8 7 6 5 4 3 2 1

ISBN: 1-886913-15-3
LCCN: 98-71628

Book design by Will Powers
Cover design by Randall Heath

Except for family members and public figures,
I have changed the names and identifying details
of all the characters in this book.

FOR GARY

Prologue

When I was nineteen and driven to the extremes of my nature by what I believed to be the extremism of the leaders of my country, I met a living saint. I had been a hippie. I had been a revolutionary. I had come, by virtue of my rebellion, to dwell in a floating wonderworld of freaks and criminals and artists. I was at that time feverish and flailing. To say I was suffering a complete mental and physical breakdown is somehow to understate my part. I was ill, but I considered my sickness inevitable. I had cultivated my distance until straight society seemed little more than a blotch on the far horizon. Madness seemed vastly romantic, politically relevant, and tremendously literary.

I was born in 1952 and came of age in a polarized America, one of millions who protested the war in Vietnam. My father, a tolerant man who also opposed the war, always said there were two sides to every story. He had been a radical in his own youth, but even then he'd read two newspapers, his side's and the other's. He'd advised me early on to do the same, but I refused. In my opinion, there was was only the prosperous war-bloated materialism of sixties America, which my friends and I called the "death culture," and its alternative—our counterculture, which offered me a job as a writer, a home and extended family in every youth enclave, and a fully furnished worldview. My opposition to the war was a way of life. It was why I left home at seventeen, why I didn't start college, why I joined the communes I did; it influenced what I ate, where I slept and with whom, where and when I traveled, and what I believed. I believed the war was wrong, and I still do. My life followed the antiwar movement's progress from resistance to rebellion, then I spun off into rage and breakdown. After the Kent State shootings, I no longer believed my dissent was protected. Instead, as I saw it, laws were enforced by the henchmen of my enemy, and it was my duty to defy them.

.   .   .

I came of age as a writer in a time of confessional poetry, journalmania, and underground newspapers. As an alternative press reporter I published page after page of articles and reviews about my life and times; and I spent hours filling journals with poetry. All those words safeguarded the secret that I really knew very little about myself. As for everyone else, particularly those unfortunates over thirty, I'd rather have cut off their heads than talked to them. The last thing I wanted to hear was how they had been young and full of promise once.

I spent my recovery in the loft of an underground impresario, who was a celebrated orgiast. Sounds of fucking wafted up from the lower floors. Exiles and displaced persons mistook my mattress for political sanctuary, and visitors on the tourist trail stopped for a peek at the ghastly and beautiful ring I wore. Out of the psychedelic gloaming, Dick Gregory, antiwar activist and conspiracy theorist, appeared, radiant, the nimbus of sainthood about him. "I want you to think about going home," he said.

All right. But where was home? Was it the hippie Amsterdam I'd just left? Chicago, where I'd been a bride of Mao? Ann Arbor, where I was a Red Star Sister in the White Panther Party? San Francisco, where I'd been an underground press reporter? Or was home my red suitcase?

I

Patriots and Liberators

The American landscape was to be planted with flowers not paved with gold.

MURRAY BOOKCHIN, "Between the 30s and the 60s"

> O pleasant exercise of hope and joy!
> For mighty were the auxiliars which then stood
> Upon our side, we who were strong in love!
> Bliss was it in that dawn to be alive,
> But to be young was very Heaven!

WILLIAM WORDSWORTH, *The Prelude,* book II

The Red Suitcase

In 1967, when the Vietnam War was playing full blast, I was slowly turning utopian. At the heart of the new world I dreamed, there was to be no war, no napalm, no lies. There was to be no racism, no poverty, no hatred. Perhaps it is instructive that my goals were not unsimilar to those of a Miss America contestant whose sappy calls for "world peace" were an embarrassing annual cliché. Miss America wanna-bes could smile thousand-watt smiles, but they were fuzzy on how to achieve peace for humanity. I suffered no such doubts. By 1968 I believed that nothing short of a revolution of the mind would achieve utopia *here*.

Writers about the sixties tend to slice the decade into two parts—good and bad, rise and decline. You read enough histories and the good sixties start to look like a WPA wall mural: muscular young folks, full of pluck, marching off to the civil rights movement and the New Left, while Beatlemania and Motown shake the last of the sleeping campuses awake. Guys grew their bangs and threw their hats away. Girls teased their hair, and hiked their skirts for free.

Then—tympani rumbling—came the bad sixties: abstract expressionism met its human form. The war ballooned. Around 1967 girls stopped combing their hair, and wearing skirts made it hard to run from cops at demonstrations. There were the assassinations of Martin Luther King Jr. and Robert Kennedy. The Black Panthers battled cops in the streets and the courts. McGovern was bulldozed. Song lyrics got weird. Drugs got druggier. Woodstock happened like a miracle, but was obscured, first by Altamont, then by Manson and the aftermath of My Lai.

The perception you carry of a time is flash-frozen by where you were and who you were when your wave unfolded. In 1967, the bad sixties still looked good to me.

Perhaps in the public imagination hippies and radicals are to the Age of Aquarius what the flapper, the bootlegger, and the expatriate are to the Jazz Age—mostly undifferentiated caricatures. But every rebel has a story. Baby boomers like myself, born more than a decade behind showmen and innovators like Abbie Hoffman, Tom Hayden, and Bernardine Dohrn, were hanging on to the sixties' coattails. In a culture that worshiped youth, mine placed me firmly in the vanguard of the revolution. On the other hand, I was always a little sister, who, like other younger siblings ad infinitum, wants to astound and overcome her elders.

I offer you one woman's point of view. It is not my intention to glorify what was often a shadowy, anxious time, but by telling you this story of the war years in terms of my own life, I hope to salvage some sense of the utopianism and the complicated vision of country and self that dazzled so many of us in the age we held in common.

I know most reunions are rarely as thrilling as they promise to be. Still, it is an irresistible, universal urge to try and reclaim something lost, track down something unfinished, show off to somebody who underestimated you.

When I was young and lived in Amsterdam, I was in love with an Irish musician named Brendan—who in turn was in love with an Italian junkie named Angela. I knew that I would be alive long after Angela had died; and long after Brendan had forgotten me, I knew I would remember him. I imagined a day in the future when I would show up on his doorstep; I was always accomplished, sometimes rich, always beautiful, always successful in love and in maintaining my independence. The promise I made to myself long ago was that no story was over until I said so. Presumptuous—but what else are historians? It's no use leaving history to experts. Champions of the dull thought and the conventional act are always venturing forth to rewrite the past. Lately, I've noticed a lot of smug pundits, many of them baby boomers themselves, standing in line to scold "the sixties generation" for its endless adolescence. Long after Nixon's death, those of us who opposed the Vietnam War are still hearing our youthful selves portrayed as the spoiled brats of a permissive age. I won't refute that. I'm sure brats abounded, as they do in every age. They disturb people with new scientific and political theories, compose symphonies, and write poetry of staggering beauty and wisdom. I admit brats can be annoying, but I'd always rather be on their side. Personally, I think it's absurd to suggest that I or anyone would automatically want to *mature* beyond utopianism.

There are unfinished mysteries in everyone's life (sorrow and terrible depth even in an infant's cries). The story of Brendan and Angela happened long ago and far away. Why did he love her and not me? Why did she have to die? Back then, I asked my journal about it, then tossed the journal into my old red suitcase. I've never been good at throwing things away. Consequently, my red suitcase is a magpie's dream, holding all the shiny souvenirs of a generation, and the volumes of notes I promised myself I'd organize—someday—when I got my life together.

In one file folder I have a little library of literary magazines; in another, yellowed newspaper articles (both mainstream and underground) with titles like "Students March for Biafra Relief," "Muskie Bids Heckler Share Platform," "Leslie Appeals Contempt Charge." Leaflets: (hand-lettered) "S.D.S. Meeting Tonight!" and (mimeographed) "STRIKE!" Here are a couple of hagiographic portraits of Che Guevara alive and gesticulating, or martyred with a swooningly romantic quotation—"At the risk of sounding ridiculous a true revolutionary is guided by great feelings of love"; and here, sheaves of poetry on onionskin—documents of unrequited love in New York, San Francisco, Amsterdam, London, and Florence; an underground newspaper I attempted to bring from Amsterdam to Paris, only to be arrested at the border as a smuggler of pornography; a photo from the Métro the day I intended to meet with the North Vietnamese in Paris and negotiate an end to the war.

I'm writing this the way I remember it. I do know I'd have to be some kind of zealot to believe that what I say is the only truth. It's a constant struggle not to turn memory into myth. Here I am with all these notes and all these journals and all these artifacts—I can only say I'll make my best effort to be reliable and maybe that is the same as getting my life together. In any case, to smell the inside of my red suitcase is to be instantly overcome by patchouli.

My parents gave me the red suitcase on a visit home in the early 1970s—to supplement the frame backpack I always carried. Maybe you saw me. In those days the American hippie girl abroad was the talk of the piazza, plaza, and square. In every train station in Europe it was easy enough to pick her out: by her good teeth, obviously braless breasts, sixty-pound pack, and the bandanna that kept her hair from the pack strap undertow. She had the pill, ten dollars a day, and a ticket to ride. At the risk of sounding like a B movie, adventure was her destination. And on her face, beneath the travel grime, was *that look*:

the glow of the unconquerable, that look of health and youth and confidence and an optimism so innocent of irony that her European companions didn't know whether to exploit or console her. Any observer cynically probing for signs of a secret Machiavellianism might be more likely to encounter a cheerful hybrid of Dale Carnegie and Bella Abzug.

.　.　.

The original purpose of the backpack was its convenience. I know I had been inspired to reduce my possessions to essentials by Isabelle Eberhardt's *The Oblivion Seekers*:

> A subject to which few intellectuals ever give a thought is the right to be a vagrant, the freedom to wander. Yet vagrancy is deliverance, and life on the open road is the essence of freedom. To have the courage to smash the chains with which modern life has weighted us (under the pretext that it was offering us more liberty), then to take up the symbolic stick and bundle, and *get out!*

Although admirable in theory, Eberhardt's zen minimalism just wasn't me. In those romantic days I never carried what I needed. Instead of extra socks, I had extra scarves: long, flowy, silky, feminine lengths of color invariably water stained, frequently torn, and excessively wrinkled. All this was, I imagine, the antithesis of the beautifully packed lavender-scented steamer trunks of those women who preceded me on the European grand tour.

"'The American girl,' the world's highest achievement," Edith Wharton wrote in *The Buccaneers* of the daughters of the men who made fortunes after the Civil War. For the most part, those self-possessed, athletic, rational young ladies had money, marriage, and fashion on their practical minds. If they were too romantic, they got into trouble.

In my own youth, money and marriage were hardly considered subjects fit for conversation between strangers. (Occasionally, fashion was discussed, as in, "Where did you get that afghan coat, Afghanistan?") It didn't hurt if your father had prospered in the boom after World War II, but unlike Wharton's *Buccaneers,* you didn't have to be rich to bum around Europe in the 1960s and 1970s. While back home, economists and historians struggled to define what working class and middle class meant in postwar America, the girls I met were, on the whole, unconcerned with conventional background or position. Independent women had traveled to Paris during prohibition to make art and drink like fish, and to Spain in the thirties to combat fascism, but never had there been so many women—traveling alone and in shoals, just to "get out."

.   .   .

"Bliss was it in that dawn to be alive. But to be young was very Heaven." William Wordsworth's idealism collapsed with the French Revolution, but his lines (embodying as they do *every possibility*) continued to inspire generations of young radicals. When I first read them in 1967, I thought maybe Wordsworth knew me. He was, at any rate, with me in spirit as I slumped against my bedroom door smoking Kents, watching over my shoulder as I alternated between reading him and *Mad* magazine, Malcolm X and Marvel Comics.

In 1967, when I first discovered Wordsworth, my father, Steve, and I had just moved from Riverhead into the house of my new stepmother, Ann, in suburban New York City. My mother had died two years before, and both my older brothers were away at college. We had been living on eastern Long Island, which was farm country then, on the other side of the tracks from the posh Hamptons (so close, my mother said, you could smell the martinis at dusk). If you summered in the Hamptons, Riverhead was where you went to get your car fixed. My father had been a labor organizer, a spice salesman, and now owned a five-acre auto-wrecking yard in Speonk where the off-duty chauffeurs of the glitterati came to buy parts for their own cars. I loved to watch my father at work as he sorted through towering piles of tires, hubcaps, and fenders. If something wasn't ready to hand, he'd set out into the yard and, like a master butcher, carve directly from a wreck.

First, though, he'd always pocket his book. An early and loyal prop of the paperback industry, my father never went anywhere without a science fiction, fantasy, or western novel in his back pocket. He always had books going consecutively in every room at home, on the dashboard of the tow truck he drove (to read at red lights), and on the kitchen counter to read during dinner—we all did that—with one ear cocked to Cronkite, reporting the death tolls in Vietnam.

Riverhead Grammar

1958–1963

Riverhead was a small town with distinctly drawn borders that my mother, as a census taker and market researcher, could transcend. After school, I used to ride around with her while she did her interviewing. Sometimes we discovered a story that began in the burgher district and ended in "The Bottom," Riverhead's black ghetto. Or we'd hear something in Polish Town that later caused reverberations out in Wildwood, the tract-housing community where we lived in a rented house. Once in a while, my mother would drive us over to Southampton to observe the rich. She admired their sidewalks, a civic amenity seriously lacking in Riverhead.

I suppose it was during those excursions that I first got the idea that the rich were a useless, vacationing tribe who had nothing to do with us. They had different customs and holidays. Their weekends, my mother explained, were always at least four days long, and just making it through the night was cause to celebrate with an afternoon orgy of shopping. As she and I walked around Southampton with our ice cream cones, my mother would point to skinny women in mink stoles. "Fur in the summer," she'd say. "Tourists." We observed their behavior with derision, while they looked right through us "locals."

My mother, who'd grown up in Brooklyn, hated being taken for a local. She was used to the complications of city life, like crowded trains and waiting in line at hard-to-find restaurants with the best red sauce. Riverhead bored her. It was the boondocks, hicksville, nowheresville, and, adding insult to injury, no delicatessen for a hundred miles. She came from a close, urbane family, in which if you couldn't say something sarcastic, you didn't say anything. My father, on the other hand, was not a sarcastic man. He liked a joke, but he was soft. At family dinners with his brothers-in-law he was shark food. I think that's one reason why my mother married him—relief from always having to be cutting and witty. They met at a dance for Jewish soldiers during World War II, and he proposed on the Staten Island ferry seven days later. She remained a joker all her life, a *sport,* a *corker,* but seasoned, mellower when the pressure was off, once she'd left her father's Brooklyn home.

Like my father, my mother loved to read, and the little public library tucked into Riverhead Elementary School offered her a temporary haven. The library suffered from the same lack of light as our classrooms, but my mother called it romantic. She drew my attention to the special shelves above the librarian's desk, where what seemed like hundreds of book skeletons—just yellow cardboard and string— awaited restoration, and to the librarian herself, whose skin was gray and whose eyes were all pupil: "If they don't get new books soon," she once said, "they'll kill that woman with glue."

In first and second grade I liked to read about little girls in China and rapidly exhausted the library's resources—there was just Pearl Buck. I sought out books about little colonial girls who saved New York from its British masters, little Indian girls who rescued lost causes, little black girls who led slave rebellions, and little Jewish girls who liberated countries. There weren't many of these. I had better luck reading the science fiction books in my father's downstairs collection. He had hundreds of genre novels without back covers, bought at discount off the revolving racks in drug stores. Other children had haystacks, I had a hill of paperbacks. In those books buxom women might be found lounging about scantily clad in furs, but just as often they led revolts against tyrants, liberated worlds, and engaged in passionate romances followed by the companionate marriages of true minds. Many of these pulp fictions were essentially utopian, their purple prose also a subversive education. Later, when I became a reporter, I felt their influence whenever I fought the urge to reverse an outcome or, on dull days, to add more romantic storytelling notes to my news.

.   .   .

Riverhead Elementary School was a harsh, dark, brick, Yankee institution full of shadows. I loathed school and the bus ride there and back (packed with bullies who broke my glasses). My early teachers were far less interested in demonstrating the pleasures of learning than in propagating a Puritan worldview. According to my first-grade teacher, Mrs. Baton, the sensible citizen got up in the morning, put in a full day at her job regardless of its conditions—no exceptions—was serious— no exceptions—was God-fearing, saved money, respected elders, family, and flag. In her comments on my first-quarter report card, Mrs. Baton observed that I "lived in a dream world and constantly had to be jolted out of it." She jolted me for losing my train of thought, falling out of line, laughing too loud, and reading with too much expression, but her jolts meant nothing to me, and in her third-quarter report she upbraided my parents for raising a "dissenting individualist and a wise guy."

Mrs. Baton's disapproval backfired. Soon I was taking pride in my defiance. I read Mrs. Baton's insistence on docility as the strongest endorsement of its opposite. Although it made me miserable, Mrs. Baton angrier, and many of the other children crueler, I began to cultivate difference. My mother, recognizing that it was horrible to be an outcast in first grade, counseled me to bend, but I kept digging deeper into new reservoirs of pride and stubbornness.

One afternoon toward the end of the school year, she and I were sitting, as we often did, in the car behind the Riverhead library. She had stubbed out her cigarette and was checking her lipstick in the rearview mirror when she said, "I think you could be a writer, if you wanted." It was a career in which being a dissenting individualist and a wise guy might function as assets, even strengths. At the same time she suggested, "You could marry a publisher." This wasn't meant to diminish my abilities, or the infinite possibilities ahead, but to cover my bets in a practical manner—along the same lines as spitting through two fingers to ward off devils, which my mother also did from time to time.

Mrs. Baton had looked ancient to me. But I suppose she was only in her mid-forties in 1960—probably about the same age as Richard Nixon that year, when he lost his presidential bid to John Kennedy. Over time those two—Baton and Nixon—have intermingled in my memory. Neither could tolerate opposition, and both were determined to crush dissent. I acted out my objections to Mrs. Baton through passive resistance (I knew it was a fight I could not win in the open). I was sixteen when I took Nixon for my personal enemy. By then I felt I had better command of my weapons, and a real chance to bring him down.

·   ·   ·

Directly behind my elementary school, "The Bottom" stretched out on dirt roads, its wretched shacks only slightly better built than the slave quarters on the farms themselves. There, nasty tin buildings served to shelter black migrant workers who'd been hired for pennies to come north and harvest potatoes. We heard five dollars was the going bribe to get on the truck to Riverhead. Sometimes, toddlers too young to work in the field would stand on the other side of our school's barbed wire fence; at recess we would watch them watching us in an indelible tableau of segregation, Long Island style.

There were no music or art classes in the workhouse world of Riverhead Elementary, but sometimes we would be force-marched to the gymnasium, for a chorus recital, a play about the Snow Queen whose eye broke into a million crystal shards, and once, in a program as important to my development and as subversive as my father's books, a visiting linguist.

It was dark, as always, in our windy gymnasium, the walls of brick and cement crumbling, the lead paint chipping, the insulation exposed, asbestos fibers here, radon gas there. We students were in the bleachers, at a great distance from the visitors' court, where the linguist gave his presentation. He talked and talked, and nobody paid much attention—we couldn't hear him because of the wind, or see him in the dark. He talked and we drowsed, or swatted each other with discreet violence, under the military gaze of Mrs. Baton.

I was halfway up the bleachers, squashed next to a girl who hummed, and impatient to know what was going on when a ripple of sound climbed the bleachers. It was shocking to see massive Mrs. Warder, guardian of silence, frantically waving her arms, whipping the sound up row after row, children whispering through cupped hands, until everyone knew the magic word was *windowsill*.

The linguist conducted our ensemble. His arms stretched toward us as each row of students amplified his Elizabethan hiss: "Win-dow-sillll," rising up the bleachers like smoke. He commanded us, and for the next few minutes we chanted "window-sill" and "whip-por-will." Words, he proved, could be used, bent, stripped of meaning, made into irresistible music, so that even odd quartets like the vast Mrs. Warder, prim Mrs. Baton, the vacant girl who hummed, and I might harmonize—in a glorious oratorio that transformed the old prison like noon light through stained glass. Words, those mundane tools, were like the potato I would read about in a haiku years later—within one humble tuber are rivers and mountains. Words, he showed us, could change things.

.   .   .

The Riverhead duck and potato farmers had for generations been the town's masters: the Warders, the Falks, the MacDonalds. They were Yankees with old Dutch and Scottish blood mixed in, and were famous for violent family feuds and tragic family flaws. Twenty years later, I was to hear the outcome of some of the rumors that had flitted around when I was a child. Freddie Falk's father killed his grandfather over a beautiful mistress, a former migrant worker whom the grandfather had kept hidden in a duck barn (or was it a potato shack?). After high school Freddie went off to Princeton. One day he jumped into his Porsche and was never heard from again. Freddie was in my grade, and I remember him because, unlike many of the scions of wealth and privilege who were the glamorous champions of high school politics and sports, Freddie was a dissolute drunkard from the age of twelve. When we were in sixth grade he once suggested that "we put aside personal differences and make out."

Years after I left Riverhead I heard that my second-grade teacher, Mrs. Warder, had been brought up wealthy. She'd led a gilded life until her husband lost all their money in a confidence scheme. Afterward, she'd had to settle for the life of an educator at Riverhead Elementary School. Perhaps, by the time we met, her home life with Mr. Warder had become a living hell. For whatever reason, she had bloated into an obese harridan whose campaign to crush the spirit of as many of her students as possible was protected by an invulnerable sense of position. To Mrs. Warder, it was Mrs. Warder and Mrs. Warder alone who was holding back the tide of anarchy, of the black and Jewish domination of Riverhead Elementary—and, by extension, of the United States of America. Next to Mrs. Warder, I found, old Mrs. Baton was a genuine humanitarian.

Early on, setting the tone for the school year, Mrs. Warder had sat the few black students in the back of the class. She took every opportunity to ridicule their reading skills and shocked us into silence once by pulling a migrant child's pants down—to show us how he'd shat himself (he hadn't known he was allowed to use the bathroom). We were encouraged to laugh. She enjoyed pulling children's pants down. She liked to hit, too. And she hit hard, as I was to discover.

That year I began perusing the daily papers for news about the "Ban the Bomb" movement, whose idealistic goals and alliterative name had seized my imagination. I expanded my own writing portfolio to include poetry as well as stories. And when I was eight I published an antinuclear prose poem—my first—in my father's old union (Garment District Number 65) newspaper. At the time I think my father was probably more excited about seeing "A WALK UP THE CAPITAL STEPS" in print. I took it for granted that people would want to read what I wrote. Here it is, unexpurgated:

> Happiness is a walk up the Capital steps. A walk through a maze of difficulties towards a country of peace and understanding. A walk which killed many men and made many others. A walk through the past to the future. A walk to a land well worth living in.
>
> This is a walk up steps of gold. Our country started with stone steps. As England faded out our steps turned to bronze, bronze as the bell of justice, the Liberty Bell. For some these steps of gold are cracked. These steps of equality and understanding are cracked. People who are prejudiced and bruised are the ones who walk these cracked steps.
>
> Who knows how far these steps will go? Perhaps we may yet have steps of diamonds for world peace. Perhaps the steps will change back to stone for Atomic wars. It is up to us. It is our Nation to preserve or waste. It is up to us to walk the Capital steps.

I was sentimental and gravely patriotic for a while that year. I remember feeling religiously awed and overwhelmed by the concept of America's melting pot, and I memorized all the words to Emma Lazarus's poem inscribed on the Statue of Liberty. I still didn't have any friends who shared my enthusiasms, so I began to tap into an incipient talent for tabloid journalism. Finally, my classmates began paying attention.

Years later I'd find myself writing profiles and news reports for the underground press that were just barely less fictional. I would always begin with facts, but I couldn't control my imagination. Both as a second grader and later as a young reporter I felt I knew instinctively the direction in which my stories should go. As in my father's pulp fiction, the powerful should be laid low, the poor and weak should triumph, and women, whenever possible, should lead revolts, liberate worlds, and engage in passionate romances.

In second grade my plots were sketchy but my readers didn't mind, as long as their names were mentioned. The more children I included, the greater my fame. There was a general interest in gossip and innuendo and a curiosity to see how far things could go. I eventually learned that if I could amuse and flatter, I could also use this new skill to wound.

I wanted revenge on Lynda Campbell, a hoarse-voiced bully who pushed me around on the bus and who was Mrs. Warder's darling. Writing a glorious half-page fantasy about our class at a carnival, I sent Lynda Campbell and Zekie Goodall (the child of recently settled farm workers) up in a Ferris wheel together, where they kissed.

I passed the story around, and it was my most scandalous success so far. Children who'd never paid attention to me before, even children who couldn't read, were sneaking looks at me and snorting with vicious laughter. Mrs. Warder could not ignore the challenge.

"Would you like to bring that note up here, Leslie? Why don't you read it to us, so we can all enjoy what you've written, Leslie."

The room was all hushed suspense. Most of the children knew what was in the story, and found it horrifying to contemplate an adult's reaction. But I stood erect, enunciating, reading with *expression*. Nobody laughed at the funny opening, or gasped at the eloquent description of an amusement park in Riverhead. And when I reached the part about Lynda Campbell I was wrenched out of the spotlight as Mrs. Warder, her face the color of boiling tomatoes, literally tore the paper from my hand.

"Disgusting! Lies! How many in this class believe this smut? Pornography! Brody, stand in the corner until I decide what to do with you!"

The children murmured in agreement as the monstrous Mrs. Warder proceeded to give testament to the brilliance and virtues of Lynda Campbell. "She is a good little girl, an obedient little girl who would never, NEVER, do anything . . . so repulsive."

"ZEKIE, do you agree that this story is a lie?"

Zekie had been one of the few kids who spoke to me in class and I'd used him terribly. He hadn't known anything about my plan, and here he was on the verge of punishment. I didn't know it, but Zekie knew: boys had been lynched in the South for less.

"Come here, you!" Mrs. Warder had worked herself into a frenzy of hatred—because I had exceeded her expectations of an eight-year-old girl, because she was caught off guard, because I had attacked her pet, but mostly because Zekie was black and I had dared to allow the threat of miscegenation to enter the halls of Riverhead Elementary.

Mrs. Warder sat her huge frame on a chair and pulled me over her knees. She pulled my dress up, exposing my panties, and as I struggled in her massive grip, she spanked me. And as she hit me she spoke with the beats, "Tomorrow-You-Will-Apologize-To-Lynda-In-Front-Of-The-Whole-School-You-Stupid-Stupid-Girl."

.   .   .

The bus ride home was surprisingly tranquil. I had imagined shrieking and stabbing. There was some pointing, and choked laughter from a few of the bullies, but the keenest torture was internal. Could Mrs. Warder actually assemble the entire school tomorrow, grades one through six, to hear my confession?

I didn't want to tell my mother. But if I didn't I'd compound the problem by having to tell her why I hadn't told her in the first place. All the way home I wondered how I would get through the next seventy or eighty years of my life. When the bus finally turned into Wildwood, I got off and walked downhill to the bowling alley: maybe I could get a job.

In the middle of the afternoon, the lanes were just a big empty hangar. There were a couple of guys practicing, and it was comforting to hear the run of soft-soled shoes, the rumble of the balls and the pin-set machines. It all seemed too normal for a girl with my demonic past. At any minute, someone would stand on a chair and point, "THERE SHE IS!" I expected hisses, and when they didn't come I grew braver.

On the jukebox, someone was playing the same girl-group broken-hearted songs we sang on the bus, and the luncheonette gave off the familiar odor of burned grease. It seemed like a regular day, but I was outcast, exiled. My mother might console me but it didn't really matter with Mrs. Warders walking the earth. I sat in the lanes for a while shivering and crying a little, and hoping some interesting company might arrive to improve the situation, but none did.

Finally, dredging up fifteen cents, I settled for a large cherry Coke, with two maraschinos.

Vildechaya

1963–1965

My mother went down to the school and raised hell with the principal for letting one of his teachers beat me up. Mrs. Warder was made to apologize to my mother, but she never said a nice word to me. I was made to apologize to Lynda. Zekie disappeared from class for several weeks, and by the time he returned, Mrs. Warder had turned the greater part of her wrath on a Polish child who stuttered.

Although school remained the same eternal jungle of cruelty, I was toughening up. So much so that in the following year, when I encountered my first episode of direct anti-Semitism, I took care of the problem myself.

The perpetrator, Desirée Sullivan (whose father was vice principal), sat in front of me in third grade. She didn't like me, and one day in class she turned around and called me a "Jew bitch." At that time, I thought just being sworn at was the overriding insult. No ten-year-old was allowed to say the word *bitch*. There weren't any worse words that I knew—maybe one—"Bastard," I rejoined.

Desirée ran to inform her father. *Bastard,* of course, was the word he least wanted to hear in reference to his own daughter.

That afternoon in Mr. Sullivan's office, I was treated to a canned lecture on how courtesy was the bedrock of civilization. "But did Desirée tell you she called me a Jew bitch?" I asked.

He hadn't known, but two wrongs did not make a right. We were made to apologize to each other.

"What did you learn at school today?" It wasn't a question I encouraged, or could have answered at the time. I didn't have the words. But I had seen that racism and anti-Semitism are to be assumed in stupid and cowardly people unafraid of reprisal; that people in power are truly surprised when their authority is questioned; and, furthermore, that people rarely mean it when they say they're sorry.

· · ·

One afternoon, on her rounds, my mother pulled me out of the car to go shopping. She was excited because during an interview someone had said the model air-raid shelter downtown was finally open for viewing. In class, we'd had civil defense drills, and I knew to hide under the desk to avoid radiation, but I'd never before considered what could happen if the bomb fell after school.

I have no idea how seriously my mother took our visit. My father said later it was a lark, simple tourism among the fortresses of up-to-date paranoia—to see up close the shining shield that could be installed in your own home. I thought it was like having a world's fair in the backyard. Maybe it meant the future had arrived in Riverhead, and we consequently were a little less hick and more New York. Maybe it just made my mother feel a real part of her time and place. She was very happy that day, laughing and affectionate. The line around the block had a high-pitched, revival meeting tone, all our neighbors chattering and clamoring alongside.

My mother and I didn't discuss the reasons for an air-raid shelter; we just inspected the kitchen and sleeping accommodations and the miraculous modern toilet facilities where a chemical would reduce what you made to smoke.

In the larder, she was tickled by all the cans on the shelves, turning them over in her hands. "Mmmm," of Campbell's soup, she approved. The rest of the food was *chazerei,* junk. In the end she enjoyed visiting so much, I thought we might be getting an air-raid shelter of our own soon. But my mother was getting sick, and we wouldn't be going on outings anymore.

.   .   .

At first our family had huddled together with the other few Jewish families in Riverhead—stranded, as my mother saw it, in the sticks. My parents didn't make many friends there; my mother thought the other wives shallow, and my father was always working. I became friends with the other Jewish girls in my class, but as my mother grew sicker our lives diverged.

I knew my mother was very ill, but nobody ever said *cancer.* Suddenly, she stopped working and began seeing a doctor. It seemed to me that whenever we started to talk, she cut our conversation short. She would push her hair back and hold her palm against her forehead, as if she always had to feel her temperature.

"Are you still there?" she asked one day, with her eyes closed.

I couldn't play my Beatles records while she was resting. Sometimes she was already asleep when I came in from school. She didn't cook anymore, so we often ate Swanson TV dinners in divided aluminum plates, fried chicken or turkey and gravy, corn in one corner, mashed potatoes in the other, or we'd heat up frozen beef pot pies. Even when she did eat, she only picked. It seemed to me that whenever I looked up, my mother was watching.

One night at dinner, I said I wanted to shop for clothes with her, as my other friends did with their mothers.

She shook her head. "Your father will take you."

"Fathers don't go shopping at Marty's Hole in the Wall."

"I'm not gonna argue with you," my mother said.

I wanted her to argue. I wanted to see her feet planted, reading me the riot act in a heated voice. I wanted to see her shrewd look, but she was listless. She'd throw her hands up, then let them fall. "Go by yourself."

I was eleven in 1963, the year before Mods and Rockers blasted away what was left of fifties fashion. I still longed for the cosy cashmere sweaters and matching plaid skirts that other girls could buy. But these were expensive outfits, and even if I went by myself my parents wouldn't countenance cashmere. My father's business was picking up, but now there were medical bills. The money that had been saved to buy a house was going to doctors.

When I was literally desperate for new clothes, my father would drive me to Robert Hall's. And that, I discovered, was almost like going by myself. I would grab whatever I thought probable and try it on behind the half curtain. My father would wait for my appearance, patiently occupied by books like *The Mastermind of Mars* or *Knights of the Range*.

"That's nice," he'd say, inevitably.

"It doesn't make me look fat? I look fat."

"It's very nice."

Back home I'd hold a fashion show for my mother, and if she was feeling strong that day she'd mutter, "You guys," shaking her head, while she pulled up the shoulders of a sagging blouse or tugged my skirt around, so the seam was on the side. Neither my father nor I ever checked much for fit.

.   .   .

Two other Jewish girls in my seventh-grade class, Meryl Sammler and Sheila Klein, also lived in Wildwood. After school we'd gather to go-go dance in my basement. Since my mother was usually in the hospital, my father always at work, and my brothers in college, there was no one to turn the volume down. We alternated British invasion tunes with Motown, Freddy and the Dreamers, Gerry and the Pacemakers, the Miracles, Peter and Gordon, Sam and Dave, and danced until the other girls' mothers called them home to eat. Once in a while I would have supper with Meryl Sammler, quietly astounded at what an actual family dinner could be like.

Both Sammler parents and children were *zoftig* and wore big glasses. At a typical meal, over huge portions of all the major food groups, Mrs. Sammler would announce her pride in Meryl's most recent A. Mr. Sammler would then try to engage little Barry. What did he think of his sister's consistently brilliant performance? Barry, a hyperactive underachiever, never thought much, and any interruption of his wolfish rending could result in food spray showering the table.

I sometimes felt that beneath Mrs. Sammler's steel-wool Afro she was measuring me against her daughter, tallying our marriageable assets. In clear complexion, breast development, and scholastic achievement, Meryl excelled. Perhaps I had a smaller tushie, but points off for messy hair, clothes that didn't match, and poor table manners.

"What do you do in the afternoon when you're alone so much?" Mrs. Sammler asked me.

"I don't mind being alone," I said. "I like to read. I have a cat named Sloopy."

"You come over here whenever you want," she patted my hand. I remember looking around and thinking her living room was a lot more than its plastic-covered sofa and its collection of decorative china plates. I would have liked to have leaned against her soft shoulder the way Meryl did. At the same time, I felt bribery in the air. I knew that this living room, though appealing, was not the kind of place in which a girl could feel free to dance. Mrs. Sammler was kind, but both she and Sheila Klein's mother were eager to break up our unsupervised go-go parties. In a confidential moment, Sheila Klein once revealed that her mother thought I was turning into a *vildechaya*, a wild animal.

Prophecy or curse? I spent hours obsessing. Did Mrs. Klein, who was very tall, and always seemed a little witchy in her unmoving helmet of dyed black hair and extreme beige foundation, think I was wild because I ate when I was hungry, danced all afternoon, read novels instead of studying math? Did she know I accidentally wore two different socks to school—and didn't care as long as no one saw; never emptied my coat pockets of used tissues and candy wrappers? I tortured myself wondering if the new friends I felt so proud of had betrayed our trust. We said we would set ourselves against all mothers. Countless times, I'd heard both Sheila and Meryl call their own nosy, bossy, in the way.

Maybe Mrs. Klein really could see into the future. Although then I was a little girl with messy habits, in just four years I would be sitting naked on a crowded hill in Woodstock, part of an open conspiracy of disorder that threatened not only Mrs. Klein's dearest hopes for Sheila, but her sense of civilization as well.

Mrs. Klein herself had been a European war refugee, and she'd landed, like my own mother, in the boondocks. They were of an age, and both had two sons and a daughter, but little else in common. My mother had let things slide, but Mrs. Klein kept her death grip on propriety and appearance. She didn't smile. All those days I'd stood on her doorstep, waiting to see Sheila, she never invited me inside.

"How is your mother?" she would ask.

"She's good," I'd lie.

"Good," she answered, duty discharged. "Tell her I said hello."

I hated her for even asking. If Mrs. Klein cared, she would have found time to visit the nursing home where my mother had to spend her final year. My mother had few visitors. Both my brothers were away at college, where she wanted them to stay, protected from the draft by student deferments. They visited when they could. Regularly, there was only my father and I, and her brother and sister-in-law, who lived nearby.

·　·　·

Every night that year, before our visit, my father and I would eat dinner at Howard Johnson—both of us lost in our novels. I read historical novels with names like *The Silver Chalice* or jokey biographies by comedians like Alan King. As my father read he'd breathe heavily. His face was very brown from outdoor work, and so were his hands. Just above the wrists where long-sleeved shirts ended was a flesh line of white. His body, accidentally glimpsed, was a ghostly white. Until he retired to Miami and started wearing stylish Bermuda shorts, my father never deliberately revealed his legs. He told me he hated his body.

I hated mine, too. Every piece of fried fish, every Coke, was a rebuke. I was sure that if we ate at home, I'd have the clear complexion that girls with mothers at home had. I blamed my father for my complexion, my weight, my failure in math, and, most of all, for the nursing home where old people in wheelchairs tried to touch me. Once, one ancient crone patting my head had said, "Your hair's like velvet. Like mine was."

My mother died in 1965, two weeks after I turned thirteen. I was in eighth grade. Afterward, our position in the community gradually became clear. There was no more pretense that we were another assimilating, upwardly mobile family. My father and I were lost souls. He buried himself in work. I slept through school, and every night we ate at Howard Johnson. I still have the old menu in my red suitcase. For months HoJo's specials were the only way I could distinguish the days: Monday, spaghetti and garlic bread; Wednesday, fish fry night; Friday, all-you-can-eat clams. I papered my room with Beatles posters, and like so many other girls my age, prayed the band would return to America and console me.

Now, when I view the films of all those screamers in the grip of Beatlemania—all those open mouths and exposed teeth—I think we look on the verge of devouring the lads. Confronted by our mass desire, I'm grateful the Beatles were such a benign force. I'm glad that instead of activating the madness of the crowd, they decided all that adulation just made it hard to hear themselves onstage. (We were defenseless, utterly in their hands, and the Beatles just patted us sweetly on the head and sent us home to grow up.) I can say as one of that mad crowd that I didn't consider myself crazy, I was weeping for joy at their famous concert in Shea Stadium, way, way up in the bleachers. People were polka dots on the stage below. Everywhere girls were panting, about to faint, recovering from fits, weeping, embracing, praying. When the band finally began to perform they were exquisite, miniature mimes. No sound system could overcome the roar of that army of sopranos. What if we'd all said one word, like *windowsill* or *whippoorwill*? The stadium would have spun away. Which in a sense is what happened.

Swinging

1966–1967

During the winter of 1967, I was reading Sammy Davis Jr.'s autobiography *Yes I Can*; watching the rock and roll variety show *Where the Action Is*, hosted by Paul Revere and the Raiders, and *Dark Shadows* (a popular soap opera about vampires); and listening to "Darling Be Home Soon" by the Lovin' Spoonful, "Georgie Girl" by the Seekers, "Penny Lane" by the Beatles, "Hold On" by Sam and Dave. I rummaged through popular novels, television, movies, and Top 40 music to build a profile of the artist I hoped to become. In my diary I noted:

> An artist has neither responsibilities nor obligations, nor are they held to rules and logic. Free love is an important ingredient in their lives, as is free and immediate access to all the major cities of the world. Above all, an artist must strive for originality. Greater than love, greater than liberty is originality.

To me, even clichés were new. "Was it better to be happy or suffer for one's work?" I asked my diary. Suffering, of course, was the nobler choice. Wasn't I already suffering? As a freshman at Riverhead High, I was surly, resentful, angry, failing my classes, and sometimes even drunk.

In contrast to the high suffering of art, school was plain misery. My English teacher, Mr. Zimmerman, marked every one of my compositions D or F, and in the margins he roared in red capitals, "ATROCIOUS GRAMMAR! . . . BIZARRE SPELLING." At the time I refused to bend or make any kind of compromise to standards and conventions. I considered Zimmerman a coward without the necessary verve to understand how I'd moved beyond mere grammar and spelling, to poetry. When Zimmerman stood in front of the room elucidating style, a deafening blood rage overtook me. Only Mr. Moritz was worse. His algebra class turned my bones to jelly. I believe I hallucinated, defensively, at every class session. People spoke in tongues. I was lost in a jungle where every equation, every axiom, every little theorem was a vine.

On the day Moritz finally suggested I drop algebra in favor of general math, I wrote the following in my diary:

> I couldn't stay in class and I felt like I was going to cry. Everything seems to be closing in on me at one time. Dad getting engaged to marry Ann. Us having to move. My marks and math, everything! I started crying hysterically. I went to Tepper's candy store and called Meryl who was home sick. She helped me calm down and told me to go to Mr. Grasso (my guidance counselor) and ask him to help me. I did, after I went back to school I went straight to him. He understood, I mean he didn't understand but he understood as much as anyone could. I was crying in his office and he said he'd help me and we should take one thing at a time. Today—English. 7th period he took me to Mr. Zimmerman to find out if I had any talent in my poetry (I brought some), and why I did so poorly in my compositions. Zimmerman thinks I have talent. To quote him, "she has something . . . a way with words." But my grammar is "abominable." He's going to help me get a style.

At first, I was just glad to set my burdens down. I needed to refuel. Resistance, though my way of life, had worn me out. I was a willful and intense child, and adults apparently did not find me charming. At first, Mr. Zimmerman was amused by my poetry, or perhaps by my conviction that what I wrote was poetry. Mine clearly was not the kind of poetry Mr. Zimmerman enjoyed. In the confessional free verse I depended on to organize daily chaos, he saw an unfocused welter. I wouldn't listen to his criticism, and after a meeting or two, he abandoned the idea that he could mold me. I did make an effort to master grammar, and I read all the books he suggested, but I always had the feeling he didn't take me seriously. That was a mistake. I was, if nothing else, a very serious girl. Zimmerman said I was too young to know what I wanted. I thought he was too old to adapt to new ideas or forms. Perhaps it was in our relationship that I first recognized the generation gap. Mr. Zimmerman, smoothing down the ends of his black mustache, was so ironic, but his irony and all his principles of grammar and five hundred years of English literature would not save him when my kind came to power. I could not have articulated these thoughts back then, but I meant to overthrow him.

.   .   .

Francine Dylewski's house, around the corner from the high school, was where my new high school friends and I did most of our drinking and fighting. In the movies girls slapped men when they got fresh. In my friends' homes, tired bullies slapped haggard drudges. In our ninth-grade crowd, boys slapped girls when they talked dirty. Girls slapped boys when their affections strayed, or when they imagined sarcasm or irony. Girls slapped other girls when they suspected rivalry, or when all else failed, to prove superiority.

Francine was slow and ripe, and boys found her thrilling. Her house, with its scratchy sofa, flaking rugs, and exhausted single mother, was our oasis. My best friend, Wanda Gacek, didn't drink, but I did—more for the listless charge of being talked about than the stupor achieved (followed as it inevitably was by several hours of sleep on any flat surface).

Every afternoon after school, Wanda and I would run back to her house to watch *Where the Action Is*. Wanda's house was right behind Francine's, and like Francine's, it was a dark box, quartered. There were two closet-size bedrooms, one for her parents and one that Wanda had to share with her twin brother, Stash, divided by a heavy drape. Wanda and Stash also shared a face, but Wanda had inherited all the blood. Wanda was charming, plump, and rosy; Stash was severe, bone and ivory. He liked me enough to delay his math studies every day in favor of silent and wishful observation.

Wanda's kitchen always smelled of sour cabbage, and every afternoon her mother could be found stirring a pot. Mrs. Gacek, a tiny wrinkled woman raised in Poland, wore a babushka and cleaned doctors' offices on the night shift. To me she looked exactly like a Rackham witch, with her pot, constant broom, and toothless mouth. I rarely went into the kitchen, and Mrs. Gacek never emerged. She spoke very little English, and in our long acquaintance I saw her smile only once.

After my mother died I spent most afternoons at Wanda's house. One day, when I was passing through the kitchen, Mrs. Gacek offered me some pierogi from her pot.

"She wants to know if you want sour cream," Wanda said, seating me beside a china bowl with a brace of boiled dumplings.

When I said yes, Mrs. Gacek's effort to smile dragged down half her face. She spoke in a musical burst, spooning blinding-white half-moons.

"She says she's sorry about your mother," Wanda translated.

The Gaceks were Catholic, but Mrs. Gacek had been in Auschwitz, and she had a number tattooed on her arm. "She won't show it to you, though, so don't ask," Wanda said.

My mother was dead, Wanda's mother had been tortured, Francine's mother was never truly awake. I think it's amazing that we weren't completely paralyzed. We read fan magazines for news of our favorite bands, played their records, and whispered to their photos. When we were in bed, these were the secret men who prowled in our yards, their pointy patent leather shoes tapping out sensual impatience in the night. Our dream lovers always had long hair and insolent expressions, wore low-slung bell-bottoms, and carried their guitars like gypsies wherever they roamed. Someday, they would arrive on our sidewalks in broad daylight and beckon silently with tickets to London, and we would swing under striped umbrellas on Carnaby Street.

.   .   .

My father had become engaged to his childhood friend Ann Taussig and was going back and forth to Massapequa every weekend. I hated the commute, but he wouldn't leave me home alone at night. Every week I would climb into the backseat, slam the door, and treat my father to a fraught and sullen silence, until something arose that I needed to yell at him about. I frequently accused him of dragging me along as a convenient baby-sitter for Ann's eight-year-old son.

"Edward's never any problem," he said.

It didn't matter that Edward was the most amiable, flexible child, rarely spoke, and didn't care much for company. He watched TV quietly until he was tired, then put himself to bed with a book over his head.

"You don't understand," I hissed, that forlorn refrain even I was tired of hearing. My father shrugged. "What would you do at home?" He couldn't possibly be expecting the truth.

If I hadn't had to baby-sit, I might be at a dance, lying to someone else, or getting drunk, or insulting someone or being insulted, perhaps by the boy I liked most.

In the backseat I'd turn up the angry silence and thrash around so that he couldn't help but note my disaffection. If my father started to whistle or hum, I'd sigh heavily.

Outside, along the road the spring potato fields were starting to blossom. Some weeks, to add variety, we'd travel by the ocean shore.

My father would point out the curling fog, or the strength of white-caps over the waves.

"Big deal," I'd say in my most dismissive, sophisticated tone. "Fog, waves. Who cares?"

Some weeks we'd drive through Stonybrook, past pretty gray farm-houses and vine-covered garden walls, to stop at the small Jewish cemetery where my mother was buried. The graveyard was surrounded by woods, and birds landed on the smaller stones, inspecting all visitors. We were always the only people there. Down a neatly raked path, my mother's grave was still fresh in comparison to those around her. We'd unveiled her stone the previous November: "Beloved Wife and Mother." My father had planted ivy.

My father didn't know it, but I'd seen grief turn him into Torquemada. I'd hidden in the basement as he'd burned all my mother's remaining papers in an iron drum. From my hiding place I heard her final wisecracks become just crackling. I saw her secrets disappear page by page until everything was gone at last: her game laugh, sharp wit, and trickster spirit; the shrewd look that had made me want to tell the truth; her beautiful white shoulders and the hands that had smoothed my hair.

At the cemetery, my father stood beside her grave staring down with a terrible watchfulness, haunted and baffled, while I descended into tears. I always wanted to visit, but I often felt tricked. I suspected he used her to reach me, when everything else failed. And I'm glad to say it worked. I clung to him, and cried into his shoulder. Later, back in the car, I sat up front, his docile daughter for an hour.

Summer of Love

1967

To my father's family, his marriage to Ann must have seemed like a dream solution. They were both recently widowed. They'd grown up together and had known each other all their lives. Ann had one young son, and Steve a daughter still at home to raise.

Ann's mother, Eva, and my father's mother, Golde, were distant relations and best friends in their youth on the Lower East Side. Eva was American-born, witty, and full of ideas. (My father cites the time she taught her dog to use the toilet. The neighbors queued up, and she let them in one by one to gawk.) My grandmother Golde was slower on the uptake, but had been a lovely Edwardian beauty. In photos as a child in the Lithuanian woods she resembles Alice in Wonderland, her long, fair hair ornamented with a bow. When she was thirteen, Golde traveled alone, freight class, to an apartment in New York City's midtown to care for a widowed brother's children. Her brother soon remarried, and his new wife was cruel to Golde, publicly accusing her of stupidity and sloth and peasant manners. My grandmother endured her trial for three horrible years, before (like the heroine in some New World fairytale) leaving in the middle of the night.

At the beginning of the century the Lower East Side was exploding with poetry and liberty, and on her first night in town, a seventeen-year-old Jewish girl with just a few pennies could buy a cup of coffee *mit schlag* in the Café Royale and be serenaded by a Yiddish anarchist. The night of her escape, Golde moved in with Eva, and before long they were working side by side in the same shirtwaist sweatshop. Golde and Eva invented a family tree, installing themselves as the great-great-granddaughters of cousins hung together as horse thieves in Lapland. Neither girl was sentimental enough to construe herself the descendant of royalty or wealth—just a simple horse thief, and in Lapland among the Eskimos. Perhaps the idea of Jews on horses riding freely and unrestricted by czarist race laws was a fantastic enough image at that time to project from a tenement flat. I like to think of Eva and Golde, after a day of sewing, drinking lemon tea and luxuriating in the romance of their outlaw heritage—two Jewish pirate queens.

I suppose they may have been impressed by the surrounding talk they heard of rights and unions, and with the vision of Jews escaping the Lower East Side for parts more American. Golde, more than Eva, was dazzled by the Jewish mob boys. They always looked so well dressed, and they had money in their pockets to spend on a girl. My grandfather Charlie was one of these bad boys, and Golde married him when she was seventeen. Born in America and gifted with a beautiful singing voice, Charlie was kicked out of the synagogue's choir for smoking before puberty. He was lithe and glum, a hood, right on the fringes of Murder Incorporated. When asked for a general description, my father remembers him with mixed emotions. He was a good provider and a great mechanic, but "a miserable human being." It's just thanks to Golde that he lived long enough to open his own garage. When he was newly married, Charlie got into a fight with some thugs down on Hester Street. He might have landed in prison or worse, if Golde hadn't persuaded him to escape with her to "the open fields of the Bronx." Although it meant leaving everyone she'd come to love behind, it was the only way to save Charlie. Apparently, the Bronx was too far off the map to drive to. Gangsters don't take the subway.

Golde and Charlie had been welcomed into Eva's sprawling East Side clan by its awesome matriarch, Aunt Hasha. And it is worth a brief digression to recall the one photo remaining that shows Ann's great-aunt Hasha holding court. Weighing in at about three hundred pounds, in this picture Hasha is surrounded by her good friends Abbott and Costello, Hasha's son (cousin Tootsie), and Tootsie's wife and his girlfriend. Over thirty years Aunt Hasha bore eight children. She was from all reports an expert wheeler-dealer and managed to care for hundreds of greenhorns over the years, as well as the lost and poor people of the neighborhood. She pulled strings and cut corners to find food and jobs. But whether everything was always on the up-and-up, who could say?

Now, to do real justice to this photo (to tell it the way Ann told it to me as her tante Rebe had told it to her), you'd need to imagine a vaudeville stage with some snare drums that go *ba-dum-bum,* and a shtick-drenched voice:

"Here behind Abbott and Costello is Hasha's son Charlie . . . He's in iron and steel . . . His mother ironed and he stole! . . . Charlie's daughter

Anna married Natie Kaplan and had a car of her own, a maid, and an apartment on Sutton Place in the East Sixties, and two mink coats . . . *before anybody else had ever heard of them. Anna's husband, Natie, was in pharmaceuticals . . . heroin, opium, marijuana . . . ba dum bum. And he had a bodyguard, an ape* (who once had asked my stepmother, Ann, out on a date; she declined). But the pride and brains of the family was Tootsie, about whom the song "Toot Toot Tootsie [Good-bye]" was written on the occasion he was sent up the river for good. *Tootsie worked out of Manhattan with the Lepke, Garrah gang, otherwise known as Murder, Inc. . . . Not a petty crook . . . he held a high position."* *Ba-dum-bum.*

Aunt Hasha's husband, Barney Cohen, was a Hebrew scholar, but there is no other evidence of religious practice, or political involvement, among that crowd. My own grandmother's shtetl life had been Orthodox, but she changed her customs in New York, where being Jewish was much more elastic. None of her children, my father and his two sisters, ever exhibited more than a cursory interest in the Jewish religion, but they all identified with its secular humanist wing. (In his teens, when my father became involved in left-wing causes, he had no trouble accepting Marx's pronouncement that religion was the opiate of the people and called himself an atheist.) My grandfather Charlie didn't concern himself much with either Old World religion or the New World passion for getting and spending. He was seized by another distinctively American goal, spiritual in its way. Charlie wanted to be his own boss. He considered financial success less important than a man's independence. My father and grandfather were opposites in temperament, but they both shared the ambition to be out on their own.

. . .

In the summer of 1967, when my father and I moved in with Ann and her son, Edward, my two older brothers were working at a resort in the Catskills. Their visits to Massapequa, either together or alone, were few and fleeting.

Only an hour's commute from New York City, my new home was in one of the bedroom communities that grew up with the population boom after the war. Most of the town had been carved into pop-up homes like ours, but the ocean shore was studded with gaudy palazzos, tinged with the mystery of the mafiosi.

Massapequa doesn't seem more likely than other suburban locales to breed celebrities and inspire their written reminiscences. Yet, it has been home to a generation of memoirists. Both Ron Kovic, the Vietnam veteran turned radical, and Peggy Noonan, the right-wing speechwriter for Reagan and Bush, went to high school in Massapequa. Both of them grew up in lower-middle-class homes with salt-of-the-earth values that they interpret in their respective memoirs in vastly different ways.

In *Born on the Fourth of July,* Kovic writes about how his ideas of patriotism were forged in Massapequa. Over time he came to realize how all the John Wayne–type heroic images he'd absorbed in his youth had filled his head so completely they'd left no room for independent thought. Noonan's memoir, *What I Saw at the Revolution,* is a thin salute to the flag-waving, brain-blurring myths that Kovic came to reject. A third Massapequan memoir, Betsy Israel's *Grown-Up Fast,* is set in the apolitical suburban ruins of the late seventies. In Israel's Massapequa, alienated kids come of age in a raunchy town full of mindless sex and nasty drugs.

In the eighties, Massapequa was home to church secretary and *Playboy* model Jessica Hahn, whose testimony helped convict televangelical conman Jim Bakker. In the early nineties it seemed the whole country was convulsed with the tragicomedy of the gun-wielding nonchalant Amy Fisher (the "Long Island Lolita") and her lover Joey Buttafuoco, a Massapequan auto body shop owner. Buttafuoco's behavior, magnified every night on the news, was reflective of a certain kind of local pride and arrogance—the "in your face attitude" of some fourth-generation mid-island males. It's related to the same kind of rash dummy demeanor and tough-guy razzle-dazzle that lies at the root of the war movie version of blind patriotism that Kovic's book bravely testifies against. In the current climate, white guys like Joey Buttafuoco act as if they're the last line of defense against gentrification on the one hand and diversity on the other. They don't know whether they're coming or going. For months Buttafuoco was a running gag on *The Late Show with David Letterman,* mainly because of his name, but also because his pride was indefatigable. This guy from "guyland" (the name, Ron Rosenbaum writes, "we expatriates like to call it"), with apparently more balls than brains, was subjected nightly to humilation in front of millions of people. But Letterman could not make him look ridiculous to himself.

Massapequa is home to a rash of other performers, including the movie star Baldwin brothers, composer Marvin Hamlisch, and comic Jerry Seinfeld, who helpfully translated the town's name as "Indian for 'by-the-mall.'"

Despite their achievements, none of the stars mentioned here can rival Massapequa's most celebrated actress on the world stage. Christine Jorgensen, born George Jorgensen Jr., was an ex-G.I. whose Swedish sex-change operation made jaws drop in the 1950s. Hacks exhausted barrels of ink describing her life as a soignée lady of fashion. Jorgensen spent most of her time in the city; but an event in her later years caught the interest of one of the century's great wits. Dorothy Parker is known to have remarked on a great variety of subjects, but this is the only recorded conversation I've found in which she addresses Massapequa. When told of Jorgensen's move from Manhattan to mid-island to live with her elderly mother, Parker quipped, "And what sex, may I ask, is the mother?"

There is a parlor game in which players put together the perfect dinner party with guests from any time and place, real or fictional. Caryl Churchill fashioned the idea into an act in her play *Top Girls,* bringing together women like the great world traveler Isabella Bird, the mythic Pope Joan, and Dulle Griet, the peasant subject of a Brueghel painting. As I write about Massapequa, and question my own place at its table, I can't help thinking we could make a wild party out of our local heroes. "Joey, dear, have you met Christine?"

In his memoir, Ron Kovic attributes a Norman Rockwell–like atmosphere to the neighborhood in which he grew up. Mothers stayed home. Sundays after church, dads cooked big breakfasts. Little boys trotted off to Little League or Cub Scouts, and played at war in their backyards. Kovic makes very clear the subterranean currents by which those little-boy games fed into the myth of the idealized warrior. He never questioned the easy sentiments of patriotism or the glorification of war he'd heard about all his life, until he went to Vietnam. Kovic came home with his spine broken, unable to feel anything below his chest. Perhaps one of his greatest achievements has been to make readers understand how *everything* one takes for granted can become uncomfortable, futile, and embarrassing. In painful detail, Kovic describes the way a broken man may grope toward awareness, and how he may find himself on the other side of catastrophe somehow, transformed by compassion.

Remembering the mass protest demonstration he addressed as a

Vietnam Veteran Against the War, Kovic writes: "In the war we were killing and maiming people. In Washington on that Saturday afternoon in May, we were trying to heal them and set them free."

That was the day he returned his war medals.

.   .   .

Kovic's neighborhood wasn't far from mine, but I was oblivious to the Massapequa that included baseball and Cub Scouts. My new stepbrother, Edward, had been born with an empty eye socket. I discovered that he, who had seemed so agreeable, or at least easy to manipulate the year before, also suffered terribly as an outsider. And he, too, was still reeling from the death of a parent. Edward didn't want to go out much. And that summer, I thought he might have been the one person in the world even lonelier than I. I couldn't help feeling jealous when, on hot afternoons, after Ann came home from work, they'd cool off together in the kiddie pool in our backyard.

I couldn't join them. I still refused to recognize Ann's authority. She was the usurper, foisted on me, melting my father's mind and memory. *"Where on earth has daddy dropped me?"* I asked my diary. In our new neighborhood next to the Plainedge exit on the Long Island Expressway, every house looked pretty much alike. Blocks and blocks of identical yards subtly distinguished by topiary follies, holy shrines lit by fairy lights, and varicolored lawn jockeys. Our yard was unadorned, and it was entirely owing to the fact that my father parked his tow truck out front that I ever found my way back at all.

"Moloch! Moloch! Robot apartments! invisible suburbs!" Allen Ginsberg wrote in *Howl*. Who knew what blasted lives transpired behind those manicured lawns? I was fourteen, living with a fright wig where my brain should have been. Winds would blow, tendrils fly (all this and I'd still only dreamed of taking drugs). I think my confusion was due less to a struggle with conformity that summer than with being generally lost. A country kid with a bad sense of direction, when I wasn't slumped against my closet door listening to Simon and Garfunkel sing "I Am a Rock," I would walk for miles under the expressway and find—wherever I ended up—that there was always another service road, another concrete tunnel or off-ramp, another greasy spoon.

Inside one old luncheonette, a man working behind the formica counter told me he'd started out jerking sodas part-time in high school, before World War II. I imagined him looking just like the kind of fresh-faced character you'd see in a Jimmy Stewart film. His face had become gray and scrunched, but he still wore a kid's white cap, and he was still selling greasy hamburgers and tuna fish on rye and egg creams and black-and-white ice cream sodas thirty years later. He could flip eggs behind his back and make a sundae with his eyes closed. He wiped down the counter and joked with his regulars while he refilled their cups with some scummy-looking coffee that had probably percolated all day. I returned there a couple of times and sat at the counter with a book, spooked by my own anonymity. Once the counterman leaned over and whispered, "If you smiled more, you'd be prettier."

That was the last time I went there. I wanted to get out of Massapequa and never look back. At the same time, I'd have given anything to have had what it took to be a regular. I wanted a place at the table, at the counter. I wanted to be someone, somewhere, even in Massapequa. Christine meet Joey meet Ronny meet Peggy meet Les.

Bringing the War Home

1967-1968

In the autumn of 1967, the suburbs were living up to their promise. Shopping was entertainment, and the malls glowed with nowness. I didn't have any new friends yet. Vietnam was my only reliable nightly companion. Trapped by circumstance, I had gradually begun paying more and more attention to the mosaic of protest that television spilled into our house.

I was curious to hear my father's opinion of the Vietnam War, although this line of inquiry, I realized later, set a precedent. In our house we hadn't gotten around to mentioning the Holocaust yet. Our dinnertime discussions of World War II had rarely gone beyond the same few cracks about my father's fortunate Stateside service in the Quartermasters Corps. It was a kind of joke, like Dobie Gillis's father's refrain: "double-you—double-you two—the Big One!" The rest my parents seemed anxious to put behind them. It would be years before remembering became as much of the Jewish suburban experience as forgetting once was.

My father was fifty that autumn. A liberal who had long admired Hubert Humphrey for his support of unions, he was surprised and disappointed that Humphrey hadn't taken a stand against the war. (Humphrey must know *something,* I heard my father rationalize on several occasions—some *secret* that prevents him from breaking with Johnson.) "It's wrong, it's illegal," he said of the war, "according to the Geneva Conventions Decree. But I don't know how we'll ever get out."

In the New Deal wonderyears, my father had come to believe that the fight for fair wages and decent hours was the same as the fight against fascism. At eighteen, he had joined the Civilian Conservation Corps and been swept up in the workers' struggle for peace and justice (and perplexed why anyone might feel less absorbed than he by those ideals). In Massapequa, his demonstrating days were all in the past, but he offered me some helpful advice: think twice before you sign a petition with your real name (a result of the blacklisting some of his petition-signing friends had suffered during the McCarthy years); *never* cross a picket line; and later, when the FBI were tracking me, *always* call from a safe phone. You're probably being tapped.

By that September there were around one-half million troops in Vietnam, and 13,000 American deaths. I was desperate to be part of the antiwar action. That October, I wanted nothing more than to join the more than 100,000 people gathered in Washington to "confront the warmakers" and "unscrew the war machine." In my head I'd already merged with war resisters around the world, while my wretched body was left to drag through its adolescence at Plainedge High.

In school, I slowly began to make friends with other misfits and outsiders. All of us were alert to the wave then unfolding, an amorphous fusion of style and politics denoted at first glance by our hair. Ours, we boasted, was longer, wilder, frizzier, and more natural than other kids'. Boys in the hippie crowd, like Davie Brillstein and Andy Schubert, were suspended from school when their hair touched their chins, while girls suffered more subtle punishments for daring to transgress school conventions. Once, early that October, a couple of pouting debs cornered my new friend Jana and me in the girls' room.

"Hippie scuzz!" they shouted, aiming aerosol cans of hairspray in our direction. Their intent was to immobilize our hair and, by extension, our minds. But the tide was against them, and just a few months later those same girls would let down their own big, lacquered hair.

Like a lot of other high school students around the country, my new friends and I had begun to focus on various ways to bring the war home. I was reading Wordsworth by then, absorbing his euphoria and urgency. "O pleasant exercise of hope and joy!" I couldn't shake the sense that time was fleeting. Che Guevara had been killed in Bolivia. I was already fifteen. If I didn't bring the war home now, when would I?

· · ·

By 1968, the fashionable rhetoric encouraged kids not to trust anyone over thirty and, furthermore, to kill our parents. We understood these to be metaphorical expressions. Nobody was planning to kill anybody, but in that unlikely eventuality (and who could say for sure?) it was much more probable that we'd kill someone else's parents. Other people's parents were easier to admire or despise. It was hard for me to see Steve and Ann with any clarity, but the insecurities of my new friends' parents seemed painfully obvious. Mr. and Mrs. Brillstein, for example, were ready to stand on their heads to buy their son Davie's love. Davie Brillstein was a chatty junior with a piercing laugh and no sense of direction who liked to drive around in his mother's Mustang getting lost. The Brillsteins' affection for their son seemed at once noble and ridiculous, and it desperately embarrassed Davie, who was a lot less klutzy than his parents imagined. (He'd grow up to become a cultivator of high-grade Hawaiian marijuana, rich beyond Irv and Dodo's wildest dreams.)

Irv and Dodo Brillstein had been active themselves in the thirties, and they wanted to know all about our movement. When they'd first heard that we wanted to organize a student group against the war, they'd purred with pleasure. But moments of such generational solidarity were rare. The Brillsteins were willing to indulge our *utopian* vision, but they never stopped reminding us that we also needed an *economic* analysis. Involved as they were, they were still somebody's parents, and eventually they wanted to know how much personal liberation was really going on. Davie would roll his eyes as Irv launched into another lecture against "that long hair, that unwashed look. Still, if Davie wants to have an antiwar meeting in our house, he should feel free."

Hippies had suddenly popped up in every part of the school. Cheerleaders, wrestlers, National Merit scholars, yearbook editors, and almost everyone else was walking around in a brand new blue daze. Over Christmas vacation, Jana, Davie, Andy, and I had begun discussing how to harness a part of the energy all these newly minted freaks were spending on finding and buying pot (overnight, an industry!) for the antiwar movement. We phoned Columbia SDS, and they agreed to send a speaker to help organize us. At the time, Students for a Democratic Society was the nation's largest New Left student organization, with chapters at most colleges and universities. High school students were routinely forbidden to organize chapters on school grounds, so seeking to join SDS automatically endowed us with the sense that our little group was a force to be reckoned with.

I recently found my old SDS membership card in the red suitcase, rubber banded together with a hand-lettered leaflet announcing an "open Plainedge action meeting," and a wallet-size photo of the British band Herman's Hermits. I never actually sent in my dues (five dollars for a year's national membership), but I remember how carrying the card made me feel that much more authentically part of the movement and terribly sophisticated. At that time I didn't know another kid who carried any kind of card. In our wallets we carried school portraits of each other, or of our pets, maybe an illicit note, rarely more money than the cost of lunch in the cafeteria. *This is to certify the membership of . . .*

Under my signature there is a brief statement describing the organization: SDS "seeks to promote the active participation of young people in the formation of a movement to build a society free from poverty, ignorance, war, exploitation and the inhumanity of man to man." What more could I add? Perhaps, just the word *woman*. All that was just around the corner.

.   .   .

Where you stood on the war was becoming as divisive an issue in school as out. Every day classes would be disrupted by teacher tirades or debates between furious antagonists. Even the walk from class to class held the promise of an argument with an acidhead like Ruthie, whose beliefs were summed up in the philosophy "Why hassle?"; or Harris, an irritating hawk, whose hatred of the Red Menace was as constant and virulent as the acne that ruined his face.

Everyone seemed to be turning on, and school spirit, which I considered at the time to be another word for blind patriotism, seemed at an all-time low. Nevertheless, we hippies and politicos didn't think our classmates understood how quickly and with what energy the war was continuing to expand. To raise their *consciousness,* to combat their *apathy* (the jargon we used), we sensed that we had to be obvious and loud, even obnoxious—as long as we weren't passive. *Relevance* was the fashionable code word my friends and I adopted to display our sympathies. Sometimes, we could be puffed up with self-importance, but underlying the occasional pose was the urgent sense that what we were doing *meant something.* Adults had to know we weren't being fooled. High school was a warehouse for soldiers. We were being treated like children when, in a year or two, the boys in our class would be expected to march off to war; we girls expected to wave them off with a kiss. The struggle against the war lured us farther afield until it seemed one of the unofficial goals of the SDS chapter in Plainedge High was to spend as little time there as possible.

Almost every Saturday Andy Schubert and I would take the train to the city, to go to museums and to see movies. Andy's whole family were avid museum- and theatergoers. They knew about art and literature and went out to see foreign films. My parents were great readers of popular fiction, but the Schuberts read difficult books, ones by Roth and Cheever and Mailer and Nabokov. Before I met the Schuberts I'd never known a family that wasn't either Jewish or Catholic. The Schuberts were secular, humanist, cosmopolites. And although both worked (Ingrid taught history, Alex was a photoengraver), there was something tantalizingly bohemian about them. Marble busts of family members sculpted by Ingrid's artist father stood on heirloom sideboards, and beautiful paintings by her artist brother hung on the walls. Ingrid's sister was an actress who also read tarot cards. Her nephew, a member of New York's Open Theater, extended their ties to the avant-garde into the next generation. Alex was also a jazz aficionado. He had all of Billie Holiday's records; it was at their house that I first heard that brave, silken contralto.

Being welcomed into the Schuberts' home meant I was able to spend less time in my own. Ann and I still weren't getting along. My father told me that she had once been a brilliant scholar. She'd sailed through high school in Brooklyn and begun Hunter College at sixteen, but I wasn't interested. From what I'd observed, she was too caught up in magazines like *Woman's Day* and *Ladies' Home Journal*. The lessons those magazines taught about cosmetics and clothes and cooking and knitting and keeping a home, I didn't want to learn. I defied Ann at every opportunity. I refused to do household chores, categorically refused to clean my room. I enjoyed being a slob, I declared. I even wore a button to that effect: *Kiss me I'm a slob*.

Ann and I had a hard time just holding a conversation, and the last thing I wanted to discuss was the state of my room. After absorbing a few months' worth of hostility and defiance she gave up on diplomacy. When one morning in a voice unused to high registers she shrilled, "Clean that cesspool, or else!" I knew I'd succeeded in driving this normally reticent woman into barking hysteria.

Later that day, while I was at school, Ann gathered my dirty clothes, scattered papers, records, leaflets, buttons—all the paraphernalia of my sloppy life—and dumped them out the back door. Then, in a final, eloquent gesture, she threw a garbage pail on my bed.

I remember sputtering, dumbfounded at her audacity. In my own falsetto response I heard how far I'd fallen from the moral high ground of global political issues. I knew her game, I screamed. She'd tricked me into becoming *childish*.

Ann was raging red hot by the time my father came home to conciliate. "Don't you have any pride?" he shouted.

"No. Not your kind of pride." His appeal to decency was completely ineffective. I had a lot of pride, but very little sense of shame. That strategy backfired further when I blamed my stepmother, the usurper, for making me the object of my father's disgust.

"Don't you think she's suffered enough?" he asked, pointing to Ann. "No!"

While Ann and I were at daggers drawn, Edward and my father were engaged in skirmishes of their own. Edward was a moody child who preferred to be left alone. His solitary nature clashed with my father's philosophy of universal amiability. The more Edward refused to participate in simple conversations, the more my father pushed him, until the little boy exploded and the friendly man lashed back. As Edward grew older he sharpened his weapons—mumbling malice and sarcasm, which my father could never ignore.

Eventually Ann and I negotiated a modus operandi. As long as I didn't deliberately confront her, she backed off. Those first few years our family dinners were tense and brief—the atmosphere heavy with hurt feelings, each of us nursing grievances that went much deeper than an evening's quarrel.

. . .

The Brillstein house became our Party headquarters. On the night of our first real meeting, while we waited for the SDS representative, Dodo handed around fresh-baked chocolate chip cookies and coffee. Then she and Irv withdrew to where they could hear but not be seen.

I knew from the moment Columbia's representative, Tim Lowenthal, entered the room with his mad eyes and furzy hair that I wanted to march in his army. I would make myself into a warrior queen if that's what it took to show Tim Lowenthal my commitment. I thought he was beautiful and that whatever he was saying was beautiful.

"Self-sufficiency," Lowenthal was saying, "self-reliance. College and high school chapters just tangentially connected . . . Of course you'd appoint one member to liaison."

I sat on the Brillsteins' sofa, ready to be of service, to the chapter and to the revolution. My credentials were flimsy. Although I always wanted to do good, more and more I was resenting having to *be* good. My heroes were often rebels to the bone. But that night I was willing to fall in line, stage a coup, do whatever it took to liaison with that man.

Meanwhile, Lowenthal was asking, "What do you want?"

We said freedom of expression so we could wear the clothes we wanted to school. We said freedom of assembly so we could talk to each other in the hall. We said freedom from illegal search and seizure so the assistant principal couldn't go rooting around in our lockers whenever he felt like it.

Lowenthal nodded, "What do you really want?" He raised his voice, "Do you want a world with peace and justice in it?"

"Right on!"

"Do you want to show solidarity with the revolution in Vietnam?"

We punched our fists into the air.

"Power to the people," Tim Lowenthal said. "Revolution takes love and devotion. Do you want to overthrow the running dog lackey? Power to the people! Do you really want to off the pig? *Do you really want to off the pig?*"

Now, we knew that Lowenthal was getting us wound up and that he was a little bit overheated, but I was thinking if it took being bloodthirsty to get his attention, I could be bloodthirsty, and I shouted louder than anyone, "Power to the people! Off the pig!" We were having a really good time when Mr. Brillstein burst into the room.

"It's getting a little late, don't you kids have to get up for school tomorrow?"

"Irv," we heard from the kitchen. "Leave them alone."

"It's not the whole picture, they're not getting—"

"Irv, we discussed this. Let it be."

"Ten more minutes," Mr. Brillstein said to Tim Lowenthal. "Then I'm driving you to the train."

Lowenthal raised an eyebrow, like Vincent Price in a horror flick.

"Dad—," the mortified Davie Brillstein began.

"Do you want to overthrow the government violently?" Irv shot back. "Because if you do, you can leave my house point blank. None of you have the first idea."

"Irv." Mrs. Brillstein emerged with a coffee cake.

"I'm prepared to let you listen. You kids. Dream, whatever. Make a better society. But be careful. Ask Davie. Davie, tell them about McCarthy."

"Dad," Davie called shrilly. *"Not now!"*

"What do you think you're doing here, inciting a riot? These kids have to be in school at eight tomorrow. Get your coat." There was a beat of silence before Lowenthal replied.

"Fuck you," he said.

Mrs. Brillstein gasped. At first it seemed Mr. Brillstein hadn't heard. "What?" he asked quietly. "What?"

"You want to know who the enemy is," Tim Lowenthal told us as he backed toward the door. "Take a good look."

If I was to point to a moment when the generation gap first seemed material, this was it. The previous year I had sensed that Mr. Zimmerman, my ninth-grade English teacher, and I were on two different sides in a battle zone, but he'd held all the weapons. This was a different situation entirely. It was as if, in the wake of one "fuck you," the ground had cracked, the way it does when spring breaks up the ice in the Arctic; and while our side remained intact, across the divide, an island holding Irv and Dodo was floating away. Soon they would just be small figures in the remote distance, waving. I suppose to a casual observer I may have appeared to be sitting still on the Brillsteins' couch, maybe biting my nails a little more intently, slightly embarrassed, avoiding the adult eye. But inside, I can tell you, I was a nubile young dragoness, soaring over Massapequa, claws and wings fully extended, snorting fire. What an erotic thrill. Lowenthal had struck the blow.

When Columbia exploded in the spring I knew Tim Lowenthal was inside the barricades, probably shouting, "Fuck you." I hovered around in the crowded streets staring ardently through the wrought iron gates (noncollege students and all "outside agitators" were prohibited from entering Columbia's grounds), squinting at the titles of the pamphlets on the information tables, at the savage student faces and flying banners. I only wanted to go to college to go on strike.

. . .

Later that year I took the opportunity of my eleventh-grade English thesis, titled "Antigone's Modern Relevance," to articulate my worldview, which careened toward utopianism with a strong strain of puritanism:

Antigone knows that to ignore the truth would be to invite spiritual death. It is hard living that way. Not too many people will truly live or die for their convictions. It is difficult to be offered joy and to choose to remain unhappy for the sake of your principles. American society, luxurious with items of joy offers young people a similar choice. It is so easy merely to join in the decadent society and enjoy the pleasures of living. It is so hard to reject the temptation to sit back and enjoy what money can buy. Today however, a great many young people are rejecting the middle class ideals of society. There are people who can see through the transparent pleasures offered them as bromides. Antigone is a modern symbol of the people who have chosen integrity, morality and justice, over law, order, and indifference.

Mr. McKay was distinctly unimpressed. He awarded me an indifferent grade, 75/83, and in his comments explained, "Your topic is 'Modern Relevance,' but that is not a subject for literary criticism. You are committing C. S. Lewis's crime of going outside the work. Suppose Antigone were not relevant, would it be a lesser work? Discussing a work as if the message were its only value is not a valid literary exercise."

Mr. McKay flattened me with his "New Criticism." C. S. Lewis! What next? T. S. Eliot? They were dinosaurs. By insisting that there was one correct way to read, he reinforced my own fuzzy beliefs that reading wasn't a matter of taste but ideology. For example, I thought Mr. McKay couldn't possibly enjoy an antiestablishment book like *On the Road*, while he presumed I could never appreciate the composed style and moral intelligence of a classic like *Middlemarch*.

During my Saturday commutes into the city with Andy Schubert, I read everything I could about the New York of J. D. Salinger, of Grace Paley, of Dutch last names, of Dorothy Day and Dorothy Parker, of jet-setters and social reformers. Somehow Ayn Rand's nervous, selfish New Yorkers in *The Fountainhead* managed to coexist with Claude Brown as he wrestled for self-awareness and justice in *Manchild in the Promised Land*. All these worlds were simultaneous, and I was a reader of many parts. Somehow, I could absorb cautionary tales about martyrs who eschewed "transparent pleasures," and still enjoy novels about bed-hopping playboys and pill-popping dolly-birds. I worshiped every kind of writer, without regard to their subject or style. Eventually I came to recognize that if I, as an admirer of great books, could simultaneously possess a deep regard for pulp fiction, might not anyone—even Mr. McKay—given the desire, transcend experience and habit, and read across boundaries?

The breadth of books I read helped me sketch an identity. After all, I wasn't just a high school radical. I was still part Rat Pack and part Carnaby Street. I was as much the girl who wanted to be in a James Bond flick (wear my hair up, sprayed to a burnished veneer, and drink martinis), as I was rebellious daughter, sister, and apprentice writer.

One weekend afternoon Andy Schubert and I went to the café next to the Museum of Modern Art, where I caught the eye of a glittering human bonbon (black marshmallow hair, almond white lips, and eyelashes as long as her nose). I recognized her from the cover of her popular book. A bad, sexy book—on the incorrect, decadent, and bourgeois book list—which I'd inhaled in a single, wanton, breath. Here was Jacqueline Susann, author of *Valley of the Dolls*, and at her feet was Josephine, her poodle, in her blinding jeweled collar.

"Jackie," I ventured.

She arched an elaborate brow.

"I just want to tell you, I *love* your writing."

"You're too young for my book," Jackie said, surprisingly practical. Did she speak that way to all her readers? For a time her flamboyant melodramas caught the trashy glamour of the age. They were devoured across the spectrum, hidden under covers and in cupboards by businessmen and underage revolutionaries alike.

I couldn't think of anything more to add to our literary exchange. Embarrassed and giggling, I ran outside. *Her writing?* Her *writing?* Andy taunted me all the way home on the train.

I don't know if Mr. McKay ever read *On the Road* or *Valley of the Dolls*. I may have greatly underestimated him. I do know that I eventually came to love *Middlemarch*. I came to love everything George Eliot wrote, and for many reasons, not the least of which is because, in the miracle of her humane, capacious prose, there is room for everyone, even a New Critic.

Sex in the Age of Aquarius

1968

Members of the Youth International Party, or Yippies, had first imagined their "Festival of Life" as a counterculture alternative to the 1968 Democratic Convention in Chicago. It was to be a utopia, in direct opposition to the corrupt and deadening values represented by the wartorn Democrats. The festival was announced, then canceled in the wake of Robert Kennedy's assassination, and then revived. Although at first it had seemed that thousands upon thousands of young people would converge in Chicago, only a few thousand actually turned up, my brothers among them. It was an excruciating time to be a little sister.

Didn't I have the same depth of courage, the same political expertise, the same sense of outrage and passion as my older brothers? My father may have been sympathetic, but he categorically refused to let me go. He seemed to think it was sufficient to remind me that I was not yet sixteen. My oldest brother, Bob, would be hitchhiking from West Virginia, where he was finishing a year as a VISTA volunteer. Ricky worked the first part of the summer in the Catskills as a waiter at Ruben's Maple View Hotel, the same resort we had visited as a family every summer when my mother was alive. I begged my brothers to intercede for me, but in the end I had to settle for watching the convention debacle on television with the rest of the world.

Ricky stopped in Massapequa on his way to the convention and regaled us with true stories about the prodigious appetites of the diners at Ruben's (where the all-you-can-eat guarantee was part of the deal). Almost every day he was amazed by a new record in gluttony. It was nothing for a guy in plaid Bermuda shorts and a pork pie hat to eat thirty blintzes at a sitting. The waiters would carry out buckets of sour cream, vats of borscht, hampers of potato pancakes, casks of applesauce, barrels of kosher dills and pickled beets; trenchers of poppy seed, sesame seed, and kaiser rolls; rye bread, challah—and all that was prologue. After a long day playing mah-jongg and pinochle in the hot sun, dinner customers would order two or three main courses at a time: roast chicken, stuffed veal, brisket, flanken. You wouldn't think there'd be that much boiled beef in the world. A waiter would race out with two hot mains with silver covers, three sides, a monkey dish, and a gravy boat, drop them on a table, then scurry back for the next person's order. It was like serving a hundred Paul Bunyans. In the kitchen they were always making bets on who could eat the most kishke, kugel, carrot tzimmes. Every table had its regulars—for instance, "the newlyweds" were famous for eating nine times a day. They'd wait outside the dining room door for the first seating every morning, eat through all three breakfast shifts ("I think I'll have some herring, pickled herring, matjes herring, creamed herring, a little lox maybe and cream cheese and farmer's cheese . . ."), and then be back waiting for the door to open for their first lunch. There were frequent moments that defied even the jaded credulity of the second-generation college student staff. Why, for example, would anyone *choose* to gorge on schav soup? Schav, perhaps more than the rest of Ruben's earthy menu, could never disguise its peasant origins. Devised to sustain a shtetl resident through the poorest times, it is made of water and grazing grass, and that's how it tastes. Anyone who consumed multiple servings of it could inspire the entire staff with awe.

Before June, Bob had favored Kennedy. In Chicago, he camped with the Yippie forces in Grant Park. It wasn't until he arrived that he learned Mayor Richard Daley had refused to issue a permit for the festival, or allow protesters to sleep in the park. Daley's refusal seemed to my brother an insult to his right to dissent. There was also an incredible party going on. Hippies and yippies (and "flippies," as Daley called them) were up all night—some getting high, some fucking, some talking political revolution.

Ricky, a devoted follower of Eugene McCarthy, worked for his candidate first in a campaign storefront, then at a table in the lobby of the Drake Hotel. While Humphrey and Muskie were being nominated, Ricky was in the hall wearing borrowed credentials. Bob was teargassed outside on Michigan Avenue in the violent skirmishes that the Walker Study Team would later call a "police riot." As word sifted through the convention about Daley's police going berserk outside, his plainclothes goons bashed resistant delegates and nosy press members inside.

Some observers have commented that "Boss" Daley was as clever at manipulating the television audience as his Yippie opposition. What better way to hammer home your superiority and invulnerability than to demonstrate utter contempt and fearlessness in the face of who-knew-how-many millions? What the hell could they do, on the other side of the screen? He was the duly elected mayor of his great city, and no technological advances tethered him. Let the viewing audience call Daley's face, frosted eyes, and red, rubbery jowls an icon of megalomania. (Norman Mailer wrote that he looked like a "vastly robust old peasant woman with a dirty gray silk wig.") In Chicago, the convention hall became a battle for Daley democracy—the hell with the cameras that showed the world Daley brutality.

Bob marched in the candlelight protest that followed. This was a solemn memorial to the hope that the Democrats would be able to end the war (or ever defeat Nixon). I remember watching it with my father and Ann, all of us outraged, searching the screen for my brothers' faces. Television mediates and mitigates. Although outraged, Steve and Ann feared for my brothers' safety. While outraged, I was also entertained on some level and on the edge of my seat waiting for the "There they are!" kind of thrill.

I was, in those days, fascinated by accidents of time and character. That night, I wondered in my diary: "What if Joan of Arc or Antigone had been on the scene?" The subtext (though still unarticulated out of residual insecurity or girlish modesty) was another question entirely: How would it have been different if I'd been there?

I asked a variation of the same question a few months later after a concert by the protest singer Phil Ochs. "And there but for fortune may go you or I," he'd sung in my general direction. After the concert, I'd wanted to follow him home. I'd wanted to surrender myself: virgin, freedom fighter, fan (if someone had mentioned Tim Lowenthal I probably would have said Tim Who?). But I couldn't even move my arm to touch him when he exited through the audience. *"How would my life have been different if I'd stepped in his way?"* I wrote.

I haven't heard much on the subject of *the moment* when a girl first feels free to open her body to a lover. I don't mean when she first makes love, but when she first *feels* that she's desirable. I suppose it typically happens close-up, under a tree, behind the house, perhaps you see yourself in your sweetheart's eyes. But music woke me—Ochs's poetic pleading preacher's tenor. I thought about that nine years later when he committed suicide. I knew more about men and women then, and I was glad that I'd resisted (although it's possible that I'd have been just as glad if I hadn't resisted. That would have been the reality, and I might have spent months rebounding from his indifference or rejection or abandonment or—in another scenario—monumental devotion). In any case, by the time Phil Ochs killed himself, I wasn't listening to him much anymore, and when I did, I thought the voice that had sounded like a prayer sounded more like a whine—or a warning to the woman who loved him that she'd never have her own life. That kind of Jane Eyre passion is fine for first love, but you realize later that there has to be somewhere you can go to block out Rochester's voice calling you back across the moors through eternity.

. . .

Watching the convention fueled my passion to be at the center of things. After their experience, however, both my brothers felt more ambivalence. After having seen the assassination of his candidate over and over in graphic detail, and experienced his right to legal dissent defied by gas and violence, Bob finished his stint in VISTA and then returned to college in upstate New York. The war was not likely to end anytime soon, and for Bob (as for many others who opposed the war), a student deferment still offered the best protection against Vietnam, jail, or exile. That autumn Ricky was a senior in college in Pennsylvania. In September, when then vice presidential candidate Senator Muskie gave a stump speech there, my brother rose to heckle him and made front-page news.

It was because he cut Spanish, he said later. He hadn't cut because he'd necessarily wanted to go to the rally, but since he had cut, he thought he might as well go. The protest was of the same sort Muskie had been experiencing all along the campaign trail. Muskie would begin his speech and those people who supported his Vietnam policy would applaud and shout approval ("Give 'em hell, Senator!"), while those in opposition would boo and heckle and chant, "Stop the war in Vietnam!" There was often a thicket of scolding McCarthy signs (for the senator now out of contention), and always plenty of Wallace for President placards from his faction.

The rally, on the steps of the Washington County courthouse, consisted of about 1,200 people. It was a college town, so the protesters' ranks—usually composed of hippies, retirees, and mothers with small children—were swelled with students and teachers. Muskie addressed the audience as he always did, and his speech was interrupted as it always was. But on this occasion, when the "Stop the war" chant (which must even have drilled into his sleep) began, Muskie chose to invite a representative of the opposition up on the platform to articulate its position. This was a startling innovation in that wretched campaign and earned Muskie credit. Whatever the heckler would say, the senator had shown himself to be a reasonable man.

"Let one of your number come up here," Muskie intoned grandly. "I'll give him ten minutes of uninterrupted time."

How my brother Rick was chosen remains a question. He had the conviction, but it was for his attitude, his mouth, that his friends pushed him forward. He climbed the platform to boos and bravos, and stood amid the potbellied Democratic hacks whose looks, if looks could kill, would have broiled him. What must they have been thinking? There was a lot at stake for them when Muskie played this wild card, my brother.

Nick Thimmesch, a *Long Island Newsday* reporter on the scene, described Ricky as "a lad wearing an Army shirt, levis, sandals, a peace medallion, a large quantity of hair, horn-rimmed glasses and sideburns." Muskie asked the crowd to listen, as Ricky improvised the following speech:

> "Everybody calls us dirty and unwashed, but we are the true Americans. We love the flag as much as anyone else. We want America to stand for what the Constitution stands for . . . everyone equal under the law, which is not true in this country . . . I am out in the streets because no one listened to us at Chicago, where Senator McCarthy showed through primaries that seventy percent of the American Democratic Party was dissatisfied with President Lyndon Baines Johnson's stand on Vietnam and domestic issues. We are here as Americans, not as commie pinkoes or whatever you think just because we have long hair . . . All three presidential candidates talk about law and order, but who speaks about justice? For too long the American public has sat around dissatisfied, keeping quiet . . . protecting the status quo. It is time things changed. None of these candidates is the answer. Only vote for candidates who oppose the war!"

When Ricky finished there was fierce applause from his friends, some polite claps from the mainstreamers, and of course furious heckling from the Wallace ranks, which Muskie tried to quiet by waves and imperious looks (but he had no influence there). Returning the platform to the candidate, Ricky said, "Since he did give us a chance to express our views, I, for one, will keep my cool while he expresses his, whatever they are."

Afterward, in interviews with just about every national news agency, my brother repeatedly confessed surprise at Muskie's action. "If politicians were less afraid of the views held by voters in their own party, there'd be less protest. I'm not a radical. I'm a registered Democrat," Ricky said.

On Walter Cronkite and every other news show that night we saw Ricky punching the air with his lit cigarette. He seemed innocent and insolent and his extemporizing stunned us. Was that our Ricky towered over by the incredibly tall senator from Maine? Nobody we knew had ever been on television before. Steve and Ann's chief concern seemed to be their son's disheveled appearance, but he really looked just like most college boys his age. You could hardly call his hair long. He wasn't even wearing wire rims.

"Youse guys call us dirty and unwashed," we teased him on the telephone that night, employing the Bronx dialect of our father's youth.

Ricky told me later that he'd directed the "dirty and unwashed" part of his speech to the right-wing Wallace supporters massed in front of the platform. But in that impromptu topic sentence he addressed the issues that were polarizing families across the country. The way it appeared then, from my side of the generation gap, parents of every persuasion were saying: clean up your act from the outside in ("Take a bath. Comb your hair. Change your clothes! What is this—a cat fur cape? Feathers from stinking birds dead a hundred years!"). Children were telling their parents to clean up from the inside out ("It's because of your silent complicity that the body politic is rotting!").

Whatever Ricky said about justice and war and politics, his *presence* as a longhair picked out of a crowd, disputing policies with passion (if not, as he insisted, the eloquence that comes with greater preparation), gave heart to the idea that our sartorial rebellion wasn't mindless or careless. Within a few years, manipulating the media would be an art form, and you'd see plenty of counterculture types on TV all the time, but in that election season it was still rare to see and *hear* on national television someone who looked even a little like a hippie.

"We are the true Americans," he had said. A patriot can love his flag and still dissent. A patriot wasn't blind to his country's dishonor or his neighbor's suffering. He offers remedies. "All three candidates talk about law and order, but who speaks about justice?"

Courageous liberals like Rick and Bob were at the heart of the protest movement. They believed in the perfectibility of the state as it was originally conceived. Their effort was to reform a system whose central principles of liberty and justice for all had foundered along the way. I approved of the principles, but, in reality—the *state* concept stymied me. The phrase "true American" was being claimed all over the political spectrum. And since I hadn't seen any compelling evidence to choose nationalism over internationalism, I preferred to call myself a citizen of the world. My brother was proud to be a Democrat. Merle Haggard was proud to be "an Okie from Muskogee." I was a pinko from Massapequo.

Adults and the uninitiated were unable to see the nuances emerging month by month as the youth culture developed. It was still unusual to see a man with really long hair in 1968. Really long hair signified a committed outsider who had stopped his haircuts ahead of the trend. Someone who had endured the taunts and sarcasm and physical violence that the straight world threatened seemed heroic to us. Someone who was taking a lot of acid was also esteemed in our new hierarchy, a pioneer.

.   .   .

Whenever a set of parents was gone for the night, we'd hold a pot party. In November, my own parents left for the weekend and took Edward along. By eight o'clock Friday night our house had filled with smoke, Massapequa's burgeoning hippie population, and enough LSD for an army.

I'd only taken acid once before, when my friend Jana had halved a tab of Yellow Sunshine with me. We'd spent that afternoon grinning wildly and occasionally starting sentences that we never finished. My early visions were pastoral, a wonderful efflorescence of ivory and rose and azure (like a rococo painting of French aristo-shepherds). Toward the end of our trip, as the imagery started to fade, we philosophized about the presence of God and the future of humanity. We'd had similar conversations before, but that day (to our own astonishment) we could both articulate our ideas in the minutest detail. I spent my last hour watching a wavy maze in my mind dissolve into a transparent web, then plink! It was gone and I was left, flushed with well-being and enormously hungry.

Not this time. As I dropped the tab presented to me by my classmate, Fred Flicker, I suppose I was expecting a trip as lovely and illuminating as the first. But I hadn't factored in the steady stream of strangers in my house, or Flicker's libido.

Flicker was a petulant boy, prone to mischief and sudden attacks of the giggles. He and I had gone from eyeing each other to a flirtation that had reached its first plateau. I wasn't in any rush to progress further. A lot of people were tripping that day, and I had no intention of pairing off with Flicker. But he stayed near. "Are you coming on yet?" he kept asking. "Are you getting off?" When I finally started to take off, he let me in on his secret. "The tab you took? It's not LSD . . . it's STP."

STP was reputed to be many times the strength of a regular trip. There was no love or one-world hippie-dippie flower thing about it. It was a *biker* drug for macho guys who wanted to test the limits of their sanity. I hardly had time to ponder the consequences of having been dosed or taking a bad drug before my brain started filling up with an electric scarlet presence. "My brain is filled with blood," I complained to Jana.

"Of course your brain is filled with blood," she said, thinking she was offering consolation. "You're right!"

But everything was too vivid, too sinuous, and too red for hours. I couldn't think. I would find a thread of thought and it would be obliterated by a curtain of hot red wool, or an overturned hamper of red scarves (they looked like snakes but I knew, *I knew,* I didn't have snakes in my head). "Scarves, not snakes! Scarves, not snakes," I told everyone within hearing.

"It'll pass," Jana said. "You're having a bad trip."

I crouched upstairs in the bathroom alone for hours until the red throbbing slowed. When I could finally face myself in the mirror I saw a red leering devil with fire over his head at my shoulder. I had no fear of Satan in the religious sense. I wasn't afraid for my soul. I was afraid because I couldn't speak to defend myself, and I couldn't think what to do because the speed in the STP was racing through my mind in thousands of random letters and unformed words. The devil put his arms around me.

"Let Flicker take care of her. He's tripping, too," someone decided.

It must have looked as if I was in Flicker's arms by choice. I'd only buried my face in his chest so that I wouldn't have to see his beast face. Strangers tucked us into my bed together like some carnival travesty of a wedding night. No wedding, though, no night, and no consummation. STP was as disappointing for him as it was for me. I was a fetus with rigor mortis. He was a flaccid devil.

That was my only bad trip. Just as the Yellow Sunshine had heightened my senses, then left me feeling full of goodwill and love, the STP had discouraged me, plunged me into despair and left me angry (but also weirdly triumphant). On acid, pettiness falls away. You come face-to-face with universal virtues and villanies. I've always been glad that I tripped before I was twenty, while I was still deeply impressionable. Afterward, hallucinogens became entertainment; but before twenty, a kid on a vision quest could be tested, exalted, anointed.

Woodstock, Here I Come

1969

"F-U-C-K. What's that spell?" Country Joe McDonald sang out.
"FUCK!"
"What's that spell?"
"FUCK!"
"What's that spell?"
"FUCK!"

Fuck the war. Fuck the system. Fuck fear. Fuck repression. Fuck the old men who make death their business, who legalize murder but not the word *fuck*. One word simultaneously encapsulated all our desire and all our complaints. Our "great refusal," as Marcuse called it, was also a rapturous, burning embrace.

> Come on all of you big strong men,
> Uncle Sam needs your help again;
> He's got himself in a terrible jam,
> Way down yonder in Vietnam;
> So put down your books and pick up a gun,
> We're gonna have a whole lot of fun.

Andy Schubert and I had gone to a Schaefer ("when you're having more than one") beer summer concert in Central Park. By the second chorus, we were dancing on our chairs, our two-fingered peace signs undulating, marijuana smoke spreading over the amphitheater like the blue dome of a mosque. The fragile peace I perceived among concert-goers might have been hard to sustain in such a charged atmosphere, but an old couple smiling benevolently nearby convinced me the whole world had transcended. (Perhaps they did agree with the song's sentiment, or just liked Country Joe's good humor, or perhaps this was part and parcel of their night out in ever-surprising New York.) I think the sensation I felt in that place must have been what an intoxicated fellow-traveling playgoer felt watching Clifford Odets's *Waiting for*

Lefty. In 1939 the audience chanted "Strike, strike, strike!" In 1969, on that hot August night, there was no doubt that we could turn things around, no doubt that we were that powerful. The act was *love,* and the word was *fuck.*

.   .   .

Not long ago I received a letter from my old friend Jana inviting me to a party over an August weekend, celebrating her graduation from nursing school. There is something about Jana's modesty and humor that has always reminded me of J. D. Salinger's Franny, stemming either from her searching nature or the fact that I spent so many hours in her family's home immersed in the Salinger oeuvre. I remember at sixteen being up in Jana's room reading "For Esmé—with Love and Squalor" (which begins when a young man receives a "letter from his past"), thinking: someday I'll get a letter from my past. Someday I'll have a past.

I wasn't getting along with my stepmother at the time, and Jana had the mother I wanted. She was a Communist, or at least an engaged leftist (which in my eyes made her both romantic and infallible). She would take Jana out of school to attend important protest demonstrations, and I would cut classes to march alongside.

Looking at pictures of myself and Jana taken in 1969, the year of our closest friendship, two questions arise: Why didn't I ever smile? And, if I'd had a more flattering hairdo, would my life be different today? I was, given my disposition, more suited to Mao's Red Guards than sunny, hippie flights of fancy. I was angry, intolerant, and brash, and my theme song was "I Am a Rock." I wrote furious political poetry about the injustice of the war against the Vietnamese and my frustrated desire to sleep with the dead Irish poet William Butler Yeats.

In contrast, Jana loved to laugh. She had honey-gold hair and a witchy cackle that attracted attention from boys. Jana also shared my affection for Salinger, but she was more an *In Watermelon Sugar* girl. Both of us were little sisters with two elder brothers; and we'd both grown up in unobservant Jewish families—the products, we maintained, of bizarre parental behavior (nobody but my father collected drugstore steel turnracks on which to display his paperbacks; nobody but her mother thought *Long Island Newsday* was full of capitalist propaganda). In 1969, I was sixteen and Woodstock was on the horizon. Jana and I agreed there'd be no better time or place to begin acquiring a past, which we would, like Salinger's Esmé and her soldier, someday recall together.

The advent of Woodstock marked a coming of age for little sister-hood. None of our brothers was able to go for various reasons. This would be our experience, unmediated and unchaperoned.

> That old system is dying all around us and we joyously come out in the streets to dance on its grave. With our free stores, liberated buildings, communes, people's parks, dope, free bodies and our music, we'll build our society in the vacant lots of the old—and we'll do it by any means necessary.

In an essay written for the original Woodstock program, Abbie Hoffman articulated a vision of the utopia that beckoned. Everyone I knew *wanted* to go to Woodstock. But in our crowd only Andy Schubert, Jana, and I were able to get our more open-minded parents' consent.

I told Steve and Ann that I'd be camping out in the Catskills. They certainly couldn't object to a party in the mountains—not when they had spent so many weekends of their own youth courting at Catskill camps and resorts. That's what their old photos showed: boys in swimming trunks pointing to the muscles in their arms; yawning bathing beauties, stretching out their painted toes. In long wooden barracks they'd eaten blintzes and roast chicken and argued passionately about free will versus determinism, business, and socialism. At night they danced to four-piece bands and listened to nasty comics. That's what the Catskills were for: music, entertainment. I was sixteen. I promised not to go alone. Well, all right, they said . . . I was lucky. Even if they suspected Woodstock would be more like the early days of the French Revolution than a campers' jamboree, they gave their consent. Their only condition was that I pay my own way.

I found a job in a Hempstead shirt factory. And beginning that June I spent hour after endless hour folding and buttoning, buttoning and folding, folding and forgetting to button; taking longer and longer bathroom breaks.

·   ·   ·

That same month in Chicago, SDS was holding its national convention. The organization at that point had become so widespread that fifteen hundred delegates represented more than 75,000 or so members. By the time the conference ended SDS had splintered over the movement's direction. Members of the "Trotskyist" Progressive Labor Party, who wanted to organize in factories, clashed with the "Maoist" Revolutionary Youth Movement and the newly minted, eight-hundred-member Weatherman faction. When the Weathermen—determined to treat "youth" as a class and utopian youth culture as the vanguard of the coming revolution—walked out of SDS, they left the New Left behind looking old.

I read everything I could about the conference. I knew about every splinter group, denouncement, and counteraccusation that the underground press reported. I was working in a factory myself, but there was no contest for my allegiance. The Trotskyites seemed too sober, and the Maoists too incoherent compared to the fleet and giddy Weathermen. Besides, somebody who knew somebody told me Tim Lowenthal had sided with the Weathermen.

In the shirt factory, I buttoned and folded. My coworkers were mostly women of Italian or Irish descent. Many had been there for decades. Most were married. Some had children my age. All of them seemed able to button and fold behind their backs with their eyes closed. The Jimi Hendrixes of the garment trade. They gave me a few days' grace before complaining: my clumsiness slowed their line, my absences threw them off. I would have walked out like the Weathermen if I hadn't had Woodstock in the distance—and Peggy Doyle to my immediate left. Mrs. Doyle, who had half-inch calluses on her own flying fingers, helped me settle in to the factory's fugue state of mindless repetition. She'd noticed I was trying to vary my buttoning and folding in order to keep interested. That was impossible, she explained. You had to yield to the line. "Do the same thing every time with every shirt or you'll never last," she instructed. After ten years the shirts Mrs. Doyle folded were immaterial. What mattered to her were the slight nuances of behavior she spied in her fellow workers.

"You see that Florence Grizzetti. You see her hair? The money she spends on her hair could buy cigarettes for every person here for a week," Mrs. Doyle said.

This Florence Grizzetti worked at the end of the line, an infinitely desirable position near an open window where the rare breeze entered between iron grills. In the searing summer light, her beehive looked golden as baroque trimming.

"And that Joseph Pelligrino's just as bad. Better not talk to that

Joseph Pelligrino. Why do you think they get to work by the window? Him and her?"

I kept buttoning, my eyes on the shirts.

"The mob," Peggy whispered. "The way she carries on. With that Joseph Pelligrino, too, half her age."

Peggy's son had been killed in Vietnam. I never heard her complain about war protesters, but she blamed the Mafia constantly. "They all got deferments," she'd shout. "Because they're in prison. I don't care who hears me."

Joey was one of the floor boys who delivered our shirts on hangers and then carted off our packed boxes. He had long black hair that fell in his eyes and wore T-shirts with the names of bands like Cream or the Who. Like Peggy Doyle, he always wore a tiny American flag pin. We hadn't talked yet, but once in a while he'd catch me looking and wink (or wince, if he happened to catch Mrs. Doyle in midtirade).

When I first described Joey to Jana, she asked if he was a "freak." She meant freak, as in hippie outsider, a comrade. I couldn't say exactly. He and I hadn't exchanged a word yet, and I couldn't label him according to my experience. I was positive he turned on, so that made him a "head," and from the names of the bands advertised on his shirts, I assumed he listened to good music. He wasn't "straight," not with that hair. He wasn't exactly a "greaser." And I wasn't sure whether he was a "jock." (If this had been ten years later I'd have called him a Reagan Democrat.)

"He wears an American flag pin," I told Jana at last. That clinched it. She didn't think Joey and I had much of a future together. Although flag pins had been worn all along by the friends and relatives of troops in Vietnam, they were becoming more and more a sign of their wearer's direct opposition to the peace movement and the counterculture. Suddenly, only hawks were certified patriots.

In the few months since his inauguration, Nixon had moved deliberately toward polarizing the country. The goal of his divide-and-rule strategy was to marginalize the antiwar movement, isolate it from mainstream public opinion. He'd helped transform the cultural and generational gap that was being argued about around kitchen tables into a national crisis. Although a Harris poll showed 60 percent of the public favored withdrawal from Vietnam, Nixon gave speeches asserting that the antiwar movement was the work of a minority trying to con the silent and, by implication, approving majority. His administration's massive campaign of surveillance, harassment, and provocation helped fragment the movement and certainly raised our paranoia. (One consequence of this campaign was that J. Edgar Hoover declared that the Black Panther Party had replaced the Communist Party, which had replaced John Dillinger, as Public Enemy Number One.) Perhaps old political hands will say Nixon's fury was practical, that it fueled his power, and that it is naive to ignore how successfully his intransigence played to a population nostalgic for the paternal whip. But from here his behavior seems less like a statesman's and more like a combination of prissy Mrs. Baton and vulgar Archie Bunker. He was supposed to be the adult in the body politic. Instead, he taunted us like a desperate schoolyard bully.

·   ·   ·

At noon every day all the factory workers would rush outside into the treeless industrial park and picnic near mounds of sand and stranded forklifts. Florence and Joey would usually eat together. I'd sit alone on the steps and read. Florence had a habit of nibbling her Wonder Bread sandwich with two hands. She looked like a clean white chipmunk with a golden head. After lunch, she'd pull out a compact and whiten her lips.

One day as they passed Joey finally stopped to talk to me.

"You see them walk on the moon?" he rasped, gangster-like.

"Yeah."

He nodded and kept on walking. Florence gave him a poke with a silvery fingertip.

·   ·   ·

"This guy she's in love with supports the war," Jana teased, as we crammed into Todd Lombardi's old sports car. "That makes *her* a collaborator."

In love. It was true. The living, breathing Joey Pelligrino had supplanted the mythic Tim Lowenthal, Phil Ochs, and William Butler Yeats in my sexual imagination. I was still unrequitedly in love a week after I'd left my job at the Hempstead shirt factory.

Todd nodded, not really following Jana's drift. And why should he, with so much else to absorb? The day had arrived, we were on our way to Woodstock, clutching our tickets like talismans.

There was just too much going on for anyone to absorb it all. We weren't in a traffic jam on the New York State Thruway, we were in a magnificent procession, slowed to a stately pace, and everywhere hung banners and signs of the great crusade. The road was thick with Volkswagens, carrying pilgrims in the tie-dyed raiment of our caste. At every ramp hitchhikers thrust up their arms in the two-fingered peace salute. Car horns pealed endlessly.

"What's a collaborator?" Todd asked deep into the afternoon. He was slower and one of the boys Jana drew. Neat and compact in his blue jeans and blue denim shirt, Todd had a mother who would iron anything for him at any time of day. He was quiet, too, and people, mistaking him for a listener, confided in him. As it turned out, Todd was a listener but not a comprehender. He would sift things through and then recklessly disclose a confidence. He always had cigarettes, though, and he was generous.

Maybe two hours of slow driving in a jam could dull the awe in other circumstances, but out there, spread in every direction, was a sea of euphoria. Many times passengers and drivers in cars alongside gave us hash brownies, wine, joints. The great roads, like everything else that weekend, had passed to us.

At first we walked three abreast, like the Earp brothers, down the muddy road, until Todd paused to engage a drug peddler in a comparative study of their merchandise. This was not the smart, bejeweled sales manager of a future generation, but a fellow in the pushcart line—an independent, before mergers and diversification; bright eyed, devoted to safety and efficacy, unambitious, fulfilling an apparently endless need. We'd all dropped some acid, and it wasn't long before Jana and I grew impatient with Todd's wrangling and left him there, where, as it turned out, he would purchase some quaaludes and sleep through the remainder of the Woodstock weekend. There was just too much else there to interest us, too many different types of people, to waste time with anyone you already knew. Soon Jana and I separated, too. We waved good-bye amid the milling hordes, neither of us in her right mind. Jana found shelter that night in the Hare Krishna tent. (Two years later she'd join a Krishna commune and live with them for a decade.)

. . .

Here's my confession: I didn't make it to the music until the end. Three days of love, peace, and especially music, and I almost didn't see a single band. The grandstand was in a valley surrounded by hills. The musicians were tiny and indescribable, but their voices were the soundtrack to our narrative. There was no way to get close to the stage; every nearby acre was claimed and congested. And every surrounding hill was covered by the swarming, multifarious, inexhaustible throng. I walked around a cottage made of umbrellas, watched a woman fan pot smoke away from her baby's shrieking face. A water seller in a dhoti offered me a wooden bucket from which to sip. Beside him worked an acid salesman, also dressed simply—tie, bowler hat, no pants. On that first night, I tasted organic food for the first time (courtesy of the Hog Farm cooks, who lived in a school bus). *Organic* was a new word. Woodstock was a new world—soaked in, saturated with, absolutely reeking of desire—and everywhere on the ground, in the woods, in ponds, in tents, couples were coupling. It was strange and pagan and biblical and beautiful and contagious. The whole place was like an enchanted Shakespearean forest, and, as occurs in comedies about such places, among the whole half a million celebrants, I happened upon Joey Pelligrino. "You're tripping. By *yourself*? You're *tripping* with strangers?" he asked. "Jesus, what'm I gonna do with you? Why would a girl like you take acid in a strange place?"

I couldn't remember, but I was glad to be shepherded, and I was glad to see Joey, at least as far as I could see him, through the grid of stars LSD had etched on his face.

"I've got to get you someplace safe," he said, taking me by the hand. "There's too many people. You'll freak."

We joined the ragged column marching toward the music. And after a while, in the same enchanted way that Joey had risen out of the chaos, we arrived at a lone, abandoned car miles from the parking lot, stuck in the mud, an island dividing the company of tens of thousands. Joey pulled me in beside him, rolled up the windows, and locked the doors.

As the sky darkened and it started to pour, we watched thousands of naked people pass. On one flank I saw a line of what looked like Eastern European refugees in shawls and babushkas. On the other, a squad of garlanded cupids (a kindergarten class?) playing kazoos. We saw a mud-pie party where all the food was worn and the shaggy guests shambled into the future on a blue-lit time line. Joey was on speed. "Enough for a thousand years," he said, shaking a film can so that

I could hear the rattle of his pills inside. He let me know what consternation I'd caused at the factory—and was quick to inform me about his relationship with Florence Grizzetti. "You didn't think we were getting it on, did you? Listening to Peggy Doyle you'd think we were balling every day. Like, we're really gonna get it on with Florence engaged to Nicky Corleone."

The mob, I thought, and tried to sit up.

"Don't move, you'll hurt yourself." He stroked my hair and neck, and put a cold hand under my blouse.

"Everybody thought Florence would marry Patrick Doyle, you know, Peggy's son, but Nicky Corleone was crazy about her. I never saw anybody crazy for a chick as Nicky Corleone. He was like out of his mind. Like Florence was this queen. He used to follow her to work with flowers. At lunchtime he'd show up with a hot lunch he'd cooked. Like veal and peppers. I don't know why. She likes a sandwich for lunch, Florence."

I remembered the little white-and-gold Florence chipmunk nibbling her sandwich in the heat-blasted park.

"Everybody knew she'd never leave Patrick Doyle, but then Patrick gets drafted, goes to Vietnam, and POW! he's dead. Nicky can't get drafted 'cause of his felony record."

"Poor Mrs. Doyle."

"Yeah, poor Mrs. Doyle, poor Florence, poor Patrick."

"What a waste."

"Yeah, how you feelin'?"

Fully dressed, we kissed and squirmed on the backseat. But it would have taken a couple with a stronger strain of exhibitionism to consummate their tryst on such a public stage. Speed is a mind, not a body, drug. Joey's hands were icy, and he kept jumping up to curse the celebrants outside as they filed past.

"Poor Florence," I said.

"Don't think of Florence now."

"Poor Mrs. Doyle."

"Right." He sat up. "You want some speed?"

Lying in the car in Joey's frozen embrace had been like practicing sex, practicing losing my virginity. It was an interesting exercise, but by sunset I was finding the car a little claustrophobic.

Joey groaned, "You're going out? With that, with them?"

To Joey "that" meant those weirdos and hippies. But to me it was *us* outside. If I was going to love anybody this weekend it was *that* and *them*. "Where'd I put my shoes?"

"Whad'd'ya wanna go out there for? It's wet. You didn't have any shoes when I found you."

Like he'd found me on the street somewhere. What Joey didn't get was that you didn't need shoes at Woodstock. He just sat there, tapping his fingers on his knee.

"You go out there, you're on your own. Most of them are naked. They're nuts! I bet you couldn't find five people here who understand the domino theory. Bleeding hearts, commie dupes."

This was the first time we'd ever discussed politics. I remembered Jana's dire prediction, and at first I thought, what a chance, what a golden opportunity to convert somebody. (Maybe, if I'd had the patience, if I'd been gentler, more rational.) But, at that moment, I couldn't believe Joey had come all that way, burrowed so far into the heart of Woodstock, and wouldn't get out of the car. "You're gonna sit here forever?" I asked.

"Maybe I will. Maybe I'll drive to the nearest recruitment office and volunteer. How 'bout that?"

"Warmonger!" I wanted to denounce him for bringing the war to utopia.

"Freak!" He pushed me out and locked himself inside who-knew-whose car, all alone, armed with enough drugs for a thousand years.

They Shoot Students, Don't They?

1970, Spring

"The staff concurs: Starting Sunday Oct. 5th, The Electric
Circus will admit girls without bras free every Sunday.
Nu? We've always had that rule."

Notice in the *New York Herald Tribune*

Whenever I could cadge the money, I'd catch a train to the city. By
that autumn the commercial merger between mainstream and counterculture music, film, and clothing seemed complete. Long hair and
peace signs no longer necessarily signified that someone was antiwar,
or even antiauthoritarian. Hippie had become the general style, and
the old, easy, superficial judgments based on hair and drug use were
meaningless. A growing polarization within the counterculture produced more hippies of the "Don't hassle" stripe, their philosophy as in-
flexible as that of any hawk or dove. The younger you were, the more
likely you were to straddle both hippie and radical camps. I often felt
too hippie with my politico friends and too political among the hippies. I was a half-and-half little sister, and as such, the only place for
me, I thought, was New York City, where distinctions were blurred by
sheer diversity and numbers.

That September I saw my first copy of the *New York Herald Tribune*
outside the New School for Social Research. Unaffiliated with the il-
lustrious daily of the same name, this *New York Herald Tribune* was a
high school underground. "They folded and we stole the name," the
kid hawking papers explained.

Nineteen sixty-nine was the peak year for the high school free
press. There had been five weekly high school undergrounds in 1967.
Two years later there were more than one hundred and fifty papers
reaching two million readers.

Some papers were pacifist, some cheerfully advertised for the revolution. Most, regardless of their political stand, belonged to the High
School Independent Press Service, which served as a clearinghouse and

wire service for left and counterculture news. As reporters, many high school radicals were often fearless about criticizing sacred cows on the right and the left. I think we took particular delight in reminding students just a bit older that their little sisters and brothers were a force to be reckoned with, that we were as impatient as we were radical.

The *New York Herald Tribune* was the witty and literate brainchild of two Stuyvesant High School seniors. Lionel, the son of limousine liberals, collected rock and roll trivia with the exuberance other boys devoted to baseball stats. His partner, Gerald, came from a second-generation Brooklyn Jewish home and wrote much of the political commentary in the paper, as well as many of its book and movie reviews. (The paper's standards were high: in September's issue you could read recommendations for Ishmael Reed's *Yellow Back Radio Broke-Down*, Susan Sontag's *Styles of Radical Will,* and Lawrence Durrell's *Spirit of Place.*) Gerald was full of puns and clever repartee that could scorch even if you were prepared. His newspaper personality seemed lifted from the play *The Front Page.* He was the only high school revolutionary I ever met who'd read the complete works of both Marcel Proust and H. L. Mencken (whose loathing of the booboisie he shared).

I had a crush on the brilliant Gerald, though from this distance, I know, it was less the man I desired than the intense intellectual tornado in which he dwelt. I gave him my poems to read and waited, puppylike, for his approval.

The paper's September cover showed a photo of a group of National Guardsmen in full riot gear, holding guns and wearing gas masks. They were surrounded by hand-drawn swastikas above a caption that read: "The Problem." On the back page, students with long hair carrying guns and guitars were pictured in silhouette over the caption: "The Solution." Perhaps it is unnecessary to add that as high school students we found such macho imagery exhilarating—a fantasy of power that made us equal to the grownups. And it was becoming easier and easier to equate Nixon's escalating persecution of opposition groups with an earlier crackdown in Germany. These swastikas, so casually drawn, were meant like most of the paper to *épater le bourgeois.*

When I first encountered the *Herald Tribune* staff, there was a slot open for a women's liberationist. Many of the women's movement's early successes were in the underground press, and the young men of the *Herald Tribune* were well aware that any up-to-date underground paper's revolutionary credentials required a visible on-staff feminist.

The woman who'd preceded me hadn't lasted long and had promptly entered the group mythology as an "ultrafeminist," a term used at the time to describe a woman who was not easily controlled, had no sense of humor, and was generally "uptight" (itself an invidious curse, and an undefendable one). On one of my first visits to the paper, as if to test my own humor quotient, Gerald regaled me with a comic description of a recent staff meeting held in the pink and frilly bedroom of the ultrafeminist's suburban home.

"Why's that funny?" I asked.

"You know, contrast," he explained patiently. The harder he tried to make me see the humor in the "you know, contrast," the more I pretended not to get it. I had a strong sense that if I laughed at my predecessor's expense these guys would never take my own feminism seriously.

Women's liberation had exploded so quickly and absorbed so much territory that men were getting vertigo. The old physical laws of space and time could seem suddenly altered. Women were growing over-night like Chia plants, and the "you know, contrast," could be hilarious. One story that made the rounds, a year or two later, was of the meeting held at an all-female revolutionary cell called the Madame Binh Collective. In the midst of planning the takeover of a major network television news show and arguing about whether or not to use guns, a mouse ran through the room. The women leaped on chairs and screamed—and those most in favor of guns screamed loudest.

At Plainedge I'd often planned and led our demonstrations. I gave myself to protesting the way other girls studied dance or music. The suburbs offered limited potential, so I looked to the city for broader range and wider employment of my talent. This was a time when great ideas and great rebellions were swarming in the air. I can't pinpoint the moment when I actually became a young feminist, but my own sense of possibility made the idea that all women should feel free seem per-fectly normal.

I knew, of course, that many women were discriminated against on account of their race and class. But it wasn't until I started attending city demonstrations more regularly that I came to hear how casually discrimination was woven into the way most people thought and acted every day. I remember being shocked to hear that according to con-ventional wisdom, women were considered less capable and generally less reliable than men. It was astounding to me to learn that some people thought abortion couldn't be sanctioned because a woman simply couldn't be responsible for her actions, that a woman shouldn't pilot commercial airplanes because her period would cause her to freak out, couldn't be president because on one day of menopausal instability she'd press the panic button and start a war. At every demonstration there were always counterprotesters arguing that women's bodies were their destiny, that their brains were naturally smaller than men's.

In those first few years of the women's liberation movement, we called each other Sister and nobody could pin us down. There were the titillating, widespread rumors that girls were being coerced to burn their bras, stop shaving their legs, charge into men's toilets, and reject chivalry forever. We didn't know why it mattered who opened the door for whom and made ourselves up as we went along. Army boots and jeans were de rigueur for the well-dressed young feminist that season. Consciousness-raising groups were for women old enough to have made mistakes. Some women were seduced by the macho adventurist, outlaw imagery. Some marched in minis and beehive hair. All the stereotypes of the bitter dyke or the ugly girl who couldn't get a date or the bluestocking or the Carrie Nation–type fanatic seemed corny and *dated*. The newer stereotypes, of the impassive amazon technocrats who'd stopped having children and earned more than men, were fascinating science fiction.

At a hint of feminist theory, the *Herald Tribune* boys would fall into line, but it was only for show. When I began working at the paper there were already three editors. Soon after, an art editor was added. I was the only woman and the only noneditor on staff. I wanted to be a reporter, but every article I handed in mysteriously disappeared. Six months passed. I was doing a lot of fetching and carrying, but had yet to see a word of mine in print.

In January, we moved our staff offices into an empty three-story building on Flatbush and Fourth Avenue in Brooklyn. The seriousness and privilege of so much space with only a couple of chairs, typewriters, and a layout table were intoxicating. I don't know how we found our way into such an impressive edifice. Its interior columns, scrolled cornices, and ornamental molding left no question that once it had been a bastion of real power. I suppose a staff member's father owned the building, or else knew the landlord (who didn't know kids used it while it was vacant). There were individual offices available for everyone, but no heat. Coming in on weekends to put out the monthly paper, we'd wrap up in coats and blankets and work by window light (no electricity, either) beneath the lobby's high-vaulted ceiling, amid the garbage pails that were always overflowing with cardboard and junk-food wrappers. The garbage went out when it defrosted in the spring. It all felt positively Bolshevik.

I didn't notice how often people made calculated moves to stake out their positions on even the smallest canvas. Behind the scenes, Lionel and Gerald were busy launching themselves into the adult world. In addition to their presence at movement events, as leaders of youth, they were regulars at record company cocktail parties and Andy Warhol demimonde happenings. They both considered themselves at once revolutionaries and entrepreneurial enfants terribles—nightmare little brothers, if you will. Gerald often told me he wanted to be a millionaire before he turned twenty-five. In fact, it took him just a little while longer. Like a number of other writers who began in the underground press, he went on to work for the large-circulation porno magazines. Later, he became the editor of a large-circulation, glossy drug magazine.

Over time, I came to realize why Gerald had delayed his literary verdict. He was more aware than I of the complexity and relative value of art and love. In my opinion my poems and articles were as good as or better than anything the paper had printed and deserved to be published. It seemed that simple, but Gerald didn't think so. He recognized our relationship for the delicately balanced psychosexual game that it was. I was still a virgin and had made no secret that I was looking forward to sloughing off what had come to seem like the burden of my innocence. I was willing to sleep with him, but not really disappointed when every plan we made was frustrated by lack of funds or cold weather or the lack of privacy in his family's small apartment. Gerald was available. He wanted me, but he was no Tim Lowenthal.

In retrospect, the relationship we attempted was a lot more like the commodity exchange of a political marriage than the casual "free love" that was in the air around us. Where was the sexual euphoria I'd encountered at Woodstock? Where, in my own life, was the equality between the sexes that I preached to others? *What* new world?

At some point Gerald's subtlety started to annoy me. Shading and nuance made me crazy with impatience. I wanted to blame my failure to be published entirely on male chauvinism, and threw myself into feminist doctrine with an intensity that surprised even my closest friends. They didn't mind the content of my lectures, but rolled their eyes at my new sanctimonious tone. "Don't say chick," I'd scold and wag my finger. "We're not baby birds, we're women." I didn't want to hear more rationalizations or take tiny steps anymore. I wanted to be swept away by faith and passion.

· · ·

On April 30, 1970, government leaks forced Nixon to admit the secret bombing of Laos and Cambodia. His lies were front-page news, and the country erupted in protest. On May 4, at the Kent State demonstration against the escalation of the war, four students were killed by National Guardsmen using live ammunition.

The demonstrations at Kent State had gone on for two days. Most of the student body had gone out on strike, and there were speeches and rallies and roving protests of varying degrees of violence. A few windows were broken in town, and someone set the ROTC headquarters on fire, but it's hard to see how any of these events qualified as a state emergency.

Ohio's governor at the time, James Rhodes, panicked by the disorder on campus, called out the National Guard. Did Rhodes imagine this show of power would so impress the demonstrators that they'd slink away? In a country raised on gun battles in the streets of Laredo, was he calling the movement out at high noon? Surely, he knew that whipping up the level of confrontation would trigger *some* reaction. In later accounts, it was noted that many students turned their opposition to the war into outrage against the Guard. It was galling for them to see the symbols of Nixon's lying government trespassing on their campus and threatening their legal right to dissent. But deep as their conviction ran and enraged as they felt, those students were no army; any intelligent eye could see that. Some of them taunted Guard members with jeers, others waved banners in the troops' faces. Somebody threw a rock, but there's no evidence that any Guard members were actually hurt. Most people just hung around, curious to see what would happen next, unified mostly by emotion. Would they have hung around if they'd known that Ohio allowed its Guardsmen to use live ammunition?

At Kent State, at noon, an officer, who claimed later that he'd feared for the Guardsmen's lives, ordered the soldiers to fire into the insolent, unarmed crowd. When the volley was over, unnamed Guardsmen had wounded eleven and murdered Jeffrey Glenn Miller, Sandra Lee Scheuer, Allison Krause, and Bill Schroeder.

Some of the victims had been committed to ending the war, but others weren't even involved in the protest. Their bloody entrails foretold the future. We had become two countries, divided not by ideas or place but, weirdly, by age. We were in the line of fire because we were young, and deluded boys our own age were being used as assassins. Worse than cannibalism, it was like a body devouring itself.

In the aftermath of Kent State, Nixon weighed in with a comment calculated to exacerbate the nation's sense of confusion and division. No one had his talent for pouring salt on a wound. He gave no comfort to the parents of the dead. Instead, by calling the murdered students "bums," he endorsed this extreme method of controlling dissent.

Ten days later, police in Mississippi opened fire on a women's dormitory on the Jackson State campus, killing two students and wounding twelve others. The lines that defined our opposing forces would never again be so clear to me. They were drawn by age and gender and race and ideology. Anyone who defied Nixon, who refused to submit, who fell outside the fantasy profile of the silent majority, was an enemy of the state.

Millions of people participated in the demos after Cambodia and the student murders. According to Kirkpatrick Sale, this was the largest strike action in U.S. history. "At least 350 institutions went out on strike, and 536 schools were shut down completely for some period of time, 51 of them for the [rest of the academic] year."

Many Plainedge students walked out for the day. Some joined the large Long Island demonstration in Old Westbury. Others took the train into New York to join the city strike. Along the Long Island Railroad, at every station platform, swarms of students in khaki coats and marching boots looked like an army assembling. I doubt that Penn Station had seen such displays of emotion since World War II. Almost every city public high school had walked out. The High School Student Union had set up a strike center at the New School for Social Research, where student organizers had been invited to camp for the duration. There were blankets and backpacks strewn in every direction, and hovering over everything the sweet, consoling scent of marijuana.

They'd used live ammunition. It hadn't really sunk in at first. In the beginning it had all been about the way they never stopped lying to us. They'd lie on television with a smile on their lips. They'd lie until they were forced to recant, and even then they'd squirm around. It felt degrading to have to accuse them all the time when it was so obvious that they always lied. Now they'd been caught, and it looked like they'd rather destroy their entire society, their own future, than admit they were wrong. What arrogance, we thought, what lethal arrogance.

At night the different offices and classrooms at the New School hummed with the sound of mimeograph machines and vending machines clanging, and kids' voices yelling in the kind of school corridors where they'd been trained to be quiet. Everyone was everybody's brother and everybody's sister in the subdued atmosphere of a late-night campfire. A kid strummed a guitar, another played a harmonica, and we sang folk ballads and protest anthems. Through the night girls and boys coupled off and thrashed around in available blankets. I was supposed to meet Gerald, but in the confusion we missed each other. A boy I'd just met and hootenannied with invited me to share his double sleeping bag. And in that eve-of-battle atmosphere, I thought, why not? If they use live ammunition tomorrow—I could die a virgin. There were no reports of live ammunition used during the Kent State protests in New York, but roaming gangs of construction workers deputized themselves to confront protesters wherever there was a demonstration. As a result there were a number of violent skirmishes. One of the leaders of the construction union was named Peter Brennan, and in appreciation of his union's vigilante efforts to control dissent in New York, President Nixon invited Brennan and some other men to the White House, where Brennan symbolically presented Nixon with a hard hat. Peter Brennan was from Massapequa, too.

· · ·

That spring I was accepted into Goddard College in Vermont, an experimental school that attracted artists and writers. Clearly, my writing wasn't going anywhere at the *Herald Tribune*. According to Lionel and Gerald, every one of my articles had been lost or was "still being read." As long as they doled out hope, they believed I'd continue to run mindless errands. I was furious with myself for sticking around. When I objected, I was told to start my own paper if I wanted things changed. Instead, I demanded that the paper publish an editorial I would write about the "contradictions" between what was touted and what I saw of the revolution.

In those early days, I really believed our success could be measured in euphoria. I didn't understand why undergrounds would want to resemble establishment papers. So, why did the *Herald Tribune* have a hierarchy instead of a collective? Why were there only men in positions of power? I took it all personally. "Why are they mean to me?" I asked my journal.

"AT THE HERALD TRIBUNE FOLKS, IT IS ALL END PRODUCT AND FUCK THE UNPAID LABOR." My editorial reads as if I wrote it in shock. It's also full of typos, misspellings, and errors in grammar. Gerald agreed to publish it, but he never said a word about editing:

> This is the *New York Herald Tribune*'s token women's article. Nothing else in this issue has been written by or for women . . . As the only woman on the staff I am writing this although I admit I volunteered and was not asked to. I WAS asked to do some telephoning while one of the men wrote an article discussing his male chauvinism (he was sure that would be enough).

In between the time I delivered the article and its publication, another young woman did come on staff. Judy Leonard joined the paper as a writer and photographer, and my colleagues inserted her first article, just opposite mine, making my editorial look embarrassingly dated.

Nevertheless, I was glad that Judy had joined the staff. She was also planning to start Goddard in the fall. I'd first met her a few weeks before when she was on her way home from a modeling audition wearing the black stockings, miniskirt, false eyelashes, and high heels that Madison Avenue expected of its teen queens. Judy was a blasé Brooklyn beauty, the same age as I, but with a much wider experience of the world. Her analysis of the gender wars at the *Herald Tribune* was astute. These were little boys used to getting their own way. You could run circles around them, as long as you kept your voice low and smiled. That was beyond me. Early on, I'd hoped to inspire Judy to abandon the sartorial symbols of her oppression, but she thought I was wasting my time with trivialities. What difference did it make whether she wore a miniskirt or farmers' overalls? They were both costumes. It was of much more importance to negotiate issues like bylines. From the start, Judy insisted that her name be listed on the paper's masthead, a request that it had never occurred to me to make.

Leaving Long Island

1970, Summer

Over breakfast at the diner one morning I told my father of my plan to leave Massapequa. Right after graduation I wanted to go up to Goddard to attend an alternative media conference. Afterward, I'd go out west for a while, before college. I tried to communicate the pull I felt to be on the road. I wasn't just leaving home, I said. I felt I was joining with, being absorbed into, *something*. I think I babbled a mile a minute about the "new world" and the future. He said he understood. The west was vast and open. He had gone to Montana when he was seventeen and remembered being in an army truck full of tough boys from the Bronx. They were forced to stop on a dark forest road nose to nose with a terrifying moose. He never forgot that moose, its size or roar.

That morning, in the cheerful mode he often enjoyed before a day of grappling with city traffic, my father offered me some puzzling advice. We were seated across a formica table in a booth covered with red Naugahyde. I was probably half asleep, draped in love beads and peace pendants. By then, he no longer mentioned things like the unwashed T-shirt I'd worn for a month straight, or my dirty neck or greasy hair. Was he worried about me? My sloppiness may have seemed insignificant compared to my abysmal grades, my hooky playing, my drug taking. He and Ann may have guessed, but they didn't ask.

I loved my father, but I couldn't see him clearly because my mother's ghost was always a screen between us. I'd belittle his tolerance, bridle at the hint of restraint. Juggling his new family, new home, and new job, he must have been as confused as I. In any case, he kept his troubles out of sight. He'd return from a day in his tow truck hauling cars between junkyards, and regain his equilibrium by reading a chapter or two of a novel set along the Silk Road or the Chisholm Trail or in an outer galaxy.

How did he look to me? His face was lined and weathered from jumping in and out of a truck in all seasons. His hands were brown and rough, and even though every night he'd plunge them into a toxic, goopy, pink cleanser that smelled like bubble gum, grease stains lodged in the ridges of his nails. He was my father, and to me he had no body. I couldn't imagine him suffering mortification or vulnerability or self-consciousness or any combination of delicate sensibilities. (But delicacy was so much a part of his nature. He was a tidy man who ate fastidiously, and the fastest way to incur his wrath was to swear or erupt in a vulgar sound.)

Now, here he was in the Hicksville Road diner with a secret to relate. "I think . . . ," he began.

He looked perfectly relaxed, leaning back with his arm stretched over the booth as if our sharing philosophical insights was an everyday thing. At first I expected some adult bromide—in one ear and out the other. But it was clear he wanted his next words to do more than hover and disappear like the smoke of our normal speech.

"I think," he sipped his coffee and bit delicately into a cheese Danish, "if it's not working out, it may not be what you want."

"Have something to fall back on," my aunt Gladys had suggested earlier. Her advice had been forthright and easy to resist. My father's words baffled me. Did he think he knew what I wanted? I decided this was his blessing: to do everything and try everything. A little later I thought maybe he'd really said: You don't have to keep banging your head against the wall once it starts to hurt.

If it's not working out, it may not be what you want.

. . .

In June, I set forth to attend the Alternative Media Conference at Goddard College. More than two thousand underground and alternative communicators in news, radio, film, art, video, and music (from filmmaker Robert Altman to Yippie Jerry Rubin) converged in fractious and free-form workshops like "Capitalism and the Alternative Media," "The Spiritual Responsibility of Media," and "Free Enterprise and the Cultural Revolution." My own memory and reconstruction of the event have been helped enormously by an article called "The Media Freaks Meet the Movement," which I long ago filed away in my red suitcase. It was published in July 1970 in *Rolling Stone* by an author with the nom de plume "The Black Shadow."

From the start, the entire conference was riven over ownership of the word *alternative*. Did its meaning extend to ventures in "hip capitalism," like the new "underground" format in FM radio? Weren't the "culture vultures" who were getting rich off the unfolding explosion in rock music undermining the meaning of *alternative?* Radio's claim to the word *underground* was considered by the radicals to be even more ludicrous. The conference was a strange microcosmic hothouse experiment in the elasticity of left dogma. The line was drawn at how subversive you were, how contemptuous of profit; and the line was always moving. In the first days, some participants tried to establish common ground and analyze what *alternative* meant, but rationality was not the conference's (or that spring's) strong suit. By the end of the weekend, almost every organization would be criticized, for flirting with mainstreamism, for male chauvinism, or both. Many of the workshops, including those concerned with issues of censorship, fragmented into arguments about sexism and profiteering. Even the Hog Farmers, who'd set up a camp similar to the one they'd erected at Woodstock (and who were said to be distributing pure Yellow Sunshine LSD), were suspected by some radicals of "working within the system." The weekend's essential word was *rip-off.* It was used to connote everything from the work of record producers (who ripped off the culture) to WBAI radio personality Bob Fass's macho domination (rip-off) of another workshop, which so enraged its participants that some of them pushed him down and carried him from the room. Later, the band Mighty Quick, seasoned in the Detroit scene's grand tradition of cock-rock, was accused of ripping off its audience by torturing them with horrendous music. As the audience yelled for them to leave the stage ("Off, Off, Off!"), Mighty Quick's lead singer willfully misinterpreted their demands and started to undress. But my favorite employment of the word that weekend comes directly from "The Black Shadow's" article:

> Someone came over with word that a bunch of videotape freaks had called for a fuck-in at a small lake on the upper campus so they could tape it. Movement sisters objected strongly, as did many of the men, on the basis that a fuck-in was cool, but a videotaped fuck-in was just another media rip-off, and exploited women as well. It was decided to confront the video freaks at the lake, and rip-off the fuck-in.

I was in paradise. Goddard, built in the middle of the woods, seemed like the perfect atmosphere for my poetic ambitions. I'd just escaped school, squeaking through my exams to graduate, so the conference's "formal" workshops held little interest. Instead, I hung around the college kitchen getting high with future classmates. When I wanted more excitement, I had only to lope over to the conference, where I would immediately find myself engaged in all the dialectics I could handle.

On Saturday, the last day of the conference, a rumor circulated that a woman had been raped the night before. Many of the conference's women participants met that morning to discuss what they'd heard. The woman was supposedly very young, maybe a student. Goddard College security had been called in, or maybe the police had been called. Nobody knew anything for sure. No one knew the victim's name or where she had gone—but there was a tremendous wave of emotion. Some movement women called an emergency meeting in which our testaments of rage and fear against rapists were extended to cover the sexist environment that bred them. In this state of whipped-up righteousness, my new sisters and I stormed into a workshop called "Cartoons and the Mass Consciousness." Its two featured speakers were no strangers to outraged feminists. Gilbert Shelton, the creator of an underground comic book called *The Fabulous Furry Freak Brothers*, and Harvey Kurtzman, who drew *Playboy's Little Annie Fanny,* had both heard their work called objectifying and themselves rip-off artists. It makes me wince to remember myself that afternoon fusing with an ersatz lynch mob on the way to confront a couple of cartoonists. Their art might have benefited from some criticism, but drawing its relationship to rape was simplistic, to say the least. Wallowing in emotion, I'd become the worst kind of reactionary—a censor, a hypocritical puritan in liberationist clothing. I didn't even know who Harvey Kurtzman was.

Our mob arrived as Shelton was speaking, and, taking the offensive, I interrupted him. "Your comics rip off women! Sexist!" I shouted. "Don't you know a woman was raped?" He might have responded, but suddenly the assembled company's attention was arrested by a naked man and woman loudly and publicly fucking on a blanket in the back of the room. The audience began clapping to the rhythm of their coitus. Finished at last, the couple walked to the center of the room, where the woman announced, "All this talk is stupid. If people would ball more, everything would be cool."

This was beyond me. In the presence of such masterful rip-off-ers, my own rage simply collapsed. I sat quietly and watched the subsequent carnival. First, a guy jumped in front of me and yelled, "I am the freak man, I am the freak man." Then, behind me I heard a group of meditators begin chanting "Om." For some reason another faction had begun singing folk songs like "Solidarity Forever." Most people were streaming out of the room.

Seeing Shelton head for the door, I had the prophetic thought that I'd probably end up caricatured in his comic book.

.   .   .

I really wasn't discouraged by my first failure in the adult world of public discourse. On the contrary, I felt even more euphoric and impatient about the contribution I could make somewhere soon. Instead of waiting, as I'd arranged, to travel with my friends to a high school organizing conference in Chicago, I hitchhiked that day from Goddard and caught a ride all the way with a couple of counterculture heroes.

Bob Rudnick was one of Chicago's underground disc jockeys. He was jolly and plump and immediately undertook what he thought were the necessities of my political education. His companion, Libby, was minister of communications for the White Panther Party's central committee. Unlike most of the other movement women at the conference, Libby wore skintight singlets and hip-hugger jeans that showed off her body. On her upper arm, like an Egyptian princess, she wore a silver bracelet in the shape of a serpent devouring itself.

As we drove through the night, Libby and Bob kept up a steady patter—much of which was for my benefit. It was flattering to be the little sister taken into confidence. In the high-spirited atmosphere of siblings preparing for a big date, I shared Libby's ideas and borrowed her clothes. Neither she nor Bob had any reluctance calling themselves revolutionaries. Libby carried Mao's little red book and read aloud to pass the time. It seemed very glamorous to hear the strange, stilted translation of Chinese dos and don'ts. "The Revolution is not a tea party," she quoted as we drove through the quiet Pennsylvania Dutch country. "Let a thousand flowers bloom, a thousand streams of thought contend," she read as we passed through Cleveland (smoking our way through various pipes and joints). We assumed all the highway cops were pigs, and since we were carrying enough dope to be popped for dealers, we made the effort in daylight to look straight. I don't know how. Perhaps we just looked straight ahead. Libby's favorite theme seemed to be *life in the postindustrial economy.* She liked the sound of the phrase, I think, and frequently reiterated, "Postindustrial. No more factories, you understand? *Postindustrial*." For Libby, a native of Detroit at the height of its manufacturing splendor, the concept was as marvelous as her own transformation into a respected counselor on the central committee of the White Panther Party.

Throughout the trip, I was a willing student. Before the ride began I'd known only the barest amount about the White Panthers' founding father, martyr, and icon, John Sinclair. I knew he'd been sentenced to ten years in prison for two joints. But soon I learned all the details of his trial, the government's effort to silence him, the work that was being done in his absence, and the party's central vision, built around its three-point program: dope, rock and roll, and fucking in the streets. Rudnick invited me to crash at the White Panther commune in Chicago for as long as I wanted. Libby said I'd always be welcome at the White Panther headquarters in Ann Arbor. I wouldn't need any money. The party would provide food, lodging, and carfare. Here was the simple formula I'd been craving: revolutionary politics and communal society, all at my feet in a twinkling.

By the time we arrived at La Salle and Division Street in Chicago, I was a newly ranked member of the White Panther Party. At seventeen, though I'd never been west of the Catskills and knew virtually nothing, I'd been promoted in the name of the central committee to assistant minister of education, White Panther Party, Chicago regional branch. Within the month I'd be phoning home to say, "Daddy, I'm not going to college, I'm going to Cuba."

II

Dogma and Catacombs

It's really important now that the people out there start organizing to defend themselves against the approaching police state and to warn the broad masses of the people about the fascist terror that is upon us.

Excerpt from a letter by JOHN SINCLAIR, published in the *New York Herald Tribune*

Not one breath of my support for the new counterleft Christ—John Sinclair. Just one less to worry about for ten years. I do not choose my enemy for my brother.

ROBIN MORGAN, "Goodbye to All That"

O Pioneers!

1970, Summer

I just fished an old photograph out of the red suitcase. The picture shows me holding a banner that reads: "Liberation Means Revolution for All People." I don't specifically remember the occasion, but the picture's background places it in New York. Its revolutionary slogan dates it to around 1970.

The banner is decorated with a stenciled automatic weapon. I am wearing a virtual armor of political buttons, and some of these are also decorated with guns. I can hardly recognize myself beneath that cloud of black hair, the dark ridge of my brow. It must have been taken sometime after Woodstock, because I'm breaking the no-smiling rule.

There's so much I'd like to ask the girl in the picture, my younger self. With all due respect, I'm curious to know if she's taken the time to read her banner. Does it make more sense to her than to me? When I first looked at it fresh, after a gap of so many years, I wondered if it hadn't been written backward. Did whoever lettered that slogan mean to say that revolution means *Liberation* for all people? Or that a liberating revolution means *Freedom* for all people? If she were able to speak, I have a feeling she'd take the offensive. "You can't *achieve* liberation without revolution," she'd say. "Of course, I've *read* the banners. What kind of idiot parades around advertising things she doesn't believe? That's as stupid as . . . wearing a corporate logo on your shirt. Why on earth would you deliberately give some rich designer a free ride?"

Around the time the photograph was taken I'd begun to believe that for all people to become *liberated* there had to be a revolution. I acted, I believed, on behalf of "the people"—in justice, equality, peace. I was never a theorist, and my terms—revolution, liberation, *the people*—were always romantically vague. This social, economic, and political revolution would be achieved, I believed, through personal liberation. It would begin with a rejection of the materialism that capitalism and the class system promoted. It would result from the rejection of the imperialist and colonialist attitudes that had escalated into the war in Vietnam. It would emerge from a relaxation of the puritanical moral codes that kept public agencies and institutions in their hidebound state of Victorian torpor. It would advance when the antagonism and inequality between men and women were viewed as a corny joke of the past. And it would triumph when persecution, discrimination, hatred, and disparity between people of different skin colors were history. The day I held that banner, I imagine, it all seemed inevitable.

By spring of 1970, the guns ornamenting the banner and the buttons I wore had become a ubiquitous decorating motif. At the *Herald Tribune* we brandished the gun icon for its shock value, and over several months it became more and more an essential part of our visual and verbal language. A gun typically illustrated the list of demands that concluded most articles: Free Bobby, Free Huey, Free Erica (these were all Black Panthers in prison).

From the party's origins in 1966, members of the Black Panthers had proclaimed the necessity of guns for their self-defense. In those early days, Panthers armed with guns and lawbooks had followed police cars around Oakland to make sure that the rights of black residents were not being violated. It's hard to underestimate the gut-level response that these uniformed and armed black men and women evoked. They were a thrilling, galvanizing symbol of black pride and power to a lot of ordinary people who felt disenfranchised and lost in urban America; and a stunning, terrifying threat to the white power structure. The Black Panthers' bravado was eventually attacked with the full force of Hoover's extensive system of surveillance, infiltration, and provocation. Andrew Kopkind reported that by 1970, police or police agents had caused the deaths of more than twenty-five party members.

In time we would discover that in their lives under siege, many in the Black Panther Party leadership were also being destroyed from within by hubris and despair. But in 1970, with the images of Bobby Seale in leg chains, forbidden to speak in his own defense at the trial of the Chicago Eight, and with the murders in Chicago of Panther leaders Fred Hampton and Mark Clark (which even the *New York Times* called a conspiracy of law-enforcement agencies) fresh in our minds, many of us felt we were being tested. "If you're not part of the solution, you're part of the problem," Panther theorist Eldridge Cleaver had written. Did we have the courage of our convictions? Was there any limit to how many or how often the government would kill to stop the progress of change? In demonstrations now we were shouting, "Power to the people! Pick up the gun! Power to the people! Off the pig!" We'd made murderous threats before, but there'd been more irony than antipathy in the suggestion that we kill our parents.

Would the girl holding the banner have fired the kind of gun sketched on the buttons that dotted her blouse? I can tell you, fortunately, that she never did. I'd never held a gun until I arrived in Chicago; but I spent much of that summer in a basement, learning how to aim and load. Was it an Uzi? I could hardly tell an Uzi from an Oldsmobile, but our guerrilla arts instructor said it was. On alternate days, he taught our class how to street fight. Fifty pounds of pressure, he advised us, would break a policeman's instep. We practiced throwing kicks; but despite my enthusiasm, I always looked less like a rowdy than a Rockette.

The recruits in this chapter of the White Panther Party had signed on as part of John Sinclair's "Guitar Army," which Sinclair defined in his book of the same name as "a raggedy horde of holy barbarians marching into the future, pushed forward by a whole new blast of sound, a whole new people singing a whole new song of ourselves." Perhaps my Chicago comrades had originally been attracted by the Whitmanesque euphoria that ran through much of the White Panther literature. Or perhaps they'd just identified with Chairman John's rumored exhortation to fuck your woman until she can't stand up. I can't tell you why they joined. But it seemed to me that they were true believers in the idea, as Sinclair articulated it, that they were part of a "people" under attack for their culture.

A former English graduate student, born to an auto worker and a schoolteacher in Flint, Michigan, John Sinclair experienced a sort of political vision through a combination of rock and roll and LSD. He believed that rock and roll had saved him from a life of mediocrity, as it had loosened up and prepared an entire generation for a revolution in values. Sinclair recognized rock and roll as a great liberating force. Used "consciously" as a "weapon of cultural revolution," he wrote, it could "blow the obsolete dinosaur order and all its institutions off the face of the earth forever," and "lay the foundation for the New World of our dreams."

Sinclair's original ideology was antimaterialistic, and he was committed to communalism as the "life-form of the future." In November 1968, inspired by the Black Panther Party, he announced the emergence of the White Panther Party and its platform in Detroit's underground newspaper the *Fifth Estate*.

The first point in the party's ten-point program called for support of the Black Panther Party platform. The second called for "total assault on the culture by any means necessary, including rock and roll, dope, and fucking in the streets." The following eight points called for the abolition of money; free food; free access to information; free time and space; freeing schools from corporate rule; freedom for all prisoners; an end to conscription; and freedom from leaders.

This heady, utopian vision struck a chord with the teenagers who hung around the charismatic Sinclair. He moved from Detroit to found the White Panther headquarters in Ann Arbor. While followers like myself were drawn to his position on politics and culture, the band he managed also grew in popularity. The MC-5 played loud, driving rock and roll. Critic Lester Bangs called their music "gut pulse." The Panthers called it "high-energy," their accolade of supreme distinction. It was unadorned teenage boy music, aimed at drenching its stoned, sexually charged listeners in a storm of pleasure. The MC-5 helped to endorse Sinclair's philosophy that his constituency—all those kids dancing, smoking, and making love in the concert halls and auditoriums across the Midwest—composed "a people" whose "natural resource" was music. At political rallies, the band's trademark intro "Kick Out the Jams, Motherfucker!" raced through its wound-up listeners like a bolt of power.

As Sinclair educated himself in the modern left canon—he credits the works of Marx and Engels, Mao, and Frantz Fanon—he and his newly constructed central committee (among these ministries of education, information, and defense) determined that their party required a "mass" base in order to survive. Governmental surveillance and harassment had also raised the paranoia level to such heights that Sinclair and his followers began to advocate "armed self-defense" to protect a culture they perceived to be under attack. After their first album, the MC-5 fired Sinclair and repudiated the party. Sinclair, meanwhile, had bigger problems. In 1969 he went to jail for selling two joints to an undercover policeman. The judge imposed a sentence of "not less than nine and a half years nor more than ten years." A national campaign led by the White Panthers and joined by celebrities including John Lennon and Yoko Ono helped to free John by January 1971.

.   .   .

Rudnick, Libby, and I arrived at the Chicago Regional White Panther Commune in the middle of the night. I felt as I imagine Gramma Golde must have felt when her steamer left its Dresden port: alone on board a ship of strangers. I awoke late to find that Rudnick was out and Libby had gone on to Ann Arbor. I could have left then, met my friends, and proceeded as planned, but high school organizing already seemed childish. I had no idea who else lived in this house or what staying on would require, but I felt as if I'd graduated into the real world of a revolutionary, and that was what I wanted.

The population of my new neighborhood was transient, mostly Mexican Americans on their way somewhere else. Directly to the west was the newly engineered Cabrini Green. And toward the lake, at Wells, Chicago's Old Town began. From across the street, my side of the block looked like a tumbledown set of teeth—high apartments alternated with condemned buildings and the vacant lots of those recently demolished. Our house was three stories tall and narrow, a wooden facade mounted over brick. It seemed huge to me, with innumerable rooms, many that I, like Jane Eyre, was forbidden to open.

When I joined them, the official party membership in the commune consisted of five young men and Rudnick, our éminence grise, who came and went at his own discretion. The Professor was an intense pedant who arrested what must have once been a lively intellectual curiosity by committing to memory what seemed like hundreds of political slogans. Joey Jim was clumsy and plump and exceedingly proud of his hillbilly background. He had the most astonishing live acne; it seemed to swarm and multiply on his face before your eyes. Desperado, who was slightly older and had been in the army, was our fighting instructor. He was neat and graceful and possessed vast reservoirs of both anger and silence. Buggy, the playboy on loan from the Flint, Michigan, chapter, had an aureole of blond frizzy hair and a sexual confidence that lit him up a mile away. Finally, there was Marvin, a mysterious character who disappeared a few weeks after I arrived, and whom we came to believe was a police informer.

Only a year before, most of the staff of Chicago's underground paper the *Seed* had lived there. But as the White Panthers had moved in, most of the *Seed* staffers, who were generally older by a few years, left. The few who remained, and the constant stream of crashers who would stay for a night or a week, seemed to inhabit a parallel universe. We might see them on their way to work in the morning or hear music from behind the doors of their rooms. But they were never expected, as we were, to participate in political education and street-fighting classes, criticism/self-criticism sessions, or to work the streets every day selling White Panther newspapers and distributing political leaflets.

Sneaks and Spies

1970, Summer

At first I felt like I'd arrived at an outpost of the Foreign Legion. My brothers, as I was encouraged to call them, had turned the house into a fortress, a shrine to "armed self-defense," where the military symbolism I'd flirted with had suddenly sprung to life. We lived on the thrilling edge between paranoia and possibility. It was an accepted fact that the revolution might come tomorrow. (It might already have been declared and the news just not have reached us yet.) We used the phone box in the grocery store because ours was undoubtedly tapped. Police cars were frequently parked on the corner of our block, and at any moment, we expected a SWAT team to burst in shooting. In preparation, we hid guns in holes in the walls. At night, when everyone else slept, one of us would stay awake and patrol the shuttered windows for an ambush.

What I wouldn't realize until much later was that I'd been recruited like a missionary, imported, with my buttons and feminist dogma, into a swamp of male chauvinism where I was expected to instruct and convert the natives. I was, after all, assistant minister of education. It was a social experiment devised by a mad scientist. And though I wish I could say that I tucked into my job with the crisp authority of Wendy among the lost boys, I felt more like young Annie Sullivan with five Helen Kellers (except I didn't have a stiff spine or a teacher's dedication). I hadn't set out on this road to be a schoolmarm or a nurse. I wanted to be a soldier too.

I realize now that what I'd actually wanted to be was a gentleman and an officer. I wanted to be Count Vronsky making witty toasts across the banquet table. Envisioning a Tolstoyan world of compassion and empathy, I'd longed for romantic, perhaps tearful, comradely conversations that would last deep into the night as we pounded each other's shoulders, pledging ourselves against tyranny. While I thought that, if the need arose, I'd be willing to fight for *ideas,* my new comrades seemed poised for the literal fight. They perceived themselves as ground troops, grunts and proud of it. Unlike them, I hadn't been brought up on war movies or played with guns as a child. I didn't have any desire to test myself in battle. Fresh from the New York suburbs, I was simultaneously more sophisticated and more naive than they. I had plenty of nerve, and very little tact. I was unprepared for my new comrades' suspicion of charm and wit. In New York I'd observed a formalized dance of politics and position on the *Herald Tribune*. These Midwesterners, at the other extreme, were so much more absorbed by their emotions. They rushed around without getting anywhere and reacted immediately to whatever they felt. They never seemed to think before they spoke, no matter how ridiculous or insulting their opinions. Speech itself seemed a lost art. Not even the Professor, the house intellectual, had time to waste on a conversation lasting more than a few sentences. Instead, they concentrated all their vital energy on the coming battle.

What about afterward? I asked, and when they were silent and opaque, I grew shriller. My sense of humor grew damp and useless in that house. As mysterious as men were, those I had known—in my family, in school, in the movement—had always seemed to make some space for me in their lives, even if it was superficial or momentary over the course of a conversation. These five members of the White Panther Party made it clear from the first that I had been imposed on them. They must have seen me as a punishment sent to slow them down, a little sister whose hand they had to hold and walk to school. We were all sullenly obedient. If Chairman John said it was right on to dig women's lib, then they'd go through the motions. They perceived our shared cooking and cleanup details, gun and fighting exercises, and officer-of-the-night duties as basic training. To me, the fight class felt like the burden of gym, and the kitchen duties were a direct attack on my feminism.

"Why didn't you do the dishes?" Desperado asked, pointing out the sink infested with a towering, clotted mess.

"Women have been doing dishes for thousands of years," I complained. "That's chick consciousness, and there's not going to be any chick consciousness around here." (My revulsion at housework has stayed as sharp to the present day.)

In the beginning, we examined our every act under a microscope. For instance, if I smiled at a brother, I was liable to be accused of invoking "women's privilege," or using my femininity to induce a man into the knee-jerk response of doing something for me (changing a lightbulb, getting something down from the top shelf). I was accused of not having the stamina or the aggression or the concentration to be a fighter, of trying to weasel out of hard work, of picking and choosing and whining. Meanwhile, I became a sneak and a spy, careful to record their every failure of language (every "chick," every "girl"); all the evidence of male privilege and superiority they employed; their expectation that I was somehow less informed; their unevolved perceptions of "strength"; the sexist comics and magazines they read. Every one of us was afraid of invoking "white privilege," of doing something, anything, wrong, and having it emerge in our criticism/self-criticism sessions. In these nightly encounters we would sit in a circle and analyze one another and ourselves according to an entirely fictional, unattainable level of perfection. Criticism was our common language, and we rarely spoke except to lay blame. I was only in that house for two months, but in that brief time I came as close to a Chinese Red Guard soldier as I would ever be. Everything was form. We stuck to the rhetoric, while the issue of how we cared for one another as we made the revolution and the details of how we'd care for one another afterward were tabled as irrelevant.

There were two critical factors, though, that impeded our cycle of recrimination and punishment. First, the endless succession of joints we smoked produced a general laziness that superseded all righteous exertion. And the licentiousness that wafted through the house like the breath of poppies got inside us, led us astray, and tended to clog our minds.

. . .

At the time, as you know, despite my own inexperience I was supposed to be the expert on relations between men and women in the new society as it played out in the White Panther Commune. As you may imagine, I was not entirely up to the task. We were supposed to be equal in every way, and we were supposed to be free. We should give ourselves freely (in keeping with the tenets of free love and the White Panther Party's overarching philosophy of fucking in the streets), but did that mean not keeping anything of ourselves? I was the only woman in the chapter. At first, I didn't know my comrades, and when I got to know them I didn't understand them. I wasn't immune to the call of Eros. I just didn't know what I was supposed to do and who

I was supposed to do it with. Should I sleep with one of them? All of them? I didn't know much, but I knew the balance of power would be thrown off once I slept with any of them. Was I supposed to make myself available but keep my mind intact like a Vestal Virgin? How was that done? Would I separate mind from body, and, paraphrasing Queen Victoria, "think of the party"? I didn't know. There were no signposts, no models, no patterns, no histories. And since we never spoke on the subject, I can only guess what my "brothers" thought. I imagine they would have preferred a more spontaneous woman, a revolutionary party girl jumping out of cakes spouting slogans—"Liberation means revolution for all people!"—a more macho chick, or a simpler one like the girls back home who'd laugh once in a while and enjoy the minute. Instead, they'd been saddled with a speedy, confused, and confusing New Yorker who agonized over every little action and for whom fucking in the streets was such a goddamn big-deal dialectic.

My friend Judy Leonard from the *Herald Tribune* came to visit at about this time. Years later, she remembered that everybody seemed to be fucking everybody. That wasn't how I remembered it. I thought everybody was fucking me, but that wasn't true either. The Professor had a girlfriend. Marvin didn't like women (he was fascinated by guns and would sit by the hour cleaning and fondling them). Joey Jim had less experience with women than I'd had with men. He was like an excited puppy who'd wheedle and chew and threaten to become vicious if you wanted to stop playing. I tried to delay what seemed inevitable. He had all those blackheads, so I asked him to use Clearasil for a month (which made him angry enough to leave me alone). Desperado and I had the most complicated relationship. He was critical of everything I did, particularly of my behavior around the other men. He didn't like me, or maybe he felt that women on the eve of battle were bad luck. Or, maybe, by keeping his distance he showed that he liked me the most. The only member of our group who seemed to be perfectly at ease in the commune's supercharged atmosphere was Buggy. Women's sexual liberation translated into a free love smorgasbord for Buggy. And no one enjoyed as much pleasure from our derelict mansion with its many rooms. Buggy never slept alone. At night he'd knock on your door. If you invited him inside, he'd throw himself on top of you. If not, he'd wander away, unperturbed, and knock somewhere else, visiting crashers, *Seed* reporters, White Panthers, girls and boys.

I'd never even imagined a boy like Buggy before. Before Chicago, he'd worked as a roadie for the UP, the MC-5's replacement as party band. He was slight and muscular, his pale blue eyes memorably remote, and his focus always elsewhere. He swaggered when he walked, and in repose he looked like a sulky angel. When he'd first come to my bed, I hadn't known about his rotation system. I'd thought he was there because he liked me. I made the early mistake of hoping he'd "be mine," as on a child's valentine. But I immediately learned that possessiveness disgusted Buggy and turned him mean. The next time he visited, he made sure I realized that he was only fucking the women's lib chick out of pity. I thought I could change his mind, but he didn't like to talk. I thought he'd stop visiting. But he was a creature of habit; as long as I was on his route, he'd make a delivery. And I, starved for ordinary kindness, told myself this was love.

Judy called the house dirty, unfriendly, and weird, and she wondered why I stayed. After she left I wrote to her in the same jargon we employed in our daily sessions:

> I want to be a revolutionary bad. I know I haven't been receptive to struggle before (I've always had a remarkable capacity to ignore things, or shall we say AVOID them when I wished to). Now, I'm finally developing an ideology. Perhaps its a bit macho, a bit "Weatherman" inspired, totally third-world directed. I've stopped writing and reading except for some party papers, political journals and of course Mao's Red Book.

We were a house full of sneaks and spies. I'd lost my confidence, my own opinions, and my ability to voice them. *"I've stopped writing and reading . . ."* Perhaps I was afraid that literature would provide too many alternatives. Books were too rational; they didn't make sense anymore. I stopped writing in my diary, and instead poured my soul into a more ephemeral genre, the exhortatory leaflet. *"BROTHERS AND SISTERS!!! THE PIG IS EVERYWHERE!!!!!"*

The Professor's girlfriend, Amy, would come by and leaflet with us sometimes, and she was a revelation. "The Professor doesn't know what he's talking about half the time," she'd say. "He can be fun but you have to admit he's crazy. Though not half as crazy as the other guys in the house. I mean really—this gun fixation."

I was surprised Amy even knew about the guns.

"That's all they talk about."

I thought the guns were a secret.

"They brag about them."

Amy was exactly my age. She had graduated from a Chicago public high school that June. Her parents were also Jewish. More than anything else, she brought the comedy of the world into the house. She was a lifeboat. She'd been a high school activist against the war, too, but she could laugh at the absurd lengths we went to for political purity. If I didn't exactly see what was so funny, I clung to her bravery. It surprised me to hear her speak of the future. After just two months with the White Panthers, I'd begun to think that life everywhere was as timeless and doomed as ours.

"Come on," she'd say, her voice warm with subversive skepticism. She was going to college in September. Wasn't I? I didn't know. It didn't seem relevant. Little by little I began to construct an escape scenario that I kept secret from everyone but Amy. A high school friend had written to say she'd joined a Quaker farm commune in Indiana. Anytime I wanted I could leave in the middle of the night and hitchhike there by morning. Having an escape plan gave me the courage to stick around.

. . .

A few weeks later, Libby returned from Ann Arbor. She burst into the house sparkling like Auntie Mame bearing gifts. I was feeling dull and drab and luxuriated in her radiance. How was I doing? she asked. "Well, there's always a period of adjustment." Rudnick made a surprise appearance, too. He rarely stayed at the house anymore, but he appeared that night and acted as if he and I knew each other inside out. He bought a bottle of wine, and we toasted over the banquet table like Count Vronsky and his comrades.

I had been chosen, Libby announced, as a young revolutionary feminist, for a very special assignment. Rudnick and Libby and I, and about fifty other people, had been invited to Cuba as part of a youth culture brigade to help with Cuba's sugar harvest and meet with North Vietnamese representatives sometime in September. Did I want to go?

Was there any doubt? My trials had been rewarded. My little-sister status, which had begun to seem like a burden, was now worth its weight in pure gold. That night, I went to the grocery store and called my father for the first time since I'd arrived in Chicago. He and Ann had been terribly worried. What was I doing? When was I coming home? College started soon.

I started to cry, happily. "Daddy, I have better things to do. I'm a revolutionary now."

Criticism and Compromise

1970, Summer

At first, the best part of being singled out was that, except for Rudnick, the rest of the men in the commune had not been. I hailed my selection as a resounding triumph for feminism, and despite my comrades' escalating criticism, I couldn't have felt more self-congratulatory. For days, I flaunted my privilege. I was the house apparatchik, the party hack ("Oh, my dacha? That little cottage in the country? It revitalizes me and therefore the Party!"), too infatuated to see that my preening made our relations worse and worse.

Meanwhile, I prepared for another phone call to my father. During our first conversation about Cuba, he'd been shocked into silence, and I'd promised to call again. Everybody I knew was dropping out of college. Nobody I respected had actually graduated. I continued our argument in my head. He should be happy I had this opportunity. Not everybody is invited to participate in a youth culture brigade. Abbie Hoffman would be going, and Jerry Rubin and Stew Albert and Judy Gumbo and Phil Ochs—all the celebrities of the counterculture. We'd all be equals in Cuba.

I don't think my father really minded the Cuba part. I think now if I'd just said I was going to Havana University, he'd have sent school fees. But he minded terribly that I would be interrupting my education. He'd wanted to go to college himself, in accounting or oceanography. After the war, when he already had one son with another on the way, he'd tried to attend night school, but it had just been too hard. After working all day selling spices, he would fall asleep in class. College, college, college. All through my childhood *college* was, for my father the atheist, a word greater than God. He himself had settled for pilgrimages to aquariums and tropical fish in bowls. But, he believed, I could do better.

This *was* better, I thought. The important thing was to help that little island constantly threatened by counterrevolutionists to meet its five-year plan. Leftist "Venceremos" brigades had already been going there for a couple of years to help with the sugar harvest. A Weather-man brigade had been there the summer before and come back with sore bodies, calluses, and photographs of themselves, fists in the air in the cane fields, or sitting on the veranda of what had once been the Havana Hilton, jokily drinking tall Cuba Libres with paper umbrellas in them. It was hard work cutting cane. But it was also a priceless opportunity to meet young compañeros from every Communist and left-leaning country from Sweden to Angola. I'd always wanted to be an exchange student, but Plainedge had had no such programs.

.   .   .

Within a few days, Libby flew off again on some central committee business and Rudnick disappeared mysteriously, as he always did. I suppose he had another place to live, a real apartment or a room in a less precarious atmosphere. All the other men were in such foul moods that, for the first time, I felt nervous in Rudnick's absence. By the end of the week he would return and, with great fanfare, seem to discover me again: his protégée.

Ours would not be a typical sugar-cutting expedition, Rudnick explained carefully. If we scythed at all it would be entirely for the many cameras that would be accompanying us. Rather, this was to be a counterculture media junket. Many of the same people who'd been at the Goddard conference had been invited. (Rudnick called it "counter-culture," whereas for Libby we were the "youth culture.") In any case, we were to consider ourselves ambassadors and would be treated as such, just like the accredited envoys of other states and "peoples."

.   .   .

A few nights after I'd called my father, when I was already in bed, Desperado, who was officer that night, roused the house. I grabbed my glasses and ran downstairs to find everyone assembled, quietly and methodically beginning to implement the armed self-defense drill we'd practiced so many times.

"There's a visitor outside," Desperado whispered. "He says he's your brother."

"Maybe it *is* my brother," I whispered back.

"But he doesn't know the password. If he's her brother she'd have given him the password, right?" he asked the others. "What's the pass-word?" he asked through the door.

"I don't know the fucking password . . . Les?"

"It sounds like my brother." I peered through the wooden slats and iron bars. "It is."

"How come he doesn't know the password?"

"*I* don't know the password," I had to admit.

"That's because you've been so busy with your damn Cuba trip, you haven't been paying any attention to house duties. That could have been a pig out there."

Right after our phone call, my father had sent my brother to rescue me. Later, in the seventies, deprogramming kids who'd joined religious or political cults would become an instant industry with specially trained practitioners, many of them ex-FBI agents or soldiers of fortune. But my father had used the resources available to him. "Go see Les," he told Bob. "Find out what's going on. Why doesn't she want to go to college?"

I hadn't seen much of Bob since three summers before, when, on a flying visit, he'd turned me on to pot for the first time. "You might as well get high with me if you're gonna get high," he had said. I'd always admired Bob for his amiability and practicality, and those were the characteristics I hoped he'd display, as Desperado and the cadre restashed the guns, unlocked the bolts, and opened the door.

A while back, Bob, in his black horn-rims and chinos, had carried himself with the remote air of a Greenwich Village beatnik. Now, his hair was long and wild, and he was dressed in the bell-bottoms and fatigue jacket of a hitchhiking hippie. He'd taken a year off school to be a VISTA volunteer and (in deference to our father's call) stopped in Chicago on his way back to West Virginia, where, as a community organizer, he was helping farmers build co-ops. A lot of the locals were viciously opposed to VISTA's presence in the mountains, and my brother was getting beat up a lot. It was hard to get people to participate in the VISTA program or even to talk to one another in the presence of strangers, he said. "It was a great time to be alive," Bob told me later, when I'd asked him to remember those days. "A great time to do things, but a lousy time to get anything done."

·   ·   ·

"It seems a little menacing here," Bob observed the next morning.

"It's under control," I mumbled into my shirt. I adored my brothers, but it was my impression, at that time, that they perceived me more or less as a generic kid sister. We'd had very little experience holding a conversation as equals. My reputation inside our family was that of a clumsy, oversensitive child who never liked to be teased. As their little sister I had always felt misunderstood, or at least underestimated. It was true that when I was at a loss for a witty reply, I would burst into tears. I wanted Bob to leave. But I also wanted him to stay, at least long enough to appreciate the seriousness of my claim on the revolution. Instead, he asked me irritating questions: Why wasn't I writing? Why was I so out of touch? How did I end up here?

"What does it matter? Don't you see how things are?" Hadn't his experience at the door last night proved that the revolution was not some game?

"No," he said. "It proves it *is* a game."

I suspected he was trying to snare me in subtlety. I guessed he'd try to reset our argument on more familiar terms. We both knew it only takes a family argument to bring you back to your family. And though I tried not to collapse *immediately* into the routine sulkiness of his frustrated kid sister, the lure and habit were irresistible. Within minutes I couldn't speak without crying. "I really want to go to Cuba."

My brother stood patiently, waiting for me to stop gulping. If Ricky and I had inherited my father's pale skin and hazel eyes, Bob's olive complexion and brown eyes were so much like my mother's I could hardly look at him. Finally, he threw his hands up and, in a youthful imitation of our father, said, "I'm not going to drag you home."

I remember feeling surprised that our fight was over so soon. Those moments without speech had eclipsed everything. I'd felt as if my new adult identity had been prematurely yanked onto a public auction block. And as degrading as that had seemed, as exhausted and embarrassed as I felt, I was glad and consoled by the protection my brother offered—and that I'd managed to refuse. Bob's presence had forced me to take account of myself; and to myself, I was frantically optimistic. It was true, I was miserable in Chicago. But that was my sacrifice. Massapequa, college, Long Island, all that was in the past. It was more and more difficult to remember, and sooner or later it would all become invisible.

.   .   .

That afternoon, before I went out to sell the Panther paper in Old Town, I heard Bob out in the garden. It wasn't much of a garden—just a postage stamp full of rusty junk and wet cardboard. He was engaged in a loud discussion with one of the *Seed* reporters whom I'd occasionally seen pass through the house. She and I had never actually had a conversation, but that day she was defending my choice to become a revolutionary. "There's reality," I heard her explain, "which is what you perceive. And then there's the objective reality."

"And that's not a question of perception, too?" Bob asked. "It seems like it would be dependent on who's perceiving reality, and where and when."

"No, there are objective social conditions and they create an objective reality," she declared.

"And objective reality, according to you, never changes?" Bob asked.

"Well, it may, but then it joins another set of objective conditions. You really don't understand this?" Her voice rose.

I could see them through the back window. My brother was shaking his head. She was sighing so angrily her breath ruffled her bangs. Then he smiled and gestured, palms up, and spoke in a lower register. I couldn't hear her answer, but in a moment they both were laughing.

He's given up on me, I thought. "See ya, Bobby," I waved from the door. "Tell Daddy not to worry."

After Bob left, my life in the commune pretty much returned to the routine I'd practiced before I'd been invited to Cuba: street-fighting classes, political education classes, and criticism/self-criticism sessions in which, because of Cuba, I was always being accused of arrogance and a tendency to adventurism. Rudnick seemed to have disappeared again. Amy was out of town, and the house was empty except for my White Panther brothers and a new crasher named Rita, who'd arrived with her three-year-old child. Rita and Buggy became lovers almost immediately, and he consequently changed his whole routine. He became suspiciously pleasant. His sudden monogamy irritated me, and in our criticism/self-criticism sessions, I called him duplicitous and untrustworthy. By then, the optimism I'd rustled up for my brother's benefit had shrunk into a dull puddle of complaint and grievance.

.   .   .

It isn't so hard for me to understand how the anti-intellectual fervor of the Chinese Red Guard so quickly turned its young participants into petty despots. If all you've got is objective reality, life can seem pretty bleak. Without books, without poetry or nature to mediate my own life in Chicago, I concentrated my resentment on the residents of our claustrophobic commune. It was only us on a desert island with the unattainable ideal. Criticism was the job we enjoyed, denunciation was entertainment. I needed a break, but perversely, I thought reading would make things worse.

Some weekends, we went to leaflet and sell political books at rock and roll concerts and dances, but even among all those blissful celebrants, among "our people," I was lost. It seemed our people weren't thinking. They were duds—a mass of electrified, richly colored protoplasm that couldn't string three words together. They'd happily grab my leaflets and then drop them on the dance floor. I threatened more than once to pull the plug and scold the band for sexism. Instead, I glowered. The men told me to relax.

Rudnick showed up one night at the Avalon Ballroom in a dashiki and jeans, his wild hair frosted with sparkles from a kids' craft set. He'd brought along Stew Albert, who had also been invited to Cuba. That summer, Stew was the editor of the *Berkeley Tribe*. His name was well known to us as one of the founding Yippies. The unrestrained glee he exhibited in everyone and everything immediately set Stew apart from my usual companions. At first I attributed this difference to California. Unlike the raging egomaniac Rudnick or the robotic Desperado, Stew looked directly at his conversational partner. Such simple kindness shocked me. He talked at length about Chicago's politics and literature—the Haymarket martyrs, Theodore Dreiser, James T. Farrell, Richard Wright, Nelson Algren, Saul Bellow, the *Little Review* of Margaret Anderson. He raised his voice to speak above the band, and, after a while, he was orating in the garish Avalon lobby on the subject of anarcho-syndicalism. This he described as a great federation of workers' cooperatives, each possessing its own means of production, and bound by contracts of exchange and mutual aid. At its heart, anarcho-syndicalism is always made up of individuals who take part voluntarily. Coercion is the enemy and authority its henchman. The minority is equal to the majority, and the people are not viewed as a mass, in the Marxist sense, but as a collection of sovereign individuals.

The lesson I learned that day went beyond the history of unionism. What struck the resounding chord was hearing about literary diva Margaret Anderson, who had started a poetry magazine from nothing, kept it running for years, met all the great writers of her time—Joyce,

H.D., Eliot, Pound—and published most of them. I was embarrassed to show Stew the graceless, uninspired leaflets I'd been scribbling. What had happened to the poet I'd wanted to be? Anderson had lived in Chicago, London, and Paris. She may have lost her way from time to time, but from how she lived and the things she published, it was clear that she'd kept a healthy skepticism, a confidence that mysteries abound, and the belief that literature could be a social force. It might even offer a way out of loneliness. It would take me years to recognize that I was simply missing some recognition of ambiguity. The house I lived in was a disordered mess, but we pretended that the universe was binary. Our great performance was to act as if an objective reality existed, and as if we all knew what it was. I was trying to fit in but couldn't. As old Mrs. Baton had detected back in first grade, I was still "a dissenting individualist." At this point, however, my individualism seemed a terrible burden.

. . .

Libby arrived on her way back from a Cuba-trip planning meeting. She looked as if she hadn't slept for days. And she had bad news to report. The Cuba trip had been postponed. "Just for a while," she said consolingly when we were alone, "but if I tell you why, you have to swear to secrecy."

Having heard that Cuba had invited a youth culture brigade, the Russian leader, Leonid Brezhnev himself, had taken a personal interest. "You must be gravely uninformed," he'd told Castro. "They will all be drug addicts. They will not be serious. They will divert and distract your youth. If you allow these degenerates into your country, you may never get them out. And you will lose the support of Mother Russia."

"You have to choose," Libby ended her story, paraphrasing Brezhnev. "Naturally, we didn't want to endanger Cuba's economy. The North Vietnamese were very unhappy that they wouldn't be able to meet us. They protested, of course, but those Russian puritans control everything," she shrugged. "The North Vietnamese sent everyone who was going to participate a present."

Digging into a small velvet drawstring purse she produced a jumble of metal rings. All were narrow bands inscribed with the number 3200.

"From the thirty-second hundredth American plane shot down over North Vietnam," Libby explained. "The Vietnamese people don't waste anything. Like Indians used to use every part of the buffalo.

Vietnamese soldiers sculpt the smallest bit of scrap metal into objects of beauty."

Was she going to give me a ring? I could sense her reluctance. I imagined her thoughts—these rings were so much revolutionary currency, why waste it on a novice who might never take vows?

"Let me try." I plucked one from her hand. "Why, look at that. It fits!"

I was impossible after that. I fell asleep when I was officer of the night and overslept morning classes. I refused to make dinner or wash the dishes when it was my turn. I hung around with Rita, the crasher, and many days we did nothing but smoke pot and play with her toddler. I was always flaunting my ring like a newly engaged ingenue. In August, as Amy was getting ready to go to the University of Michigan, I told her that I'd be moving on to national headquarters in Ann Arbor myself.

"Not the Quaker farm in Indiana?" Amy asked.

"No." I felt I could serve the people better in Ann Arbor. I had a secret hope that the party newspaper there would publish my poetry. I wasn't ready to jump ship for anarchism yet. Instead, I was starting to feel more confident about the contributions poetry could make to the revolution. Wasn't Chairman Mao Tse-tung himself a poet? I'd never felt drawn to Mao's poetry the way I had to Yeats's, but I found Mao a lot more useful. If I couldn't exactly be a writer on my own terms, at least I could get some respect by claiming the leader of hundreds of millions of Chinese communists as a model. I kept the faith, and referred religiously to his little red book. In exchange, his blessing made my occupation as worker-poet more honorable. At the time, I knew nothing about the thousands of intellectuals forced into exile in the countryside; the imprisonment, censorship, and humiliation of artists; and the Red Guards' abuse of human rights in Mao's name. I just knew that the red book's appearance in my hand could instantly stave off criticism. I could use the chairman's words to explain why I hadn't done the dishes, why I'd slept until noon, why I'd missed one class or another. None of my comrades was ready to object to the chairman's words. None knew them as well as I. They were easy enough to imitate, and when memory failed I could make up my own Maoesque epigram on the spot for any occasion.

·   ·   ·

I look back now and see the girl I was in Chicago moving spasmodi-cally, from plot point to plot point, like a character in a melodrama. The period of not writing that I suffered there was a template for many sub-sequent episodes. Over the years I've stopped periodically, not because I feel I can't write, or have nothing to say, but because everything else seems more important. I've watched years pass in this way. When I finally emerge, it feels like rutting season. I'll want to write so badly I don't care where I am or who I'm with.

In Chicago as an insecure kid I thought I had to justify myself. I would have used any weapon at hand. As it happened my faith coin-cided with my need. I exploited my devotion to Mao, and found my-self rewarded. I wasn't sleeping with the chairman, but I might as well have been. Once I began writing again, I wrote nonstop, blissfully unaware that all the revolutionary odes I wrote as the Bride of Mao still sounded a lot like leaflets.

Red Star Sisters

1970, Summer

Ann Arbor had developed a reputation over the past five years as one of the hot spots of radical thought and action. Early SDS had started in Ann Arbor, and its university had contributed a disproportionate number of participants to the Weathermen (now called the Weather Bureau). By the summer of 1970, opposition to the Vietnam War had created a superconscious student population. The news was full of escalating violence, and Ann Arbor, like other radical bastions, was divided a thousand ways on the subject. In Berkeley, James Rector, a visitor to People's Park, was shot when police opened fire on demonstrators. Jonathan Jackson was killed in a wild effort to kidnap a judge and exchange him for his brother, the jailed political philosopher George Jackson. The leaders of the Black Panther Party were imprisoned on what appeared to be an epidemic of trumped-up murder charges. And most of the White Panther Party's central committee was in prison, on the run, or under indictment. Meanwhile, the war continued in Nixon's new strategy of "Vietnamization."

That August, in nearby Madison, Karl Armstrong and three other men, plotting independently of any other organizations, bombed the Army Mathematics Research Center at the University of Wisconsin. The bombers, like other leftist provocateurs in the months to follow, claimed they targeted only property associated with war research, not people or animals. But Armstrong's poorly planned explosion unintentionally caused the tragic death of Robert Fassnacht, a scientist working through the night. A couple of years later, during Armstrong's trial, witnesses for his defense tried to place his act in historical context and provide some explanation for the rapid escalation of the left's militant turn. After "seven years of failed efforts to stop the war by peaceful means" and "the failure of the political machinery to respond to the cries of the people," radical historian and professor Harvey Goldberg said, "Fassnacht's death and the injuries to innocents had to be set against the daily annihilation of Southeast Asians under American bombardment."

That summer the White Panthers, as represented by the *Ann Arbor Argus,* lambasted local "peace-punks" and "peace-creeps." In a column published after one frustrating demonstration, "David & Darlene America" complained that just trashing stores and cars wasn't working anymore. They rejected "the notion that we are merely 'vandals in the mother-country,' that our only task is disruption." They wrote that "merely cutting up and trashing windows is not enough. We have to get into offing pigs, fighting the man any way we can!"

.   .   .

When I first arrived in Ann Arbor, I went straight to the White Panther headquarters commune on Hill Street. Libby and the few other central committee members still at large lived communally in a huge, rambling house they called "Trans-Love." John Sinclair was in prison and most of the commune's resources were bent toward obtaining his release. There was a growing national awareness of Sinclair's case. *Free John* graffiti was ubiquitous in most counterculture enclaves. But by the autumn, his picture and writings were being less frequently published in the underground press. Nine months before, Robin Morgan had published a landmark feminist essay titled "Goodbye to All That," in which she'd dismissed Sinclair as a fraud and called him "my enemy." Now there were more women in editorial positions than ever before, and the trend was to distance their papers from Sinclair's embarrassing history of "male chauvinism."

In earlier days Sinclair had been a mover and shaker—so in tune with the zeitgeist he had invented a party and been proclaimed its leader. The world turned. Prison hardened him, and he couldn't feel his people's pulse the way he had. He was slow to perceive the depth of passion women's issues evoked or recognize their importance in *his* world. When he finally acknowledged the new tenor of the times in 1971, it took the form of a poignant wallow called "Free Our Sisters/ Free Our Selves!," in which he recounted his own struggle with sexism and declared (kind of late in the game) that opposing sexism was in everyone's interest:

> If we don't work to make sure that everyone is equal on all levels then we're just perpetrating the same sickness we call ourselves trying to get away from when we reject the death culture of the honks. Sisters and brothers have to work *with* each other

on every level and in every aspect of their existence to purify our culture and make sure that what we are building is a truly liberated culture for all people.

Libby, Sinclair's devoted minister of communication, responded more quickly to Morgan. In a piece of masterful spin control published in a number of undergrounds she tried to defend the chairman, scold Morgan for being less than revolutionary, and still admit that the central committee lagged behind the vanguard where the women's issue was concerned. Libby's essay sounds like a sad little fog horn in the distance compared to the peal of Morgan's liberty bell. Morgan's vivid, raving rationale for feminists to separate from the male-dominated left still carries an emotional punch:

> A genuine Left doesn't consider anyone's suffering irrelevant or titillating; nor does it function as a microcosm of capitalist economy, with men competing for power and status at the top, and women doing all the work at the bottom (and functioning as objectified prizes or "coin" as well). Goodbye to all that. . . . goodbye forever, counterfeit Left, counterleft, male-dominated cracked-glass-mirror reflection of the Amerikan Nightmare.

Libby's response is sweet and vulnerable when she writes about how she misses her absent husband, who was underground at the time, running from the FBI. She yearns to merge with him, not separate from him. In the end, this wistful description of torn loyalties paints the sad picture of a young marionette putting her head on the block to save her puppet master. I don't remember reading Morgan's piece when it came out. I think I'd have appreciated her rage. But honestly, I was philosophically closer to Libby. I wasn't ready to separate from men—probably because I hadn't had much experience uniting with them yet. I wanted to attract them on my terms. I wanted to be in love.

Whatever Libby wrote back then in defense of her party, her own practical solution was to recruit some young feminists. I was her prize. Chicago might not have been my greatest success, but Libby was positive that the party had a place for me. In Ann Arbor I could be the in-house authority on everything regarding the women's movement from behavior to ideology. I could start by helping to organize the White Panther Party's newly conceived women's wing: Red Star Sisters. The very first Red Star Sisters national program, Libby told me, would be a network of community schools. She didn't have details yet, but she imagined the program would begin with preschoolers. I think I must have groaned or rolled my eyes.

"What's the matter?" she interrupted herself.

I confessed my disappointment. Nursery schools sounded like old-fashioned women's work to me. I had hoped for more range. "I think I'd rather work on the newspaper."

The minister shrugged. She had only so much patience, and it was dwindling. I never saw her much after that. She came to one Red Star Sisters meeting and we posed together for a photograph. She held her fist in the air, Vietcong souvenir rings on every finger.

. . .

My two months in Chicago had prepared me for a certain kind of commune life. I was used to being closely watched by my housemates, and at first I was delighted that everyone in the *Argus* house seemed much too busy to pay attention to me. The paper came out every two weeks. We were always either planning it, writing it, composing it, laying it out, or selling it for the money to put out the next issue. Our commune was precariously supported by the few ads we sold in the paper, and the change we made hawking it. We weren't expected to have personal expenses. All private money was supposed to be pooled.

The year before, the *Ann Arbor Argus* had been one of the liveliest undergrounds in the Midwest. Its editor, the teenaged Ken Kelly, was a good writer and conscientious editor who made some effort to keep knee-jerk rhetoric at bay. "We will not be intimidated by anyone," Kelly wrote in an early issue. "A lot of the stories will take the form of interviews, because it's the most direct way of getting straight at what's happening, without the reporter or the editor sticking in his objectivity."

For many, including myself, the concept of journalistic objectivity was suspect. In the underground press you could see counterculture and mainstream worldviews colliding on the subjects of truth and morality. I thought that whatever their code of ethics, mainstream journalists, like historians, could really only imagine the truth under the surface. Various reporters and editors might position themselves as watchdogs of First Amendment rights, but their employers, the huge papers like the *New York Times* and the *Washington Post,* were as vulnerable to the laws of supply and demand as every other business in a capitalist country. The suggestion that these corporate concerns never accommodated the interests of their advertisers seemed absurd to me. Their reporters wrote from whatever angle of "objectivity" their experience and training permitted. How could we possibly accept their objectivity when their positions so often contradicted ours?

By that summer the *Argus* had come to reflect the party's commitment to armed self-defense and Marxism-Leninism. Within a commotion of new Communist dogma and jargon, the *Argus* became a different paper entirely. Suddenly, the old masthead was gone, and in its place was a White Panther poised to spring. Ken Kelly left the *Argus* to begin a national White Panther paper called *Sundance,* which, reflecting the party's increased fame and apparent good fortune, featured creamy white paper and full-color illustrations.

The post-Kelly *Argus* often seemed more assembled than written. It came to rely more and more on the counterculture Liberation News Service, which had also grown increasingly dogmatic. In their early days, LNS provided a diversity of left opinion. The articles written by its own staff were generally characterized by a largeness of spirit and quirky humor. Under its new leadership, LNS distributed by-the-number graphics, and its writing about domestic bombings, trials, demonstrations, and third-world revolutions became numbing and predictable.

The new *Argus* may have lacked the spark of its more original or imaginative siblings, but it almost never missed a deadline. Verna Lipton, the paper's new manager, was one of the revolution's master bureaucrats. Only twenty years old, in another time and place Verna would have commanded shipyards. A careerist in a world of amateurs, a zealously devoted party member, she was quick witted and supercritical. She juggled bills, placated creditors, and kept the paper and commune together with the despotic force of a captain of industry. Her own métier seemed to be less the articles we published than the slogans that so emphatically punctuated them: Power to Good Dope! Power to the People! Life to the Life Culture! Death to the Death Culture! Seize the Time Outlaws!

In rare moments of repose, Verna would turn her attention to reorganizing the commune's domestic conditions. "The dishwashing roster has got to be maintained!" she'd demand. "The upstairs hall must be swept!" Once, in a cold fury, Verna announced that the punishment for any commune member failing to wash the dishes on schedule would be to recite Mao's eleven points of liberalism before the assembled house. I'd never succeeded in improving my house-keeping habits, and my standard defense (washing dishes was sexist role-playing) made Verna's one blue eye and one brown eye go dead. But, thanks to my experience as his bride in Chicago, my "Mao" was almost letter perfect.

I didn't have much use for Mao myself anymore. Now that everyone seemed to be on a Mao kick, divorcing from him offered a new way to assert my individuality. It was hard to tell just how serious the new conspicuous carriers of the red book were. Some, like Verna, used him as a stick with which to beat you, whereas for others, he was a relic, evolving into a pop star. At demonstrations, you'd hear people substitute M-A-O-T-S-E-DASH-T-U-N-G for M-I-C-K-E-Y-M-O-U-S-E, sung to the tune of the "Mickey Mouse Club Song." Mao was becoming more and more like other celebrities, like James Dean, Marilyn Monroe, or Che. Andy Warhol knew it when he made that silkscreen of Mao's portrait—the same steroidal face you saw on all the pancake-sized badges everyone was wearing. Even John Lennon was caught up in the fashion. "I really thought that love would save us all. But now I'm wearing a Chairman Mao badge, that's where it's at," he said.

After several months of personal intimacy with Mao's writing, I'd come to the conclusion that the chairman was a big windbag. His poetry wasn't even very good. Ho Chi Minh's, I thought, was far superior. At the time, I wasn't brave enough to say anything outright. But when, having failed at dish duty, I was required to recite the eleven points of liberalism, I put my own spin on the occasion. With the commune assembled, I sang all eleven points in falsetto: to let things slide for the sake of peace and friendship . . . to indulge in irresponsible criticism . . . to let things drift . . . to hear incorrect views without rebutting them . . . I flapped my arms in a silly interpretation of Chinese opera gestures.

All it took for me to divorce myself from Mao was a wave of my hand. At the time it never occurred to me that in China another girl my age and disposition would probably have ended up with a dunce cap on her head, reciting the eleven points of liberalism during ten years of hard labor for a similar display—that is, if she missed being executed for hooliganism in the first place. It would take a while for me to make that connection. Back in Ann Arbor that night I had to endure the censure of my own peers, who judged my performance both "creepy" and "racist." "You're jive," Verna accused me. "You better take those points to heart."

That may have been our longest conversation. The only thing Verna despised more than liberalism was irony. I was never serious enough by her standards. Always an outsider, a carpetbagger, an East Coast sharpie, an imported ultrafeminist, my presence insinuated that she'd been somehow lax in revolutionary conduct. She suspected my enthusiasm for feminism was an attention-getting "ruse" and, in her favorite word, "bogus." Feminism was one more hoop to jump through to show one's dedication. Look what she'd achieved already. In Verna's cosmology (where only bands achieved "high energy"), unrestrained enthusiasm led to extravagance and time lost from work. Flamboyance led to idleness, decadence, and, ultimately, parasitism. I'd offended her, and her response was to dismiss my revolutionary pretensions.

I wondered who Verna really was. The face we saw was resolute and forbidding. She never smiled in front of rank and filers, but we'd hear her giggle with her sweet-natured boyfriend, Lon, who spent much of his time on his back smoking pot. Every couple of weeks, after the paper was put to bed, Verna would change out of her hard-core worker's regalia of jeans and work shirt, and, freshly costumed in minidress and heels, leave us to visit her sick mother in Detroit.

.   .   .

The *Argus* commune rented a two-story house on Ann Arbor's residential Arch Street. Layout and production absorbed the living room and dining room. The kitchen was small, and the table seated only four or five, so we never ate together in one place. We'd usually scoop brown rice and vegetables from a big pot and find a place somewhere on the floor.

Upstairs, Verna and Lon had one bedroom to themselves. The rest of us, a frequently changing number averaging between six and ten, shared two small carpeted bedrooms. There were a few mattresses, but most of us slept in sleeping bags. Some people insisted on claiming sections of a room for themselves and slept in the same place every night. Others objected to such bourgeois "territorialism."

In September, Amy, my dear, practical friend from Chicago, left behind her boyfriend, the White Panther "Professor," and began school at the University of Michigan. After three weeks she dropped out and moved into our commune. Amy found a job at an ice cream parlor and kept her dorm room for the semester, so she could escape from the closed world of the *Argus* from time to time. Buggy had also migrated back from Chicago. The other members of the commune were all from Ann Arbor. Even if they were estranged from their families, they had friends in town, other places to go. At night, our house would become a hive of activity—communants and friends crowded into the little bedrooms to smoke pot and drink rotgut wine, waiting for Verna to call us downstairs as she whipped the paper forward. But afternoons could be lonely. In the morning, I'd leave with a bundle of papers under my arm. (I loved to cry the news at the top of my voice. It was never an easy sell, but it got me outside.) Then it was home to an empty house. In Chicago, where nobody had left me alone, I'd pined for privacy. In Ann Arbor, I felt neglected. The term *ultrafeminist* had provided me with a ready-made identity. But the term was generic, and I wasn't. I'd used it to position myself in a strange place, much in the same way I'd used Maoism. It functioned as a magic cloak, offering the illusion of power to me and its threat to others. But the boys stayed clear. If anybody, in the party or out, was fulfilling the third point of the party platform and "fucking in the streets," I didn't know them. In our commune, Kenny Danz was the only boy not wary of me, and he was a gentle femme.

Kenny walked with his back arched and his wrists deliberately limp. He had a great heart and the habit of wisecracking to protect it. We kept each other company—neither of us eighteen yet, and in so deep—swinging giddily between wild spirits and strict ideology. One evening he painted the ceiling of the center bedroom with the red star flag of the National Liberation Front. I officially named it the Vietcong Lounge. The house's other semipermanent occupants included Randall the Teenybopper, who at sixteen bounced back and forth to his parents' suburban home, and eighteen-year-old Violet, who'd been purged the year before from the Weathermen as a "weak link." A few days before beginning college at the Art Institute in Chicago, Violet had phoned her parents in what, I came to discover, was an increasingly common ritual, to say, "Mom and Dad, I can learn more from my brothers and sisters in the party than at any bourgeois art school."

All these strangers thrown together, expecting to make a revolution together. I recorded their names and biographies, and hid my notebook under my pillow. I was sure that if they found out I was writing about them they'd think I was a narc. We were all so tense about the possibility of infiltration.

Soul Saving

1970, Summer

Tucked into Ann Arbor's downtown and counterculture neighborhoods, among the student radicals and revolutionaries, were various pockets of "street people." The term was loosely applied to a cross section of humanity, from homegrown hustlers, bikers, battered wives, and hapless hippies to newly arrived runaways, zonked-out vets, drifters, and grifters. Street people might be homeless or crashing in alleys or living ten to a room in a run-down downtown home. They might also be the children of professors or executives, like Randall, who would spend a few days flirting with drugs and danger, and then go home to sleep off his hangover. The local merchants called them "street scum," but the White Panthers officially framed the street people population as noble savages. They were the "peasants" of our revolution. We considered hippies and freaks already part of our "nation within a nation." So, when the party leaders directed us to create a mass movement, street people seemed the most natural target for our conversion efforts. Let the Trotskyites organize factories. Our work would be to bring political consciousness to the spaced-out, stunned, addicted, and unemployed. In Ann Arbor that summer, the Guitar Army and the Salvation Army shared its potential flock with the Hare Krishnas, Jesus Freaks, and a few new gurus. From the start, it was clear to me that I wasn't very good at street work. Proselytizing without appearing to be patronizing or condescending wasn't a skill I came by naturally. I was not adept at the art of persuasion. The more excited I'd get, the less articulate I became.

One evening, I arrived home to find a contingent of bikers in an argument with Violet. Their leader, a greasy-haired bantamweight in leather and gang colors, held a woman on his lap. Another woman was ostentatiously entwined around his leg. Both girlfriends were young, plump, overflowing their identical halter tops inscribed with the gang name "God's Children," and looked like the models for a sailor's tattoo. Apparently, the biker artist, Red, had come to our house in response to a recent *Argus* ad inviting illustrators from the community.

It had been Verna's idea. "Bikers are culturally alienated, too," she'd lectured one night. "They're outlaws, too. They hate the system that fucks them over, too. They fight each other and us instead of the real enemy: the capitalist system that perpetuates their macho myths."

Verna had faith in the biker population, so it was a shame she wasn't there that night to help. She'd gone on one of her periodic junkets to Detroit. In her place, Violet, the ex-Weatherwoman, wasn't building any bridges. The sample cartoons Red had brought to show were all of the same characters: a demented-looking black man with bugged-out eyes in various states of sexual arousal with a number of equally lascivious, big-bottomed, white hippie chicks. His drawings were clearly in the tradition of R. Crumb, but without Crumb's irony or satire.

I'd arrived as positions were hardening on both sides of the argument. "It's racist!" Violet was sputtering. "Is that clearer? Sexist, oppressive, exploitative . . ."

"So fucking what?" Red countered. "It's good drawing. You didn't say what to draw. I thought this was the *free* press. Free my ass," he said to his girlfriends, who both scowled harder.

At first, I confess, I stood speechless. I wanted to say something conciliatory, something that would contribute to building a united front between bikers and freaks. Although I thought Red's pictures were disgusting, I was more shocked by the fact that he obviously didn't mind that he was racist. It didn't matter to him. What kind of revolution would we make with these guys? Red was twice as old as Violet, and just tall enough to stand menacingly above her, though she held her ground. And while I should have raced to her defense, I could hardly squeak out my objection. He ignored me, anyway. He wasn't going to listen to more criticism of his art from another teenaged chick. Spitting out a final curse, he gathered his coterie and departed.

"Why don't you come back for a Red Star Sisters meeting?" I shouted to Red's companions.

Immediately, Violet turned her frustration on me. "You can talk in sisters' meetings, but not in social practice. Why? I really felt alone there. Really up against the wall!"

Later, she would tell everyone how I'd clammed up in the clutch. The upshot was my demotion in the collective *Argus* house mind from my "ultrafeminist" status. At first, I couldn't apologize enough. I'd lost the only position I had held in the house, and my pride was wounded.

But as it worked out, having been denounced as a phony freed me to be more myself.

. . .

Ann Arbor, with its leafy streets and fair-haired folk, was a strange and foreign planet. I wanted to leave. But the easiest way, calling my father and asking for plane fare, was the first thing I rejected. I had become completely compulsive about not going backward. I wasn't going to fail as a revolutionary. I wasn't rejecting *revolution,* but these midwestern communes left much to be desired. My forward momentum had taken on a life of its own. Besides, my body was trapped in a cycle of scabies. Everyone in the house had them. We shared sleeping bags and could never properly organize a complete housecleaning in which we'd all wash ourselves and our bedding simultaneously, then do it exactly the same way the following week to kill the eggs. I had scabs all over my body, and I couldn't stop scratching long enough to plan my escape.

The Midwest, as I perceived it, was cold and unimaginative. The White Panther Party was not, as I'd observed it so far, the rainbow of folk its literature promised. Anyone not midwestern, light-haired, and born Christian stuck out a mile. Siddhartha, a tall, thin, ornately decorated hippie, and the only black White Panther, proved the rule. The utopia I'd envisioned just six months before in high school seemed generations past. Marxism-Leninism had become the party's leading ideology (though creating a "Woodstock Nation" still remained our objective). Others took the contradictions in stride, but I was losing my way in a babble of slogans and new daily directives. Despite my personal divorce from Mao, I was still devoted to the idea of internationalism; but among other things, it seemed, the third-world vanguard remained rather inhospitable to Jews. I considered Israel, like the United States, an imperialist country. So as a Jewish American I was, apparently, doubly cursed. I blocked the subject of Israel out to the extent that I could, and raised Leila Khaled, a Palestinian hijacker, alongside Bernadette Devlin and Bernardine Dohrn into my pantheon of women freedom fighters.

I'd never been religious and never really given Israel much thought. At home our Judaism had been vague, exotically tied to lighting candles for the dead and holiday meals. When I was seven, at my brother

Bob's bar mitzvah, I had fallen on my head and left the party in an am-
bulance. My entire family, I was later told, ran alongside it for blocks,
Gramma Golde moaning that I had died. I have always liked that image:
the women in their chiffons and high heels, their chignons coming un-
done; the men in their tight-fitting suits; and all the children in shiny
black shoes, like a Marc Chagall painting about us. Since I'd given up
my home and family I supposed I could slough off being Jewish—
except that my speech and face together apparently fit some general
notion that prompted Midwesterners to ask if I was a "New York Jew."
So what I learned that autumn was the old lesson: whether or not you
remember you're a Jew, a Gentile will remind you. When I thought
about it, I was confused whether Red the biker had more of a place in
our "United Front" than a revolutionary who was also a Jew.

When we were together, Amy and I would occasionally talk about
being Jewish. We'd joke about the stereotype of wealthy Jews. Was
there some way we could turn the myth to our advantage? We didn't
know any wealthy Jews. If we did, we'd probably eat better.

As it was, I was always hungry. The commune barely provided
enough food for our evening meal, so I was constantly shoplifting
candy bars and hunks of cheese. I hated the brown-rice-and-celery
meals that we took turns cooking. As healthy as they were, as vegetarian, as organic, as third world, they tasted like nothing. It was always
surprising to me how much was left over. Many of my comrades
seemed to have no appetite at all. Later, I was surprised to discover that
my housemates were filching the newspaper receipts and sneaking out
to a fast-food dive called Mr. Ham and Mr. Pig. I went there myself
with Randall one afternoon, and although the thrill of stealing and
lying to the commune soon turned into guilt, the protein high lasted
all day. I became more and more obsessed with food. When Violet's
birthday arrived in October, she was invited home. Her mother, an ex-
cellent chef, had promised to cook duck à l'orange. I tried to invite myself, but Violet still hadn't forgiven me for the biker incident. I wanted
that duck so desperately I considered following her home with a gun
and occupying her family's kitchen.

After our foray to Mr. Ham and Mr. Pig, Randall the Teenybopper
invited me (with a bag of ginger cookies) to play hooky in the town
arboretum. We took his portable radio and a blanket. It was a warm
October day and as we lay side by side, he told me about his love for
Lana, who, at fifteen, was already a junkie. I'd met Lana once. She'd

even stayed at our house, but she'd ripped off some money and hadn't been allowed back. She was a runaway from Detroit who looked like Ophelia, so frail and delicate you wouldn't be surprised to see her rise up and drift off. Randall had tried to help her. He'd given her money and found her places to crash, but now she was hustling, too. Could I help? he asked. I cared so much about women, couldn't I help Lana?

I didn't know what to say. Maybe she could get into a drug program. "She doesn't want to kick," he said. "Maybe you can talk to her."

"All right," I agreed. But then, and this was the breakthrough for me, I said, "Remember, I'm only seventeen myself." I was afraid he'd take it as an excuse (a cop-out, we would have said), but it made as much sense to him as it finally did to me. Maybe I was a revolutionary, but I was also only seventeen. I wasn't a miracle worker. I hardly knew who I was myself.

He didn't argue: another miracle. I wouldn't have to defend what I didn't know. We just lay like a couple of ordinary, prerevolutionary teenagers, enjoying the heat and the moment and the radio. A Detroit underground station was playing John Coltrane's "Central Park West." Later, I would read James Baldwin's story "Sonny's Blues," and in Sonny's performance find a description of how I felt that afternoon, listening to Coltrane: "It was very beautiful because it wasn't hurried and it was no longer a lament. I seemed to hear with what burning he had made it his, with what burning we had yet to make it ours, how we could cease lamenting. Freedom lurked around us and I understood."

The General Harriet Bus Trip

1970, Fall

I started writing in my journal again. I recall that this was a great plea-sure, though I now find some of those journal entries disconcerting. More often than not, the evidence contradicts my memory, and I'm not sure which to believe. I remember being miserable in Ann Arbor. I re-member thinking that I didn't have friends and that nobody listened to me. I just wanted *out,* I recall, but that October I wrote:

> I've been happier here than any other place I've been. My sense
> of humor really developed in Ann Arbor. I laughed an awful
> lot and my social practice was revolutionary. It's a tremendous
> unifying feeling living with people you love and working with
> them.

Was I writing for an audience? I don't remember expecting people to flip through my journals or feeling that I couldn't write what couldn't be read aloud. I do remember being confused, and I say so, often, in my journals. I was absorbed in finding some kind of balance between "the personal and the political," and the early journals seemed to exist for me to work that riddle out. The women's liberation movement was putting more and more emphasis on personal expression. "The per-sonal is the political," I wrote as a mantra, but I gave myself a hard time when I was too "internalized" or "self-indulgent." My writing, I sus-pect, was as much ventilation as truth. I suppose I took liberties, but to what extent? Confessional poetry was all the rage, my journal predictably therapeutic. I poured teenage angst, political ardor, and feminist fury into my poetry "for the people," but the questions re-main: Was I constructing myself as I imagined I'd want to be remem-bered? Would I have bothered to write all those pages to myself if I'd imagined how suspicious a reader I would become?

The girl I remember myself to have been was not fixated on ideol-ogy—infused with the utopian spirit of Woodstock, she was more of a hippie than her comrades. But, in a letter to Judy Leonard, my Teen

Queen and staff photographer friend from the *Herald Tribune,* I represented myself as someone quite different: "I just don't agree with the Woodstock Nation ideology," I wrote. "I think Woodstock was, in objective reality, a white sexist scene, elitist in being expensive, and that being inherently exclusive, dig?"

I also thought that I'd made the decision to work on the paper because I wanted to write, but in the same letter I confessed to Judy that Libby had invited me to live at Trans-Love but I'd followed Buggy to the *Argus* house.

Buggy, I'd forgotten. I thought the crush I had on him had hardened into anger. Could it be I was still sufficiently *in love* with Buggy to want to live where he lived? My letter to Judy says yes, but I can't remember. Did I reject the trappings of power that accompanied residing at Trans-Love to show off what a lumpenprole I was? I was seventeen and believed power was potentially everywhere. Buggy, though, would only be at the *Argus* house (where he'd continued his casual disregard for the minions he fucked until he wandered back to work as a roadie with the UP, and his minions supplanted him in their beds with one another).

The *Argus* commune was more social and far more feminized than the Chicago White Panther house. There were no regimented classes, but we still had an officer of the night whose job was to stay awake and baby-sit the office files and equipment.

Ours wasn't unfounded paranoia. We were all tense about the possibility of infiltration. Before I'd arrived, a plainclothes cop had insinuated himself into the *Argus* community, and consequently several staff members had been busted. All across the country, agents of COINTELPRO, the FBI's counterterrorist campaign (instituted around 1969 as a counterintelligence program to repress black militants and the antiwar movement), were specifically targeting underground papers. (Since the passage of the Freedom of Information Act, many investigations have proved that the FBI took us as deadly seriously as we took them. Thousands of such pages provide a perverse relief—they really *were* following us!) Many newspapers were under secret observation, and some were actively harassed. FBI surveillance and harassment took many forms. Narcs spread paranoia, dissension, and suspicion in the various paper collectives they infiltrated. Police raids were directed at finding the taped or written sources of underground communiqués. The printers of dissident papers were harassed and papers of limited income tied up in the courts for taxes or on issues of source protection. Several lawsuits were also pending in which underground reporters and editors accused the FBI of illegal wiretapping, using undue force, and illegal search and seizure.

Paranoia itself was a resource, necessary to surviving in a place like the *Argus* house. Years after I left the commune, the anxiety of being constantly watched stayed with me, and some sense of paranoia figured in the things I did and the places I went. I sometimes wonder how the rest of the staff coped with their paranoia. Over time most of us drifted out of touch. I heard that Lon was paralyzed in a car accident. Kenny contracted AIDS and died. It took Amy years to shake off the feeling that someone was following her. Violet still thinks someone may be. She recently told me that out of the current atmosphere of sixties bashing, a new McCarthyism will certainly emerge specifically targeted at aging radicals.

One night at the end of September, it was my turn to guard the house. I was probably stretched out downstairs on the scratchy, torn corduroy sofa. From my journals I can tell you I was confused. I'd either never been happier or more miserable. I wanted to get away from the regime of the revolutionary, and I wanted to get better at it. I wanted to go "on the road" in the best Kerouacian sense, but I was still trapped in the cycle of scabies. There's a good chance I was scratching my scabs at about three in the morning when I opened the door to six sunburned revolutionaries on their way back from the Sky River Rock Festival.

"The Lost Kidz Tribe," as they called themselves, were making their way across country. They'd started in Berkeley (where some of them had worked on the *Berkeley Tribe*), and all seemed to carry that California joie de vivre. Phyllis, whom they called Bear because she looked like a plump, plush teddy with Veronica Lake hair, seemed immediately to find my company fascinating. While the others slept, Bear asked if sisterhood was growing in our collective. And what was I doing personally to further its growth? Over the next few days she listened to my enthusiastic plans for overhauling the sexist attitudes, still so pervasive in our party. She seemed to thoroughly understand my complaints against ardent Maoists and dishwashing. Bear herself was dedicated to a whole new level of sisterhood. "Lesbianism," she explained, "was a logical extension of women's struggle, of getting tight with sisters." Everyone in their Lost Kidz Tribe was "dealing with their sexuality." Bear made it clear she'd be happy to help me deal with mine.

So far—I'm not sure why—I'd colluded with the few lovers I'd had to extinguish romance from the act. In Ann Arbor, I was having a miserable time reconciling the ideals of unlimited personal freedom that Woodstock Nation promised with the puritanical dogma of communism. (Add to this the typical horror of those early mating games: Does he just like me because he can have me? Does he even think I'm pretty? *Am* I pretty? Is it counterrevolutionary to want to be pretty?) It seemed we might do whatever we wanted, but if what we did gave us either pleasure or pain we couldn't discuss it (that would be self-indulgent). We had to move on. We felt *guilt,* not in the wake of any particular encounter but about *feeling* guilt. (I feel guilt, therefore I haven't purged all my middle-class impulses. What's wrong with me?) Whenever our desires exceeded immediate gratification, we deliberately suppressed public acknowledgment of them. And though we pretended to eschew the debilitating romance of the rescuing knight on his white horse, our private fantasies were as humbling. Who didn't want a lover to sweep her away from scabies and brown rice and celery? (Although in our dreams perhaps he wore Che's face or Huey Newton's.) Whatever the utopian ideal of free love represented at the start, it became eventually a bunco game run by men. A young woman's resistance was labeled "bourgeois" (an insult as undefendable as frigidity). What a perfect time for sisters to start "dealing with their sexuality."

Bear was a charming, old-fashioned rake with a new-woman's portfolio and I was curious. She told me the whole Lost Kidz Tribe would often *all* make love together. They were older, they'd traveled a lot, and I figured it was a compliment to be invited to their orgy. As I discovered several nights later, being at the bottom of a heap of writhing strangers was more about avoiding elbows in your eye than new heights of eroticism. I remember thinking their orgies were ridiculous, and giggling about them with Randall. But in my journal I wrote that the Lost Kidz Tribe were "the furthest out people I'd ever met." This was high praise.

When I consider it from here, I think there was certainly a generational difference. Little sisters and brothers like Randall and myself had come into sexual awareness, so to speak, in the second wave of the revolution. The activities that the Lost Kidz Tribe viewed as experimental, we already perceived as commonplace. They weren't, of course, but we persisted in the delusion that the world had already been remade, and we were its newest stewards. No one could tell us or teach us anything. The orgiasts thought they were breaking new ground. We were already rebelling against it. They wanted action, and we wanted love. What a muddle. They seemed ridiculous, and we seemed prudish.

. . .

Bear and her friends were not traveling idly. They'd bought a bus on Michigan's Upper Peninsula for two hundred dollars and planned to become a traveling media collective—a liaison between underground papers around the country. Eventually they'd make tapes, films, become a political Hog Farm! Did I want to travel with them? Whether I was happy in Ann Arbor or not, this was my chance to withdraw with honor, and I seized it.

The old school bus needed a lot of work and it took about a month to make it roadworthy. We pulled out its seats, put in a new floor, built cabinets, and painted. No one knew much about engines, so one of our first purchases was a step-by-step manual. Our greatest problem was a generator that wouldn't recharge the battery. With the dogged conviction of those days, it was a point of pride that we women concentrated on rebuilding the engine, while the men sewed curtains made of tapestry and tie-dyed sheets. After some consideration we named the bus *General Harriet,* after Harriet Tubman, and planned our eastward route. Our first stop would be the Underground Press Syndicate convention in Pittsburgh.

I've hardly thought of that bus trip in the years since. (I recall that I was just grateful to escape Ann Arbor without it looking as if I were running away.) In my memory, the experience was brief and confusing, and I might never have written about it now if I hadn't discovered a notebook in the red suitcase that tells a different story.

Her Own Words

1 9 7 0, Fall

It seems that the upcoming adventure stimulated my sense of self as documentarian. In stark contrast to the rambling, introspective tone of many of my other journals, I chronicled our bus trip in a neat and detailed daily log. Since finding this notebook, I've wanted to edit it a hundred times. I'm worried about leaving that younger self exposed without the defense of irony (which she would have rejected—I should know). I also know there's no better illustration of the youthful diarist than her own words.

Ann Arbor, Oct. 16
Things seemed to be dragging. Everyone's bummed out, unproductive today. I guess I'm impatient. We haven't lived all that long together and we're used to different things. We've got to develop a discipline/self-discipline for our meetings and apply more constructive criticism/self-criticism in our sessions so they don't get so subjective/intense. The bus has a lot further to go, and we've got a vast amount of shit work to do. We should have breezed through a division of the work that had to be done. But people are sick with an intestinal flu. Dan has the disease now and Bear just got it. They, and Teddy, Sue, Roy, and Mary are all staying at the Argus house because of it (creating a really crowded situation). There's only three bedrooms, and already 16 people—chapter and information cadre—living there.

Ann Arbor, Oct. 17
Under me is this tremendous treetrunk hundreds of rings/years old. It's covered by small daisy-like flowers that have still resisted the almost freezing weather that's making it so uncomfortable for us to sleep in the bus.

I thought all of us being bummed out was only us, and only our fault for letting our tribe fall apart. Not being conscious that forces (disease, weather) were natural fuck-ups that we weren't dealing with. But everything we did was necessary. Sick people had to live at the Argus, healthy people (just me!) on the cold, cold, bus.

What I found when visiting the Argus and just trucking around was that the general political sentiment is disconcerted, disharmonic, fucked-up, awful, vague, and despairing. The repression is getting heavier. A violent surge of repression is pressing Canada with the encouraging leadership of liberal Trudeau, his true colors flying. He's picking up every member of the Quebec Liberation Front and popping them for 5 years. John Mitchell commented (of course not to be outdone) that (here) the vigilantes would take care of the rebels.

Ann Arbor, Oct. 18
I slept heavily for the first time in days thanks to the cocaine last night. Sleeplessness had added to my three day self-indulgent depression. I'd been getting high without much food. Finally I was so wrecked, I crashed and it did me good.

We're leaving Friday. Before then we've got to get a stove to fucking heat the bus. Build a second cabinet to store all our stuff—make curtains—make it livable and most important/I think/make the documentary on the Argus house.

We have to be in Pittsburgh at Carnegie-Mellon on Saturday. We've been asked to give a presentation or something, so we're making a documentary of the Argus house—saying how the paper is created and showing how people live and work so well together—collectively/communistically.

Everyone in the bus really loves the Argus people. I've lived there for 2 months and feel really close to them and to the White Panther Party. However, I won't be in the party any-more/ because I won't be relating to any particular chapter. That's the criteria for membership. The party is a community based organization. We haven't many members at large—not yet. For the past month I've had a number of differences with the party especially over the name Woodstock Nation. I don't believe you can build or organize anything on an unreality/a hype something that in objective reality is racist/exclusive/sexistsexistsexist. I also don't agree with the colony theory.

Nor youth as a class. We are a New Nation, we're building an international revolution. Everyone/Women—Men—Black—Indians—Tupermaros—Vietcong-Pathet Lao (and they weren't at Woodstock) we're building a new woman, new man & new world INTERNATIONALLY. The ideology of the future is international & the old Woodstock concept is changing.

Underdog's in heat and we've got to keep the door locked so she can't get out and get fucked. She's less than a year old and if she gets fucked by a big dog there's a good chance that the puppies would be too big and she'd die. I'm writing this locked in with her. The bus door doesn't lock from the outside so to keep Underdog in I've got to stay in too.

Ann Arbor, Oct. 19
Almost everything we've gotten for the bus and for us this past 3 weeks we've ripped off. Either personally stolen or charged on Mary's Mastercharge. Shoes, stove, radios, tools, food everything . . .

We ran through the streets of Ann Arbor, 7 of us singing, ("The Best things in life are free/When you steal 'em from the bourgeoisie . . .") laughing, our arms around each other on our way to pick up the twenty-five Red Books we'd ordered from the Centivore bookstore. We sang Power to the people (off the pig) Free Bobby Seale (Erika Huggins/Angela Davis/Los Siete/John Sinclair/Women Power to Women People/Gay Power to Gay People PERVERT POWER TO THE PERVERT PEOPLE/

On our way home I saw Lana, (Teeny bopper Randall's love) hanging out on the diag, waiting for a John, and I felt real weird. Wishing I knew what to do.

On The Road, Oct. 20
So we started. At about 5:00 p.m. I fell asleep after about an hour on the road. Around 8, while I was crashed out several things happened. We stopped at a gas station and Sandy brought on board a straight looking dude who was hitching. There was already one hitchhiker on the bus by then. A guy in the Navy/a brother who hated the service/and kept talking about leaving it.

Bear was driving, Mary was staying up with her, everyone

else was asleep. Somewhere Bear took a wrong turn and instead of going East, she went South.

I woke up about 2 in the morning/half dreaming that we'd been stopped by the pigs. And surprise—it was true. Mary woke me. "The pigs want your ID." She said.

Meanwhile the pig had been checking everyone else's ID— Seems there'd been a Post Office heist recently and we were prime suspects.

We were in Marion, Ohio directly South of Ann Arbor and not much closer to Pittsburgh than when we started. We'd been bussing along at a swift 40mph in the wrong direction for about 4 hours. Apparently, the highway pig had been attracted to our bus because one of our front headlights had blown. He'd pulled us over, and at first there was no real trouble. Then the hitch-hiker disappeared. (The Navy brother had been let off just a while before but the straight dude had still been on the bus— when the pig first pulled us over).

The pig got suspicious. He wanted to know where the hitchhiker was. Laura didn't know either, and at that point he told her to turn off the engine. She did, the battery died, and wouldn't start again.

This wasn't cool. We were bound to be busted. The consensus about dope before we'd started out had been to take only easily eaten psychedelics and to keep them on your person. Mary gave us the sign to eat our mescaline.

It would have been catastrophic if we'd been busted for dope on our first night. But dope wasn't even our greatest problem. Roy (from Switzerland) had overstayed his visa. When they asked for his passport he couldn't produce it. Meanwhile, our bus was dead on US 23. We were all swallowing psychedelics and cursing Roy for not having prepared an alternate set of ID. Worst of all, we were all dependent on the pig to call a tow truck.

The last two things were serious indeed and since then we've undergone severe criticism/self-criticism. But there's only so many times you can say, fuck-it, we're fools. We're idiots.

Roy understood his situation. He'd known that the first time we were stopped and our ID checked he'd be fucked-over. He'd had a 6 months permit to be in this country as a tourist. After that time he was supposed to either get a student visa—meaning pay money to go to a university or a work visa (how absurd) get a job and be eligible for the draft. So Roy had decided to just hang around Amerika, working on the *Berkeley Tribe,* learning how to put out a newspaper that serves the people so that when he went back to Switzerland he could start a right-on paper there.

They took Roy to the Marion police station, a dip shit sterile place to check him out, and we got towed to a gas station. It was not the place anybody wanted to trip in, but we couldn't help ourselves. NOTE TO MYSELF. Never take hallucinogens in a police station again!

By around 10p.m. the bus was fixed. The pigs had called the immigration office in Cleveland, and it looked like Roy was going to be deported. Beside that, they'd found the mail sack that Roy used as a knapsack and called in the postmaster from Columbus, as well as the local FBI agent, who was most interested in the missing hitchhiker.

All of us were interrogated separately. They showed us FBI wanted posters and questioned us about Bernardine Dohrn, Huey P. Newton and Karl Armstrong. Because I was from Ann Arbor (not a Berkeley radical like the others) the questions they asked centered around John Sinclair. 'Did I ever meet him when I was at the National Headquarters of the WPP?' 'How well did I know him?' The fact is I never met him. John was in jail by the time I joined the party.

They told Dan they knew more about where he'd been the last two months than he did. They evidently knew I was a White Panther. Mostly we refused to answer their ridiculous questions. They were tremendously interested in the *Ann Arbor Argus,* and the Postmaster who was still hanging around was fascinated after Bear told him that she had seen other mail bags like Roy's at the *Berkeley Tribe*—where they were used to take the papers to the Post Office.

"Yes the *Berkeley Tribe* is another Underground Paper like the *Argus,*" she told him.

"You mean," he asked. "You people go around starting newspapers?"

The chronicle of our trip ends there, abruptly. By the next entry on October 28, I was in Boston, where I'd hitchhiked to visit my brother Rick. In a letter to Amy back in Ann Arbor, I explained my departure from the bus. It had become a "weirdo scene," I wrote.

Before we'd set out, Randall the Teenybopper had casually observed that the Lost Kidz Tribe seemed to be held together more by sex than politics. At the time I'd considered his statement undermining, almost counterrevolutionary. Hadn't he learned anything from the women's or gay liberation movements? He didn't understand, I said. It wasn't sex or politics, it was sexual politics. He couldn't understand because he was a man. But by the time I escaped to Boston, the artificial intimacy, lack of all privacy, and constant fumbling in duos, trios, and heaps had made me a nervous wreck. Refusing any one person was considered an offense against the group. As punishment you would be severely criticized but never, unfortunately, shunned.

For years, I didn't think about that bus ride. Eventually, I started to recast the story as a dark fairy tale, another adventure from which I was lucky to escape. Once upon a time, I was the innocent in a wood full of sexual predators.

Of course it was much more complicated.

By the time I came on board the bus, the three men and three women of the Lost Kidz Tribe were in the midst of a long-playing soap opera. Bear was the gay seducer, a happy-go-lucky, love 'em and leave 'em type of gal, constitutionally unable to be faithful. She was also, for all practical purposes, entirely dependent on Mary, with whom she had a long-term relationship. Long-suffering Mary, trying her best not to be threateningly possessive, threw herself into promiscuity, too, in a joyless, self-sacrificing way. The third woman in the cast, the brooding Sue, also loved Bear. They'd had a brief affair that had left Sue feeling rejected and miserably jealous of Mary. Of the men, Teddy had been gay since he could remember. He and Bear had been best friends since high school. Teddy and Roy were a couple and not particularly interested in making love to women, but willing to do their bit for the collective. I noticed that in every orgy they would roll away on their own. Of all the Lost Kidz, Dan seemed the most lost. He had joined the bus after his own dalliance with Bear. Once on board he'd made love with both Teddy and Roy, but was racked with guilt because he couldn't enjoy gay sex. On this point, the rest of the collective offered little sympathy. Dan's lapse was considered more a failure of "consciousness" than personal taste. Dan hoped to find some consolation with Sue, but she was his worst critic. At every opportunity Sue excoriated the poor bastard for his sexual and political performance, which in both their minds was magically the same.

At first, I hadn't paid much attention to the interrelationships of my comrades. I was dazzled by Bear myself and willfully ignored her other attachments. She had never denied her relationship with Mary, but she made so little of it. I followed Bear around like a puppy and resented the fact that I could never see her alone.

In that hothouse atmosphere, orgies were the collective's only solution for sore hearts. But even on drugs, those sweaty clusterfucks were more work than fun. At the bottom of every nocturnal heap lay Bear's plump naked body, supine, as if staked, while her many lovers fed upon it, like wild scavengers.

"I have to split," I wrote to Amy.

Where would I split to? I didn't want to go to college, and I didn't want to go home. So I hitchhiked back to Ann Arbor to find the party collapsing and the *Argus* in chaos. In the two months since I'd left, the house had become a crash pad. Even Verna had lost her faith. Now she wanted to become a radio DJ. The remaining staff had flirted with the concept of reforming into a community-based media collective, but, as I wrote Judy Leonard at Christmas, "IBM has repossessed our composer. We no longer have a phone and if we can't pay 1500 dollars by the end of January we'll lose our mortgage." We were "depending on the community for absolute support," I wrote. That was either a joke or a dream. Covering my bets I added, "Write and tell me about Goddard College. I think I may either see you in Vermont or move to California. All Power to the People,

Love, Leslie."

Journalism

1970–1971, Winter, Spring

On Tuesday, I checked out the University of Michigan ride board and Wednesday I was on my way to California with two students on semester break. We'd planned to share driving, but early on they'd objected to the way I merged lanes and left me to my own devices. At night I slept in the car while they shared a motel room. By day, as the West unwound, I ate through a five-pound bag of red pistachios, drank from a jug of tap water, and plowed through *The Golden Notebook*.

Lessing's novel was the right sacred text at the right time. ("It will influence your life," Mary had predicted on board *General Harriet*. That was a safe bet. What *wasn't* influencing my life?) Readers with more experience than I knew there wasn't another book like it: an overtly left-wing intellectual puzzle that gave voice to the messy lives of difficult women. My first reaction was surprise at finding Lessing's two heroines still alive at forty. I didn't expect to live to see middle age myself; counterrevolutionaries would kill me or I'd become a vegetable rotting in jail. So, imagining a future as an independent artist, alive and still "dealing with my sexuality," came as an entirely new and fascinating idea.

All the adult women I knew—aunts and the mothers of friends, even those who were politically conscious—seemed to me to have surrendered by thirty. Of course, all along there'd been rebels and eccentrics among them, but back then I couldn't recognize how getting drunk or disorderly in the suburbs constituted rebellion. There were no women in my immediate world over twenty, and I was pretty much stumbling around unhinged when I discovered *The Golden Notebook*. Lessing's suggestion that a person could dig herself out of emotional chaos without forfeiting her ideals had a bracing effect on the warm suggestible jelly I'd become. Her character Anna's reliance on a series of notebooks to reconcile the personal and political aspects of her life sent me springing to my own diaries. I recorded page after page of the most intimate details with the conviction that my daily life must be a rough draft for art. Then I read Anaïs Nin.

Nin had her problems, and her obsession with her notebook may have been one. But she was definitely sexier, more intuitive, the yin to Lessing's yang. Lessing had moral authority; her book had an aura of *virtù;* her "Anna" brandished prose like a whip to tame the world, but she lacked the sense of mystery in which Nin thrived. Daily life might exist as the source of fiction, but as Nin's example proved, it wasn't quite sufficient. A writer needed to have unforeseen adventures and insoluble problems. In a century gone mad, the writer had to be a little mad herself. Nin declared that she was "in accord with the surrealists, searching for the marvelous."

By the time I read Nin, she and Lessing together had spawned a cult of dedicated diarists. I remember sitting in cafés and looking up to find women at tables all around writing in their journals. If all the "I's" on all our pages had fluttered up on wings, they'd have blocked the sun. What were we writing about? I can only guess that others like myself were gaining and losing perspective; making true confessions and false ones; slowing the world down and quieting it; writing in fever or desperation or ecstasy and even rarely at a cool remove; indulging in grand delusions, self-improvement, and self-loathing in the service, possibly, of self-knowledge. In a whirlwind of creativity, this army of obscure diarists were valuable witnesses, the heroines of our own lives.

.   .   .

I didn't know anyone in California except Bob Rudnick, but a toehold seemed sufficient. Rudnick had left Chicago after an argument with radio station management over the radical content of his *Kocaine Karma* show. In his final act he'd cued up "Street Fighting Man" and walked out, leaving the song to repeat, some fans say a hundred, others a thousand times in a row.

The suburban San Jose where I found Rudnick was California on the verge of its silicone expansion. His new radio station was an isolated building plumped down on a mat of yellow grass and surrounded by an immense parking lot in which every space was filled. The receptionist, who was around my age, was dressed in frilly pastels. After four days in a crowded car, I was stinking up her beige lobby. My jeans were stiff with dirt, I'd lost my hairbrush en route and accidentally torn my T-shirt. I was dead tired, but so wired from lack of sleep that

I couldn't stand still. She stood, arms folded, smile unwavering as she sized me up. Was she, I wondered, a sister under that thick-caked makeup, those ruffles and bows? Just a nod of sympathy and I'd have dropped weeping at her feet. Was it my imagination or did her eyes keep wandering back to my unshaven underarms? I clearly remember being under the illusion that the traveling life was everyone's secret ambition. Perhaps I thought all she needed to escape her servile job and the dress of a baby porn star was encouragement. Confusing her fear with envy, I tried, in the friendliest way, to assure her that the pleasures of the road were free and available to all. But she wrinkled her offended nose, and whispered, "You're a drug addict. And I'm calling security."

Rudnick was crooning on the air. Later, called to claim me in the lobby, he acted as appalled as his colleagues. "What's this?" he said, making the receptionist laugh. I may have smelled, but he didn't have to make such a show of calling for a fumigator. I don't know why I hadn't thought it necessary to phone him ahead of time. Maybe I was afraid that he'd say, "Don't come." I hadn't considered that Rudnick, like me, might have wanted to elude his past in California.

To his coworkers, Rudnick was the previously big-time underground DJ. They knew he had a dark history, but this was California, and the past another universe. In San Jose, he had high hopes. He wanted to be liked, he wanted to do well at his new job, and he expected to be the sole architect of his reconstructed identity. Now, here I was, standing in the lobby, "Cousin Itt" among the blond shags, sports shirts, and frozen smiles of his new life. "Better clean up," Rudnick said, hustling me toward the ladies' room.

I don't know what I'd expected. Rudnick and I had never been close, but I felt he owed me for the misery I'd endured in Chicago. And then there was the code of the road. I wasn't sure how that worked yet, but at least he had to harbor me. I was tired and hungry, and I'd just gotten my period. In typical fashion, I didn't have any sanitary napkins or change for the tampon dispenser, and I wasn't going out there to ask the receptionist if she could cash a dollar. Maybe Rudnick thought he could choose his new bourgeois lifestyle over his old friends, but I wouldn't make it easy. And what about this Kotex company? The monopoly they had and their manipulation of women's needs were criminal! I started banging on the tampon machine. I took out my penknife, scratched the outside with interlocking women's signs, then proceeded to tear its hinges apart.

When Rudnick asked why I'd vandalized the ladies' room, I shrugged. "It was only because of me that you weren't arrested," he boomed in another mortifying public display.

That afternoon, I hitched to San Francisco. Rudnick didn't stay in San Jose much longer. The dark, druggy side of his character found a more honest berth in Los Angeles. Eventually, he went back to Chicago and came to be revered there as a grand old man of rock and roll. He died in 1995, at age fifty-two. In the obituaries he was described as a "combined Peter Pan, Pied Piper, and Lenny Bruce," remembered as "the inventor of free-form radio," for his work on *Playboy,* as a pioneer of the eighties poetry slam, and for his "baritone chortle." I never saw him again.

. . .

San Francisco in 1971. Can it have been as glamorous as I remember? Hippies, of course, were thick on the ground. It was admittedly a matter of perspective, but everyone seemed young, attractive, and stoned. The street was a perpetual parade, and we were floats rolling past. Within a year styles would change. Most of the youth on parade would trade in their buckskin for polyester. Hot tubs were a shot away. AIDS was galloping nearer. The "me generation" was the rumble underground, but who would have imagined? On that January day it was still "us" and "them."

I stayed for a month in San Francisco and my notes are full of superlatives. Everything was *far out,* everybody was *too much.* I didn't know anyone, no one knew me, and I found that distance liberating. My stay in a crash pad in the upper Haight was a vacation from the feeling that I always had to judge things politically. I'd sit on stoops writing and sketching in my journal. And although I was playing dumb, my hippie companions said I must be a genius, to read and write so much. At night I'd smoke pot in one strange pad or another. Most were rudimentary, the rooms of people passing through, a few pillows, sleeping bags, some coffee cups. But I remember one room decked out in gingham, ruffled curtains and tablecloth, another decorated entirely in tin can lids—a folk visionary extravaganza. Every day I panhandled and shoplifted junk food like all the other street people. Our late-night communal dinners, held on one stoop or another, would invariably consist of huge sugary collations catered by Hostess.

"San Francisco was where the social hemorrhaging was showing up," Joan Didion wrote in 1968. Her book of essays, *Slouching Towards Bethlehem,* published two years before I arrived, is still the best portrait of that time and place. Except for the time lag, I could easily have been one of the self-absorbed girls-in-the-crowd she interviewed about the hippie movement. I was just as sentimental and unwilling to look under the sink. Didion's observations are cool, ironic, and unusually sympathetic for an adult twenty years older and a world of experience away. When she describes a bizarre interview with Huey P. Newton (admitting his charisma but finding a creepy, machine-like precision in his rhetoric), though I wasn't there exactly, I sense myself in the background, demonstrating with a "Free Huey" sign. While California was becoming my new land of mystery and wonder, it was Didion's native landscape, damaged by crime, cruelty, and paranoia, a place where all the neuroses of the modern world boiled beneath the sunshine. Didion's California is so charged with anxiety that when she first heard of the Manson murders, she wrote, "I remember that no one was surprised."

Didion reviewed *The Golden Notebook* around the same time I was first enraptured by it. She called it the "diary of a writer in shock," and took it to task for almost all the reasons it had moved me. Lessing's voice was "exhortative," "laborious," "easy." Didion was unimpressed by the novel's moral lessons and frustrated by its lack of ambiguity; in her essay she stalks Lessing like a jumpy young gunfighter. I can't help wanting to impose myself.

I'm back in 1970, reading Lessing's novel, jumping up and down in the background. Interview me, Ms. Didion! Let me be your champion, Ms. Lessing! I want to talk about journals! Didion, I know, has strong opinions on this subject, too. Her own notebook is a sensible prophylactic against the ghosts of past selves, who "come hammering on the mind's door at 4 A.M. of a bad night and demand to know who deserted them, who betrayed them, who is going to make amends."

I want to invite both women to the great Massapequa dinner party with Christine Jorgensen and Joey Buttafuoco. Joan Didion, the awesome philosopher-queen, would wear, I think, something sleeveless and black. In conversation she'd track the immensity of all that's equivocal, random, unknowable. I'd try to keep up. Doris Lessing would arrive, sword drawn, clothed in mail. Perhaps Anaïs Nin would show up, too, her hair loosened. Of course, she'd be welcome. Her own notebook swings madly between analysis and ambiguity. If it were a beautiful human, she'd make love to it.

.   .   .

I was relieved to discover that the *Berkeley Tribe*'s offices really were offices. Unlike the *Argus,* housing didn't come with the job. And this close escape made me realize how reluctant I was to leap into another political commune. There were only a couple of things I knew for sure: I wasn't much of an urban guerrilla, and I was entirely sick of submitting to collective discipline.

By the spring of 1971, the *Berkeley Tribe* was a very different paper from the one begun two years before as the *Barb on Strike.* The original *Tribe* was the result of a struggle between generations of leftists. Most of its radical staff had worked previously on the *Berkeley Barb* for Max Scher, a longtime Berkeley activist. In the summer of 1969, after an article in a Berkeley magazine reported that Scher's gross profits exceeded five thousand dollars a week, the *Barb*'s staff, whose reporters were making twenty-five cents a column inch, cried exploitation. On their own, the salary issues might have been negotiated, but the mostly counterculture staff, attuned as they were to communalism, expanded their protest to demand that Scher open his editorials to more staff involvement and make donations to community programs. At the same time, the women on staff objected to the nature of the paper's personals. This was the argument that brought the clash between generations into greatest relief. To the women protesting them, the ads were sexist because they exploited and demeaned women by reducing them to only their sexual value. Scher, on the other hand, had marveled as the Free Love generation replaced the puritanism of the fifties with a new puritanism. The personals were voluntary, he argued. Why kill the goose that laid the golden egg? At first, there was some hope of a staff buyout, but negotiations broke down and Scher (in a dramatic move that asserted his authority but lost him the sympathy vote) commandeered the *Barb*'s subscription lists, typewriters, and supplies. Radical Berkeley threw its support behind the striking employees, and the early *Berkeley Tribe* was famously successful.

Undergrounds all over the country were experimenting with various ways to blend cultural radicalism and left-wing revolutionary ideas, but for most the recipe was elusive. Time and time again, when those two equally powerful substances were forced into the same beaker, the result was indigestible. The secret of the *Tribe*'s success seems to have been its ability to hold both interests in equipoise. But, like an acrobat standing on a ball on the head of another acrobat, on the top of a pyramid of acrobats balanced on a tightrope, this wasn't a pose that could be held indefinitely. The early *Berkeley Tribe* lived fast, died young, and wasn't an easy act to follow.

A year later, after many of its original staff members had moved on, the *Tribe*'s second-generation leadership (several of them ex-Weatherpeople) didn't deliberately jettison wit, irony, and objectivity, but those were just some of the consequences of becoming vanguard propagandists. The new *Tribe* was more radical than most of the other radicals in the most radical city in America—and that was the whole idea.

Perhaps more than anything, the vanishing byline projected the paper's new attitude. It is possible, given the time and place, to construe the resistance to bylines as a by-product of utopian communalism. The staff tried in their work to *model* a kind of postrevolutionary society, in which there would be no "star trips" and where everyone's talent would be equally appreciated and equally rewarded. I admit that, early on, I endorsed these ideas freely. I wanted to be a writer, so I assumed everyone did. But everyone's talent wasn't equal (and who could possibly regulate appreciation?). We never actually had any "stars" whose "trips" were smothered, but the sense that individuality was somehow *unsavory* contributed to a general atmosphere of mediocrity. By the time I arrived, there were some fine reporters and other resilient and eccentric contributors, but the question of the quality of their writing, even the necessity of it—why write when photos, cartoons, and graphics can do the job?—was dwarfed by an arrogance subtly inherent in anonymity: under a pseudonym, you can be as nasty and dismissive as you like and never have to own up to it.

Meanwhile, as editors came to be seen as the standard-bearers of bourgeois convention, privilege, and ego, editing became less important, less consistent, and less often employed. Only the most perverse radical wanted to grow up to be an editor anymore.

· · ·

The *Tribe*'s final decline was still a good year away when I first walked into its offices. I'd already survived the White Panther Party and the *Ann Arbor Argus*. The fact that I wouldn't be required to live on-site with the rest of the staff gave the enterprise an unexpected sheen of professionalism. Besides, the men at the *Tribe,* deep in the process of examining their male chauvinism, seemed, at first glance, a new, more agreeable, and more malleable breed.

According to Mason Monroe, one of the young men who greeted me that first afternoon, the scope and opportunity in Berkeley were beyond anything I could imagine. Himself a recent arrival from back East, Mason wasted no time confiding his own observations concerning the local passion for looting. During a violent protest, he explained, your experienced looter might pull things directly from the windows of stores or scavenge them later in the streets. What things, I asked? Toasters, gooseneck desk lamps. And if my interests ran to art, he continued, there were also great opportunities to silkscreen political posters and T-shirts on the Merritt College campus (where Huey Newton had been enrolled). Mason had read widely and had educated himself in the lives of the anarchists. He was eager to lend me Emma Goldman's autobiography, *Living My Life,* as soon as I wanted it, and, he assured me, I could rely on him for anything else I wanted to read (books were considered sacrosanct, unlootable, but he had his own large library). Mason Monroe felt he could confidently invite me to start work at the *Tribe* that very day. In fact, there was nothing the staff would like better than a young woman writer with my kind of experience.

.   .   .

As the staff of the *Berkeley Tribe* bent to its weekly task, a few blocks away on Telegraph, a new wave of peddlers hawked the ephemera of the counterculture. Everything was for sale or available for barter—candles, tie-dyes, mobiles, jewelry made and imported. Julia Vinograd wandered "The Ave" selling her poems. Everyone was everyone's friend or potential customer. It occurred to me soon after my arrival that although the *Tribe* staff prided itself on representing the culture it served, they were barely able to penetrate its topsoil. Who were the people promenading on "The Ave"? Why had they migrated here from everywhere else? (A few years later I met a woman who'd moved from Minneapolis. Why had she come to Berkeley? She was going mad from the cold, she said, and from the custom of restraining one's emotions. If she was going to go mad, at least she wanted to go mad where mad was "normal.")

I didn't have much enthusiasm for the *Tribe* as a paper. Like the *Argus,* it preached only to the converted, and the converted were starting to bore me. I hadn't lost my conviction that the war was terribly wrong, and I didn't want to be any part of the destructive and dehumanizing system that perpetuated it. For the past year I'd believed that the country was on the verge of revolution. I thought it would be bloody and long. But by that spring, as I looked down Telegraph, I wasn't sure anymore. My faith was breaking down.

I was finally at large, without the protection or influence of a party line. Even more than when I first left home, this next step constituted a leap into the unknown. Of course, I wasn't exactly like Alice, tumbling down the rabbit hole in complete innocence. I could still write for the *Tribe.* I wasn't risking everything as Gramma Golde had on the day she'd climbed on board the *Queen Frederika*. Or, as my mother had, when she'd accepted the marriage proposal of a soldier she'd only known a few weeks. Still, down the rabbit hole I went. And since this was Berkeley, it followed that my adventures underground would begin with a subway ride to Oakland.

Wonderland

1971, Spring

Oakland seemed broad-shouldered and salt-of-the-earth. It might not have been *there* for Gertrude Stein, but its hunkering, working presence appealed to me. It was far enough away to escape the inner-Tribal warfare, but close enough so that I could drift in and out on my own terms. The lively entrepreneurialism on Telegraph Avenue, Berkeley's counterculture Main Street, had encouraged me to come up with my own imaginative hustle. First, I'd tried to sell poems, but the competition had been fierce. It then occurred to me that fortune-telling might provide a steadier income. In the past, I'd displayed some talent as a tarot card reader, and, fishing from the pool of great narratives, I could always put an interesting prediction together.

The day after this brainstorm, I dressed up like a gypsy and sidled through the buskers and crowds at Sproul Plaza. My first few days I even faked a sort of Middle European accent (an interesting exercise but hard to maintain). I asked fifty cents to a dollar per reading, and every customer left knowing they would eventually travel, stumble upon money, and find the love of their life after a period of "transition."

I was certainly aware of, and pretty excited by, the irony involved. There I was, an unemployed revolutionary spinning fairy tales about love and patience and wealth and prosperity. Although I had a detailed story worked out to justify my activities to those revolutionary comrades who happened by (hadn't Emma Goldman resorted to prostitution to finance an anarchist action? So what if her first trick had recognized her as an amateur and suggested she go home?), I never saw my revolutionary comrades on "The Ave"—they inhabited another Berkeley.

At first it seemed amazing that no one called me a phony to my face and suggested I go home. Soon enough, I had to remind *myself* that I was pretending and didn't really have a gift. Telegraph Avenue was full of people pretending. Its con artists and characters worked a deeply tolerant floating world where, as long as your game wasn't recognizably subversive, you could be anybody. You could sell poetry, and people would actually buy it by the page. You could be a fortune-teller or a nineteenth-century anarchist or the Mad Hatter or a time-traveling visitor from the USS *Enterprise*.

Telegraph provided the approximate boundaries of a magic circle. The problems came with *knowing* about the magic circle. Unless you were on drugs (at which time you might forget anything), you really couldn't forget how easy it was to live in Berkeley, how unlike anywhere else. And although an atmosphere of cheerful indulgence presided, the threat of violence was always close to the surface. Sometimes the police would be called on stage to end that day's performance. Or perhaps you'd step back yourself, and, viewing "The Ave" through a rip in the magic fabric, suddenly recognize it as a sort of zoo under pressure.

.   .   .

In the Berkeley radical community, it was a truth universally held that the old days of white male dominance were gone for good. As gay men and newly collected groups of women weighed the consequences of what seemed an absolute rout, the future promised a world of experimentation.

I found a room in an Oakland apartment with Melissa and Andrea, two Jewish women from back East. Melissa was an aspiring chanteuse. When it was just we three "girls" at home, she wouldn't walk if she could stomp or speak when she could bellow. But when her "boys," her entourage of gay men, appeared, she became immediately and weirdly serene (like a TV evangelist whose smile is reserved for the camera). Melissa adored her boys, and they worshiped her.

Her roommate, the beautiful Andrea, had been a good girl back in Brooklyn. One day, envisioning her future as the good wife of a suburban doctor, she had bolted. She was very beautiful, and men, women, entire families, stopped dead on the street to tell her so. An animator might have drawn her as a bosomy hummingbird with tiny waist and sultry eye. Andrea knew she was a *character,* never more so than when she invoked her other identity as the bad girl, "Juanita." (It was de rigueur to have another name in that house—a kind of atavistic belief in the way alternate identities divert bad luck.) Melissa, a pianist, was "Baby Grand"; her "boys" were the Eighty-Eight Keys. Before I'd lived there a week, they'd renamed me.

"You need something organic," Andrea said. "How about Kasha!" She translated it from the Yiddish, "Buckwheat Groats!" It seemed absolutely wrong to me. It wasn't romantic, it was comic, like the name you'd pull out of a hippie grab bag on your way out the door, a good-natured name that reminded me of dressing up on Halloween as a goofy lampshade instead of the far more preferable Queen of the Nile. The name reminded people of *Little Rascals* movies or a kind of honey or a grain most had never tried. Andrea obviously had no talent for language. At first I resisted, but there was a certain cachet in receiving a new name as opposed to inventing one's own.

It took me a while to learn how to live with my new clown's name. Suddenly, I was funny; I only had to say, "I'm Buckwheat," to get a laugh. The name was frivolous, but I wasn't, entirely. Sometimes I'd pretend great gravity to balance those first impressions. And there were moments, sunk in poetic melancholy, that I felt ridiculous being Buckwheat Groats (on that score, it's tough to be any young writer). I think I kept the name because it was thrilling to see how little it took to puzzle people. I had an unusual name, and it set me apart. Over the next four years, I never introduced myself as Leslie.

. . .

While I struggled to reconcile with my identity, my roommate Andrea/Juanita submerged herself in a fantasy world of tango and mambo where everyone looked like artfully disheveled Spanish ballroom dancers and life whirled in a mad *ronde* of flirtation and passion. Andrea could be tranquil and contemplative. Some days she would watch out the window, drinking chamomile tea and eating matzos with butter and salt by the hour. But Juanita was a free spirit, the Queen Hummingbird gathering love from the male flowers of the field. Everything and everyone around Juanita had to be high, glorified, dramatic. "I want to go down to Mexico where the poor people live. When I need money after a while, I'll turn tricks."

Juanita spoke about turning tricks as casually as someone else might talk about temp typing. Her fantasy was not that she would do it but that she *could,* easily, and on her own terms. Before I'd met Andrea and Melissa, prostitution was not a subject to which I'd given much thought. But as their roommate, I found it an enterprise impossible to ignore. Madame Melissa ran a little gay prostitution ring: nothing fancy, but it tied up the phone.

I was learning that everyone had a California creation myth of her own. Melissa had felt oversized and underappreciated back East. Her mistake, she confessed, had been expecting straight men to love her as she was. She spent entirely too much time pining over a certain type of neat, handsome man with beautiful hands whom she inevitably terrified. She knew it sounded extravagant to recount, but after careful analysis she'd come to the conclusion that she looked like a tall gay man in drag. To some extent, she was a gay man in spirit. She knew this sounded odd, not to be taken at face value, but it was one explanation why she felt so comfortable with her "boys." They understood the torments of exclusion she'd suffered and they loved her for her outré inner self. Before she could make any progress as a musician or as a person, she first had to purge all the residual desire she'd felt for neat, handsome heterosexuals with beautiful hands. So, for several weeks she'd hustled tricks in San Francisco's Tenderloin. As she tells it, her costume was all-important: three-inch spike heels (which brought her to six-four), black, off-the-shoulder velvet gown, and a miniature devil fetish on a chain around her waist. Is it possible she did it for three dollars as my notes say? Turning tricks was a crucible from which she emerged triumphant, with complete contempt for the male sexual response. She could do anything after that, she insisted.

Melissa made her way to Oakland and organized a low-key but profitable business among the "boys" who occupied the two apartments below ours. Andrea, whose powers worked only on straight men, was jealous of Melissa's gay retinue, but I was enchanted. I was Melissa's sorcerer's apprentice, the new doll, and if no one else was home, the occasional message service. When the boys were bored, they'd make me over and fix me up. And I'd hear about the complex web of sexuality that lay beneath one tiny piece of Oakland.

Most afternoons as Melissa sat on her bed strumming her guitar, four or five young men from her extensive circle would lounge alongside waiting for the phone to ring. "Mine!" one or the other would trill, reaching for the neat square of notepaper that served as a "date booking."

"Don't believe what you see," Melissa's special confidant, Scott, explained early on. "We're not that excited, but Baby Grand likes to see our enthusiasm up." (He always said *Baby Grand* as if her name were in italics, implying an affectionate insider code in which we all conspired: *Baby Grand* had suffered so much heartache, what harm did it do to allow her this illusion of control?) "I only turn tricks to pay the rent," he told me. Scott was the most politically active, often asking if I wanted to stuff envelopes for one left-wing cause or another.

No one in that company was unaware of the Bay Area's super-charged politics, and any afternoon's idle dishing and bitching could turn to the change in the air. Even Jay, perhaps the most domestic of us all, complained about how often he ended up cooking for his purport-edly communal household: "I don't know if it's oppressive, but it certainly makes me think more about this role thing." The boys were always teasing Jay's roommate, Sidney, about how hard he worked to save money. "Does it mean when this revolution comes I have to give up my car that I worked for?" Sidney asked me, the revolution's on-site representative.

One day, Tony, who'd been in the Peace Corps for five years and was a little older and sadder, pulled up a chair opposite me at the kitchen table. He had a hangover and had taken the day off. I was too young to know how bad things had been before, he said. Cruising was a "bull-shit game you had to play because everyone else did." It could be ex-hilarating, but there was a destructive side. You might pick up the wrong hitchhiker and instead of a blow job, get your head broken. The baths were all about beauty, and what if you didn't feel beautiful? But in the old days he was never honestly himself. Now, he said:

Write this down in your notebook so you'll remember how things have changed. Now, we can be out on the streets and kiss each other. We can be in drag if we want. Because there's strength in numbers.

Politics was idle gossip compared to the hours spent interpreting signs of love and discussing the terrible pain men caused. "I want to be in love desperately, but I don't want anyone to have that control over me," Tony wept over the chamomile tea and buttered matzos.

The boys managed to keep their professional and domestic lives compartmentalized with a tidiness that Andrea as "Juanita" eschewed. She was always dragging home a bizarre assortment of lovers, and depending on Melissa to bounce them out. I had a feeling that I could learn about human nature by documenting Juanita's love life. She said she was delighted to be followed around. She volunteered to pose for photographs and would introduce me as her biographer. I wasn't much of a biographer, but it felt wonderful to be called one. In the beginning, everything about Juanita seemed equally remarkable and worth documenting, from her breakfast cereal to her push-up bra. In a certain light the whole enterprise might seem a little sordid and voyeuristic. But at that moment Andrea felt like a movie star and I felt like a genius.

In the red suitcase I found the notebook that I kept for Juanita's biography. There were only a few entries and they all sound pretty much alike. This one could stand as representative:

> Mason Monroe, hitchhiking back from the April 24th Demonstration got a ride with David, a 28 year old dope dealing crazy, crazy dude. Mason brought him upstairs then split. Everyone else was gone except Juanita who spent the night rapping and eventually balling David. She didn't see him again 'till tonight. He came over asking her to STAR in some fuck films, his eyes bulging and squinting alternately like he hadn't any control over his faculties. His tongue hung out like a lizard. Melissa and Juanita and I were home alone all sitting on the bed surrounded by guitars and pillows, Melissa had been singing and I'd been reading the Tarot. Juanita took off her pants and David leaned over. "Are you masturbating in front of me?" He asked her. Then immediately let his pants fall to the floor, his cock shot up. "You don't mind if I join you?" He sat there jerking off and talking about a friend of his who'd lent him a car to do a cross-country dope deal, and how he had a chance now to pay him back. Would she do the film. PLEASE Juanita. Juanita said, "not without the girls," meaning Melissa and me.

None of us did that film shoot. Later, though, Melissa would become involved in the porno industry, first as a performer and then a director. She made some money and eventually left Oakland to try her luck as a country-and-western singer in the Rocky Mountain states. The last thing I heard she was back in Brooklyn training to be a dental hygienist. Andrea lived in Taos for many years. She said she left Juanita behind and always missed her.

After the biography project ended, I remember sitting in my Oakland room, reading and rereading the poetry of Sylvia Plath, searching in it for the mystical concordance to my life. If I wasn't the revolutionary I had been before, who was I?

In my journals I had become much more interested in recording events than interpreting them. But I still relied on letters for self-analysis. Writing to Amy, I confessed that I didn't know where Andrea/Juanita fell on the political spectrum. "We're awfully liberal with each other here," I wrote.

Meanwhile, I flitted in and out of the *Tribe* offices, bringing them movie reviews, bad poetry, and a gossip column, "On the Ave with Buckwheat Groats." As the paper's entertainment reporter with a nom de plume I was even allowed a byline. Day after day, I engaged the mind-numbing Stalinists at work, the libertines in my living room, the grifters and fantasists on Telegraph. And every contact, every conversation, might make what had seemed clear murky, or on a good day perhaps, a little bit clearer. Like Alice, I was coming to learn which side of the mushroom made me small and which large.

There is a cartoon from around that time of a smiling man with the very top of his head sheared off, pouring coffee directly into his brain. If pure experience could be liquefied, then that drenching-the-brain image is emblematic of what happened to me in Oakland. Every device deserves a motto, and mine would read: Maybe it took a chainsaw, but her mind's open now.

Leslie and Leslie

1971, Spring

"I dare say I fancied myself in short a remarkable young woman and took comfort in the fact that this would more publicly appear."

HENRY JAMES *The Turn of the Screw*

"We didn't do it, but we dug it!!"

JUDY GUMBO

According to the report in the *New York Times,* on March 1, 1971, at 1:32 A.M. a bomb exploded in an unmarked, "out-of-the-way" men's washroom on the ground floor of the Capitol building, about a hundred feet from the rotunda. The anonymous voice in the phone warning, received half an hour before the explosion, claimed the bomb had been set "in protest of the Nixon involvement in Laos." Six rooms were damaged and some "priceless glass" shattered in the Senators' Dining Room, but there were no injuries.

This was one of many bombs that spring. I didn't pay particular attention, until someone I knew was arrested in connection with it.

In the previous year, bombing targets had extended from property associated directly with the war, like draft boards, to property that represented the underpinnings of the system that supported the war, such as banks. Left-wing bombers targeted property, not people, and the Army Math Research Center in Madison remained the great tragedy of this campaign. By 1971, the United States had been involved in Vietnam for about half my lifetime. The Paris peace talks were stalled, and all the reports were discouraging. It seemed unbelievable that the Nixon and Kissinger we knew would ever deal fairly with the Vietnamese. When word had slipped through a news blackout in February that the United States had begun a new massive bombing campaign, a wave of protest and more violent demonstrations had followed. It seemed clear that the U.S. negotiating policy would be to continue to ignore opposition voices and try to pound Vietnam into submission.

It was definitely not a conspiracy, Attorney General John Mitchell commented on the Capitol washroom bombing. While the Justice Department publicly interpreted the bomb as a one-time, isolated instance, the FBI tore through the files of hundreds of radicals to establish links. Across the Mall, the senators were surprisingly sluggish despite their shattered glassware. Several expressed surprise that there was a washroom in that area. It was, all agreed, shocking and deplorable, but no one rushed to push through bills demanding higher security and heavier penalties. Was this a different kind of senator from the type I am now used to, who whines and bellows for longer sentences and more executions? Or was there some kind of gentleman's agreement abroad not to get ruffled? A different kind of stiff-upper-lip machismo that refused to be diverted by adolescent terrorist pranks? Could the senators have been expecting something like this?

In his statement to the press, Senator George McGovern broached the subject of the inevitability of a bomb in the Capitol:

> The massive bombardment we are continuing year after year against the peoples of Indochina has its counterpart in the mounting destruction of humane values in our own land. It is not possible to teach an entire generation to bomb and destroy others in an undeclared, unjustified, unending war without paying a terrible price in the derangement of our society.

Alone among those senators interviewed, McGovern, who would run as the Democratic candidate for president the following year, connected the Capitol bombing directly to what had become our national habit. As recent history showed, bombs were now an all-American way of attracting attention. McGovern's words rang with determinist theory: our children are *that* way because we are *this* way, he said, rather courageously. I admire him now for making those connections. But back then, parents and children both seemed tired of the effort it took to bridge the generation gap. All that psychological justification (that "Officer Krupke" song and dance) just painted McGovern pinker in the eyes of the so-called moral majority. No bleeding heart was going to blame this bombing on *them*. And their children weren't buying it either. On the day it occurred, the Weather Bureau claimed responsibility for the Capitol bombing. They didn't want their action excused, either. They wanted it celebrated.

While the government's policy was to play down the scope and connectedness of the national antiwar movement, the Weather Bureau continued to act as if they were the inspirational vanguard of a juggernaut. In their second communiqué explaining the bombing, they described themselves as part of a truly great conspiracy. They had "attacked" the Capitol, they wrote, for three reasons:

> 1) to express our love and solidarity with the non-white people of the world who always happen to be the victims of 200 years of U.S. technological warfare; and 2) to freak out the warmongers and remind them that they have created guerrillas here; and 3) to bring a smile and a wink to the kids and people here who hate this government. To spread joy.

The bombing occurred at a time when activists from across the antiwar spectrum were winding up for one more mass protest and a chance to reunite at the April 24 marches. Another demonstration planned by the May Day Tribe in Washington, D.C., called for civil disobedience at the Pentagon and Justice Department and in cities around the country that would "stop the government until it signed the *people's peace treaty.*" It's important to note that that spring, many longtime movement people were feeling worn down. A lot of antiwar activists were frustrated by the public's general apathy, tired of being harassed for their convictions, and weary of butting up against an indefatigable opponent with bottomless resources. Just how many people the Capitol bombing made smile and wink, it's impossible to know. The Weathermen weren't terribly popular with the over-twenty crowd, and many devoted activists publicly repudiated them as a completely irresponsible and maniac faction.

I hardly paid attention to the Weathermen myself anymore. It's possible that familiarity had bred contempt. Several former Weatherpeople worked at the *Tribe,* and for the most part, they seemed too straight, too old, and flaunted their secrecy too much.

·   ·   ·

On April 29, the FBI arrested nineteen-year-old Leslie Bacon as a material witness in the Capitol bombing. On May 1, the Weather Bureau addressed their latest letter from the underground to Leslie Bacon's mother. It began with compliments for the outspoken support she'd already demonstrated for her daughter: "Your confidence in Leslie is justified, because she is completely innocent of any involvement in the bombing of the US Capitol. We know this for a fact because, as the FBI and Justice Department well know, our organization did the bombing."

Leslie Bacon wasn't quite the solitary mad bomber the Justice Department had anticipated. In an early profile published in the *New York Times,* her friends describe her as a "serious young woman committed to social justice and peace causes." She and I had met the previous summer when our paths crossed on the way to opposite coasts. We were the same age, traveled in the same circles, knew many of the same people, and worked for the same kinds of papers. I followed her story for the *Tribe,* and the more I wrote about her the more intensely I came to feel that our situations might easily have been reversed. Her arrest was less the FBI's big break into the underground than a new level of harassment of envelope stuffers and leaflet writers. She wasn't a leader or a courier for the underground, as the FBI had originally hoped. She was a protester, a face in the crowd.

In brief, the facts are these: on Tuesday, April 27, Leslie Bacon was taken into custody as a material witness in the Capitol bombing. At that time she was not charged with any crime. The following day, she was judged a flight risk and her bail set at $100,000. On Thursday, in the custody of U.S. marshals, she was flown to Seattle and forced to testify before a federal grand jury convened to investigate the links between recent bombings, including the Capitol restroom.

Leslie was sequestered in Seattle for a month. She was granted immunity regarding the Capitol bombing, but as a result of her early testimony the government filed a complaint naming her in connection with other bombings in New York. She then refused to testify further and eventually served a sentence for contempt of about a month. When she was finally free on bail and appealing the contempt sentence, she stayed with her parents in suburban San Francisco until she had to answer questions in connection with an alleged plot to bomb a Manhattan bank. At the San Francisco airport she was met by fifty reporters and photographers; speaking in "bitter" tones, she declared, "The only freedom in this country is the freedom for those with fat wallets. Don't ever trust the government. Whatever they tell you, they are lies."

In the Bay Area, Leslie Bacon was a celebrity. The *San Francisco Chronicle* portrayed her as a sort of rootin'-tootin' hometown cowgirl. She was good copy. Born and raised in the wealthy suburb of Atherton (never merely a suburb, in the press, it was always a *wealthy* suburb) and the product of a Catholic school education (at Sacred Heart School she'd been taught that "you don't put a white tablecloth on the table when a boy is coming to dinner because it might remind him of bed"), she'd left California for New York, and like other independent-minded young women, had become involved in various political activities in different cities. In New York, she'd worked for the Underground Press Syndicate. In Washington, D.C., she lived and worked with the May Day Tribe.

When she returned to the Bay Area, I joined her growing entourage. I'd never written a story that was as close to me as this, and I became instantly territorial, guarding Leslie's reputation as if it were my own. I didn't believe that any of the other reporters, some of them only a few years older, could possibly understand Leslie's life the way I did. In my first article I lambasted the mainstream for trying to

> reduce her to its own objectifying terms, "Buxom, tall, blonde..."
> It seems impossible for the media to understand her. Paragraphs
> have been spent on her dress ... "Miss Bacon wore a red maxi-
> skirt at today's hearings," blah, blah. There is a real fascination
> with her alternative lifestyle, shown by the constant question-
> ing about hitchhiking. The concentration on the "commune" she
> lives in, we would have said collective, so alien to them. Her
> youth.

It wasn't until years later that I came to understand how good stories *do* emerge from scrutinizing a person's past and even the clothes she wears. Good reporters dig through garbage and, like good stand-up comics, have to be able to endure huge amounts of embarrassment. I eventually learned that the best reporters always have open minds and enough heart to feel shame in the presence of terrible things. But back then I didn't know any of this. I wanted to cover Leslie Bacon to pub-licize her case, and to make sure the radical community heard her voice and opinions to the letter. I thought she needed me. I doubted that any other reporter could have been as involved or as concerned about the outcome of her story.

Did I think she was heroic? I thought she was fascinating. She was tall and sturdily built, and she had great posture, which seemed no-table in a crowd of slouchers. She was always rushing somewhere, and her long blond hair seemed to fly behind her in cartoon-speed strokes. She had the sort of embonpoint that Joshua Reynolds often painted: "Miss Bacon as the Tragic Muse," perhaps as her own ancestors were painted in their towering wigs and iridescent gowns with spaniels at their feet. Did her family wind back to Francis (it is Francis, not Leslie, you find in the encyclopedia). I have no idea how many generations her family had been in America: you didn't speak of that, of course. She was lace-curtain Irish, the news profiles implied, but mostly she was a native daughter, born and bred in top-drawer California.

I liked the way Leslie would wisecrack out of the side of her mouth. She almost always had a quick answer (while I was a slower staircase thinker). She seemed fearless, a characteristic she attributed to grow-ing up with many brothers. She seemed brave and poised, in a way I was not and wished I could be. Mason Monroe had a crush on her. Up until then he'd had a crush on me. That should have been a sign of something.

Once I accompanied her to court in San Francisco, and a picture of us together was printed in the paper. In the photograph she is charg-ing forward a step ahead of me. Her head is up and she is speaking— I know what she's saying: *here we go* . . . We are passing through the crowd of photographers who follow her every public appearance. Lights are flashing. As she plunges forward I follow, less practiced, shyer, smiling to myself. I am dressed in something that looks like an Empire waist burlap bag blouse with spaghetti straps. I'm looking down. Resigned to the furor, Leslie puts on a good show; she always has a quote for the reporters now, and they like her. "Leslie over here, over here!" A photographer shouts and she gives him the shot he wants without posing or smiling. It's *The Day of the Locust* meets *Joe Hill*. When the photograph was published, I clipped and saved it. It's in my red suitcase now.

Then there was the coincidence of our names. The caption accom-panying the photograph reads: "Leslie Appeals Contempt Charges." Both of us were Leslie, both Leslie B——. Of course, Leslie was my secret name (I was entirely Buckwheat by then). But as I continued to trail her and scrutinize her and note all our similarities, I came to find that we really weren't much alike. She was much more sophisticated than I, and occasionally even bitter. In her place I think I might have

felt much sorrier for myself. Sometimes I was frustrated, even disillu-
sioned, but bitterness, like despair, was still outside my palette.

Did I want to be her? Did I think I needed a bigger drama than the
bohemian life I was leading? Wasn't writing poetry and telling fortunes and answering phones for a gay prostitution ring enough? Did
I have to be arrested, too? As I followed Leslie for the *Tribe,* I came
to recognize that she was my subject in one way, but I was hers in
another—the dark soubrette to the blond heroine. I came to see us as
sidekicks in a way she never did. The truth is, we weren't even friends.
We couldn't relax in each other's presence. We never had real conversations, just interviews. She was as on guard with me as she was with
the other reporters who trailed her. In fact, the mainstream reporters
were much better positioned to raise public sympathy for her case. Before long I began to brood over my part as a minor character. She'd
been culled from the crowd—she'd acted while I agonized. Would I
have had the nerve she had to face down a grand jury inquisition? I'd
have cried, probably. How could I know, when I never *did* anything?
(That originally she hadn't *done* anything, either, no longer mattered.)

In the middle of this my father phoned. We hadn't spoken much in
the past few months, and when we did our conversation was spare, out
of habit. He was glad to know I was fine, I was happy to hear he was
fine. Everyone was fine in Massapequa. My brothers were both fine,
too. Did I need some money? Whenever the subject of money arose
he'd lower his voice. Normally, he spoke in an amiable tenor. But when
he phoned that night in the middle of everything, his voice sounded
deeper and more serious. "Listen," he said. "Les, we had a visit from
the FBI."

There it was. Two agents in raincoats had knocked on the door. He
hadn't let them in any farther than the hall. "They had a newspaper
picture of you and this other girl," he said. "Leslie Bacon. I think they
thought you were her, because one of them kept calling me Mr. Bacon."

"What did they want?"

"I don't think they knew. They were just fishing. I didn't tell them
anything. I wouldn't give them your address. I'm in a phone booth
now."

Oh, Dad, I thought, how brave. Thanks to Joe McCarthy he was
thoroughly educated in radical paranoia. Had Dad thought, when the
Rosenbergs were arrested, How close? I'd never asked.

"Do you need some money?" He was glad to hear I was working for a newspaper, but he could help me out a little. "Between us, no need for your stepmother to know."

Over the time I was covering Leslie Bacon I would sometimes imagine people getting us confused. The idea delighted me for its trickster value. In my mind the experience would be like *The Prince and the Pauper,* or perhaps *The Parent Trap* with Hayley Mills. I thought less of a soul exchange than of the celebrity: I would be queen for a day with none of the aggravation.

Now that I had proof that the FBI were really involved in my own case, I felt at once thrilled and disappointed at their ineptitude. If they were coming after me, I wanted it to be for something I had done to end the war. There were people I knew who said they were going underground. Most of it was talk, but the sense of risking everything seemed closer and more possible than before.

In the *New York Times* profile of Leslie Bacon, one of her neighbors, "who described himself as a political conservative," called her a girl "starved for recognition." This was a common charge from the right. Starved for recognition? Starved, rather, for meaning. A minor character myself, I was poised to leap, waiting for the call that would be pitched to my ears only, the mission impossible that would supersede fear and loneliness, the incandescent moment.

Years later, I was not entirely surprised to find my earlier aspirations described in *The Turn of the Screw.* Of course, the governess in Henry James's novella is possessed by an entirely different mission. She may or may not have been a social crusader or a paranoid schizophrenic or a true medium. Her story ends in tragedy, but early on, when the future is all beautiful potential, all a rehearsal for glory, she is "literally able to find a joy in the extraordinary flight of heroism" that she anticipates. She thinks she's on earth to be asked

> for a service admirable and difficult; and there would be a greatness in letting it be seen—oh in the right quarter!—that I could succeed where many another girl might have failed.

Girl Cracks Head:
Another Split in the Movement

1971, Spring

I got my head split open at the May 5th San Francisco
action. 6 stitches—by some pig some 2 or 3 pigs. Found
myself forced into a strategically insane predicament.
AND THIS IS MADNESS. Doing nothing/and I wish that/I
had been doing something to get my head shaved this
way—have the hair fall out everytime I touch my head.

BUCKWHEAT GROATS

The paragraph above is an excerpt from the article I wrote after the
May 5 "People's Peace Treaty" protest in San Francisco. In the past, I'd
made deliberate choices about how and when I'd put myself in harm's
way. After my street-fighting lessons in Chicago I hadn't much confidence in myself as a soldier. I'd been teargassed, but I'd never fought
back. This time, I thought I was prepared to put myself on the line,
whatever that meant. I was sure I'd be arrested. About ten minutes
after I arrived at the demonstration, I was knocked out and bleeding
from a hole in my head.

Was revolutionary violence necessary? At the *Berkeley Tribe,* we
were constantly discussing guns (which were everywhere) and bombs
(which were nearly everywhere). The Weatherpeople on staff called
the frequent explosions radicalizing, but the more authoritatively they
spoke, the less they convinced me. I couldn't bear their expert analysis. Perhaps, at first, I'd debated the point just to show off how original
and independent minded I was. I argued the anarchist view. Not
Alexander Berkman's bombs but Emma Goldman's "liberty without restraint," her anarchy of love. As my own resistance to authority turned
into a loathing of coercion, how could I countenance bombing—the
epitome of coercion? We argued and never convinced one another.
And no matter how much I argued, I always felt the vague apprehen-
sion that I wasn't doing enough to stop the war. Bombs seemed so de-
cisive. I worried that I was all talk.

The only violence I'd ever experienced was internal—beginning with the grief I'd suffered over my mother's death. I had a terrible temper. I harbored grudges over small slights and fantasized great revenge scenarios. But I was physically impulsive only in my mind. I felt susceptible to rousing speeches and inspirational music, but at the same time resented my sentimentality and indecision. I wished I could be remote and arch and bloody-minded and brave. I wondered if I was a coward.

All along, it had driven me nearly crazy to hear about villages being bombed and children napalmed. I had marched and protested and picketed and written and spoken out, but the terrible war progressed. In the spring of 1971, I was eighteen. The war was still metastasizing, but it seemed to me as if the body count on Cronkite had become background music. Public dissent seemed weaker and ineffectual; the "moral majority" was inert and numb, while the government grew more and more indifferent and arrogant.

In fiction there is often a moment of discovery, an unanticipated flash of self-awareness that propels the protagonist in one direction or another. Sometimes the moment is barely perceptible, a word, a look; at other times the discovery is everything and the protagonist is completely overcome by his or her need to change utterly. You see this in movies: the gunfighter defends his honor—*it has come to this;* the young woman realizes that she cannot live without her one true love—*it has come to this;* the cop has to bend the law to get justice—*it has come to this;* the idealistic lawyer risks his career to try a case that seems impossible to win—*it has come to this.* Spartacus leads a slave revolt: *it has come to this.*

I think many people experience an *it has come to this* moment over the course of their lives. They may call it a crisis, make small adjustments, and carry on. Others go mad, and some kill themselves. Most don't strap on a six-gun, hitchhike across the country to reclaim a lost love, turn into outlaws, risk their careers, or lead slave revolts. But some do. As a matter of record, you're usually either really deluded or beyond the pale when you slough off your daily life and answer the call.

I had come to believe that I was required, or rather entitled, to have an *it has come to this* moment. In anticipation I had imagined the moment itself as a metamorphosis; when pushed to my limits I would become . . . what? I tried to imagine myself entirely different, under a spell, no longer trapped in the snares of this world. It wasn't a happy thought, but a political necessity, a moral obligation. When it did occur I hoped it would make me happy. All that spring I felt on the brink of my *it has come to this* moment, but nothing seemed as clear as it was in the movies. Meanwhile, I tried to take stock of who I was and what I thought.

Although I admired the self-possession of those who were, I knew I wasn't a pacifist because whenever the question arose—would you have fought against Hitler?—I had to say yes, of course. I worried about paralyzing myself by thinking too much. But I wasn't willing to be pushed precipitously into a violence that frightened me. Could I act despite fear? Really, only mythic heroes were fearless, I assured myself; it's not a human gift. Most of those mythic heroes were half-gods. The warrior's trick was to suppress his humanity while fighting for it.

Worrying again that I was intellectualizing too much, I decided to participate in the May 5 protest. Unlike the huge, mass April 24 demonstration, there would be no monitors with black armbands directing people back into orderly formation. Everyone involved in this leaderless action knew that its aim was to disrupt business-as-usual in San Francisco's Embarcadero.

Two friends and I declared ourselves a revolutionary cell. We were "running partners." We even devised a code word that, when called out in distress, would bring us like musketeers galloping to each other's aid. Hitchhiking to San Francisco the morning of the demonstration, we whispered together about tactics. One organizing faction had proposed nonviolent disobedience; another, tactical civil disobedience; a third, creative disruption. We all expected to run through traffic, and we took it for granted that we would destroy property. We thought we were ready to fight.

The radical community may have been divided about its tactics, but San Francisco law enforcement was entirely in sync. Our protest had been advertised as a chance to trash the state, and the state had taken us at our word. As we arrived in dribs and drabs at the Bank of America building, we were met by a battalion of visored riot police in full regalia: on foot, motorcycle, and horseback.

I was carrying a gas mask from an army-navy store in my backpack. It was pre–World War II and looked like the head of a huge bug. It was utterly useless and weighed a ton, but I was reluctant to dump it. My insistence on lugging it around, as we hitchhiked to the city and walked across town to the demonstration, was a further example of how unrealistically I'd prepared. Even confronted by all those police, I persisted in thinking in terms of my performance. The gas mask was my costume. At first sight, I didn't think of the police as my enemy. I wasn't intimidated. In fact, I felt a little superior. We laughed at those police trapped by convention—they had to march in formation while we were free to run.

"Be light," a boy running by advised. He paused to quote Muhammad Ali: "Float like a butterfly, sting like a bee." But I still held on to that gas mask.

There was no beginning mark, no starter's gun. We swarmed over the sidewalks and into rush-hour traffic. The cops had closed the streets to cars, but some pedestrians cursed us. Others took shelter in nearby buildings, and others sailed along, pretending to ignore us, determined not to be diverted from their daily routine.

"This way to Shell!" someone yelled.

"No, Shell is this direction."

My group shot off in several directions. Within a few minutes, I'd lost my "running partners." Then, I lost my way and ran around the same block twice. I yelled out our code word, but no musketeers appeared. Then I dumped the gas mask.

I was standing on a corner completely at sea, when a wave of about twenty protesters bore down on me. I heard screams, and suddenly there were motorcycle cops driving on the sidewalk, herding us forward toward an open police van while foot cops patrolled alongside. Anyone attempting escape got whacked with a billy club. Eight of us jumped out of line and took shelter up some steps in the triangular entranceway to a bank. The bank door was locked, but when a teller inside gave me the peace sign, I thought for a moment he'd help us escape. He didn't, he just shrugged. What were the customers who watched us from the lobby thinking? That we deserved a beating? We kept banging on the glass door, hoping we could break it open.

Five cops in full riot gear surrounded the entrance: three were on horseback, two more on motorcycle, and all spread a few feet apart in strategic positions.

"It's a trap," the boy wizard next to me whispered.

We were such easy targets. Why didn't they just grab us and arrest us? It was obvious by then that we didn't have any weapons. Instead, they played a game: we were the "hot potatoes" that they flung between themselves. As each protester ran out of the enclosure, a waiting cop would whack him or her and then fling the reeling body to another cop for another whack.

"You'd better get out of there!" They brandished their sticks (as if that was some inducement).

I didn't know how not to play. I was sure if I stayed where I was, the cops would gang up and murder me. But everyone who attempted to run was flung about and clobbered pitilessly. The boy wizard said he'd calculated a geometric escape and told me to do as he did. (This might have worked in the movies, but it was gruesome in reality.) I watched him zigzag under a horse, but the furious cop on its back rode after him and hit the boy wizard until he fell. I was one of the last left and the cops weren't getting any less enthusiastic. Eventually, I just ran, and like everyone before me, the cops flung me to and fro. One slammed my back, another my leg and arm, and as I tried to escape, that one furious cop on horseback leaned over and cracked my skull.

At first, I could still run, and I kept going. I remember that minute well: the uninterrupted screaming and the blur of other casualties holding their broken heads together with their hands. I was in the middle of the street, and I looked over to the sidewalk where men in business suits with places to go were trying to get out of the way of the rioters and police. I felt inexpressibly sad, and, as I sank down, I could not resist the melodrama of my situation. Perhaps, I thought, if I called it tragedy, I'd be overcome and die. As it was, with the shred of energy I possessed, I yelled at the businessmen, "I am your daughter!" Who knows if they heard, or even if I spoke out loud. None of them moved to help me. Perhaps they would have if I hadn't scolded. And then I lost consciousness.

I was only out for a moment. A medic took me to a free clinic where they shaved my head around the wound and stitched me up. I wasn't arrested, the medic told me, because that would have slowed the cops down, and they would have had to explain why they'd been so brutal. They might have arrested me at first, for any number of things, but once they'd hit me, they could only justify themselves by saying I'd assaulted them first. So, I was lucky, the medic said. I wasn't in jail.

For days afterward my head hurt and I cried all the time. My friends sympathized, and some were disappointed that I hadn't hit back. One visitor at my bedside suggested, with the arrogance of our kind, that my wound wasn't much compared to what others had suffered. After all, I hadn't been beaten for my skin color or burned by napalm. Another turned it into a moral tale—my personal watershed: "What a radicalizing thing it must have been for you," she said. Didn't it just "prove the contradictions"?

As I lay in bed, I thought about the contradictions and the statistics. It was *my* head, not, as the newspaper had reported, just one of "many injuries." I really didn't care about revenge, but I wanted to know who'd hit me. At night when I couldn't sleep, I thought of those visored faces and I *was* frightened. I remembered how much those cops had enjoyed their job. They didn't have to torture us, but they did anyway. I knew I was never going to make a good soldier, and I worried that the violence I'd experienced had already changed me. And it was my own fault because I'd cracked the door. I thought about how those cops had seemed fearless, invulnerable, and how once I'd wanted to be fearless, too. But it was no longer a virtue to which I aspired.

In my bed, I thought about alternatives. "I want to be high," Juanita said, paraphrasing Anaïs Nin. "And I don't want to be less." Les? Was she talking about me? I wrote an article about my experience and titled it "Girl Cracks Head (lives to tell the tale): Another Split in the Movement."

I wanted my mother. Well, of course I did, but there was no profit in that. I didn't call my father. I didn't want to alarm him, and I was afraid that if he took me back to Massapequa I'd lose my momentum along with my independence. So I did without his consolation. Instead, I wrote to my brother Rick and he wrote back, "Sorry to hear about your head. Is everything OK now? With your head that is. It's hard to write about the things you feel sometimes—like how I felt when I read your letter." I thought about how lucky it was that as a writer I could observe as well as participate, and that maybe a little more observation would now be in order. Then I panicked and thought there were only three choices available to me: I could stay and fight from the underground; I could land in jail; or I could leave the country and cool down. Eventually, as my head healed, I conceived a brilliant idea about the kind of nonviolent contribution I finally felt able to make.

I decided to go to the peace talks in Paris. I would speak directly to the Vietnamese delegation, and I would end this wretched war myself.

III

Good Fairies and Freaks

———————

"I never travel without my diary. One should always have something sensational to read in the train."

Gwendolyn to Cecily in OSCAR WILDE,
The Importance of Being Earnest

"We have kept our appointment and that's an end to that. We are not saints, but we have kept our appointment. How many people can boast as much?"

Vladimir to Estragon in SAMUEL BECKETT,
Waiting for Godot

I Get Sidetracked

1971, September

> Out of the ash
> I rise with my red hair
> And I eat men like air.

SYLVIA PLATH, "Lady Lazarus"

For three hundred and sixty-five dollars, Icelandic Airlines offered a roundtrip fare that was good for a year. Some student fares were even cheaper, but Amy and I were not students, a distinction we took pains to make clear. We were now generally perceived as "hippies," though we preferred the appellation "travelers." Amy had dropped out of the White Panther Party in Ann Arbor around the same time I had. In an exchange of letters we agreed to fly to Luxembourg via Iceland, together.

I was on the road, finally. To tell the truth, I felt I'd dodged a bullet. I had a mission, of course. I'd become someone who always had to have a mission. But first things first. I planned to see a little of Europe on my way to the Paris peace talks. To prepare, I turned to the few literary models I knew of enlightened adventurer-writers. What could they show me about being an independent-minded woman traveler?

Isabelle Eberhardt, the author of *The Oblivion Seekers,* had been raised in a family of Swiss anarchists at the turn of the century. She'd dressed as a man in Bedouin robes and traveled across the Arabian desert by camel. Her "Pencilled Notes," though inspiring, didn't offer as much practical advice about scrimping on the edge as George Orwell's *Down and Out in Paris and London*—although that too felt dated. I read Jean Rhys's cautionary novels about hapless heroines at large, and from Rhys I learned the names of sophisticated cordials and how, for even a few coins, a taxicab can offer sanctuary in an emergency. I read Colette's novels and discovered that wit, charm, and sex might help a girl out of a jam, but that an older woman needs humor and resilience and some of that *je ne sais quoi.*

The book that I settled on as my most sacred text had been out of print for decades. I'd first read *Sister of the Road* when it had circulated through Berkeley in a photocopied manuscript. Supposedly the true confessions of a hobo named Boxcar Bertha, the book had been co-authored by Ben Reitman, one of Emma Goldman's lovers. Reitman's involvement gave the text its anarchist seal of approval. Boxcar Bertha had ridden the rails during the depression and, moved by the presence of so many homeless women in the nation's hobo jungles, had tried to organize them into a union. These sisters of the road came from farms and towns and cities. They traveled because there were no jobs, or because they'd been misused, or because they were surrounded by petty people who didn't understand them, or because they were looking for somebody, or they'd had a fight with somebody, or they wanted to find something, or they wanted to lose something, or they felt in the way, or just stifled. For a brief time Bertha's invention, the Women's Itinerant Hobo's Union, provided hostels where a traveler could find a meal, tips on local employment (domestic and sewing work mainly), and at least a temporary sense of security. Bertha may have been entirely glorified by Reitman in their book, but I bought it all—heroic spirit and sisterly zeal—and I wanted to live like her.

The plane was in the air. I had my books and two hundred and fifty dollars. One hundred and fifty I hoped would last the month as I wound my way to the Paris peace talks. The other hundred I planned to double in a traveler's check scam.

When you know you are under surveillance and nevertheless trip through the meadow picking wildflowers, it is inspired madness, ignorance, or supreme arrogance to also pick and choose the laws you will obey. I suffered, or enjoyed, at the time, all three characteristics in some constantly mutating combination. As a White Panther and underground newspaper reporter I had taken for granted our glorification of outlaws. In terms of graphic illustration, the rule was, the more bandoleros the better. You could always rely on portraits of John Dillinger, Billy the Kid, and Belle Starr to pep up an otherwise drab edition. In the public consciousness and the public domain these were the endlessly *available* images of our history: wild west and shoot 'em up. In that intensely romantic atmosphere we imparted a benevolence to these outlaws that they would hardly recognize. It was sufficient to say that Billy was young, Belle an independent female, and Dillinger against the G-men.

While some on the hard edge of the movement followed the outlaw mythos into guerrilla armies, I remained a freelancer, bent on defying the mighty monolith in any way I could. Morality had come to seem the privilege of those who experienced a certain stability in their lives. Was it immoral to steal? Was it immoral to bomb Hanoi in the midst of peace talks to gain a stronger negotiating position? The outlaw life I anticipated in Europe would be exhilarating, literary, and unmistakably erotic. A scam in my mind was a crime but jollier, a rip-off but not so rough, a con without extensive research. I took for my models both the international pirate queen, Ann Bonney, and Pretty Boy Floyd, the American Robin Hood. And while the Symbionese Liberation Army planned kidnappings and bank robberies, Amy and I (in keeping with my more cautious postwound mentality) planned to inaugurate our European crime spree with a feet-wetting exercise: in the Luxembourg airport, I would pick up her suitcase, and she, claiming it lost, would request reimbursement. Later, in England, after we had become more experienced swindlers, she would cash in my traveler's checks and I would declare them stolen. Who doubted that American Express was in some way, directly or indirectly, contributing to the war in Vietnam?

The flaw in my argument was that, as an outlaw *outside* the United States, I'd be striking blows first against Iceland, at whose airline terminal we would arrive, and later Great Britain. My sense that all corporate systems were ultimately one may not have been completely offtrack, but to think that conning *any* authority would eventually result in a strike against Washington was quite stunningly American. I may have wanted to be a cosmopolitan internationalist, but I was still deeply Massapequan.

·   ·   ·

Emerging from the long flight, the fifteen or twenty hippies aboard descended on the airport like a litter of white mice. The Luxembourgeoisie pulled up their skirts as we scurried to retrieve our huge, colorful frame packs. We women, in keeping with the style of that autumn, wore yellow, red, or blue bandannas around our long hair; our male counterparts tied bandannas around their necks or to their belt loops or their packs. In subsequent months those bandannas, the flag of westerly advance, would be among the first symbols of Americana to disappear. Eventually, we'd recognize that the packs themselves read like neon signs flashing *innocent abroad* and exchange them for something dustier, dirtier, and generally more neutral.

America held no cachet on the hippie trail that autumn, and New York was at the nadir of its popularity. The city's reputation was at once that of a supermechanized factory town where soulless company men manufactured money—the decadent home of the materialistic jet set, and the source of the mysterious darkling bankers who pulled all the strings (an image stinking of anti-Semitism). New York City was "the belly of the beast," and its existence was an insult to the anti-materialistic, rural-centric, if not agriphilic, fantasy that played in the minds of the foot soldiers of all nationalities on the hippie circuit. Only the con men and crooks among the traveling hordes still saw New York as the land of golden opportunity. (Is it any wonder I found a home with them?)

I would discover over time that the hippie diaspora created its own taxonomies and hierarchies based on where you'd traveled—and how long you'd been on the road. Eventually, I'd come to reject that class system like any other. In those early days, though, I was always running into someone eager to weigh and judge me in what could seem like a contest of competitive free-spiritedness. Around the corner there always seemed to be someone, often French or German, usually a man, who'd take it upon himself to inflict a kind of anti-American hazing. In that atmosphere of ritualized and diffuse dogmatism, I'd be held personally responsible for the Vietnam War and two hundred years of racism. It didn't matter that I'd fought against the war or that I wasn't rich or even a student.

From this distance I think it's likely that I arrived in Europe completely paranoid after a time under FBI observation and routinely mistook curiosity for surveillance when it wasn't one or the other. Later, I came to understand that one of the great pleasures of arriving in a strange place is the freedom to reinvent yourself, but early on, while I priggishly censured my compatriots' choice of travel guides, clothing, and luggage, I envied their ability to, as Henry James put it, "glide." Many of them could laugh off the stereotypes (rich, vulgar, materialistic, gullible) in which Europeans had pigeonholed traveling Americans for two hundred years. Some said, "Come on, how can they love our movies and music and hate us?" Some countered with the Groucho Marx response—they wouldn't want to be a member of any club that wanted them. Some were Ugly Americans and didn't know or care.

But I wanted to penetrate and *merge* into the international hippie demimonde as soon as possible. I didn't think I could do that as an American and a New Yorker. I was so eager to deracinate that I was shocked to encounter any evidence of national pride anywhere. But first impressions showed that not everyone felt the same. Irish hippies, though cynical, tended to be sentimentally patriotic; Canadians pasted maple leaves on their packs to distinguish themselves from us; Italians sighing "Che bèlla Itàlia" would tear up over the beauty of their distant homeland. The source of my pride came from the belief that I'd successfully *escaped*. I was no longer complicit in America's crimes— but still I couldn't "glide." Instead, those first few months in Europe I lurched through so many exhausting arguments about growing up in the poisoned atmosphere of America that, like Quasimodo crying sanctuary, I pasted a maple leaf on my pack and cried *Canadienne*.

·   ·   ·

What an opportunity for a writer. What would Doris Lessing have made of it? I was at that time still besotted by Lessing and often mused about her possible responses to one thing or another. My journey to Europe had brought me physically closer to her, and I spent many hours those first few weeks composing what I hoped was the perfect letter of introduction. Ours would not be like my brief encounter with Jacqueline Susann, but a sort of family reunion. If I could just convince her to see me, she couldn't fail to recognize her literary heir. I wrote:

Dear Ms. Lessing,

I am 18 years old, and The Golden Notebook is the first book I've read that seems to have been written for a woman's reality. Most novels I think have been written for men or according to a male oriented consciousness. Your book has come the closest to my experience. I've been through a "party" too. So different, but "similar" to yours. After I emerged from my stint with "The White Panthers'" dogmatic and internalized collective, I lived in communes and traveled across the states, living out my politics.

I think I may be having the modern version of your characters' experience. I find myself filled with satisfaction, extraordinary happiness, contentment. Then, for no reason losing myself to a powerful unhappiness or worse, a fog-like space-out. In those times I lose touch with reality. My eyes will stare at

something, but I won't see it. I'll bite my nails incessantly, drop
things and leave them where they fall, I'll ignore people, and in
absolute powerlessness, dreaming in color, robbed of any particular reality, become a lump of hot body wax.

I write poetry and hope to write novels. I'd like to meet you
and talk to you about politics and literature at your convenience.

Sincerely,

Buckwheat Groats

Having constructed a letter that I felt best represented my literary
talents as well as my social engagement, I was stymied over whether to
sign my real name or my nom de plume. From this distance, the condition I describe sounds suspiciously like the final throes of malarial
delirium. And though I can't imagine that Ms. Lessing received many
letters from fans comparing themselves to "hot body wax," back then
I decided that only by signing myself "Buckwheat Groats" could I be
assured of setting my letter apart in her mind. If being different was
becoming a bit of a fetish, at least I could claim consistency all the way
back to Mrs. Baton in first grade. Surely, the sympathetic Ms. Lessing
would appreciate the extent to which I was prepared to surrender myself to art.

There was one other writer in London whom I wanted to meet, but
I was years too late. Sylvia Plath had died in 1963. I went twice to pace
the street outside the house in which she'd committed suicide. I suppose I thought, like others who worship at the tombs of their idols, that
I could get a glimpse of some purer essence if I walked where she had.
Beyond all my expectations, on my second visit the current occupant
of the house emerged. She was very pleasant, but graciously demurred
when I requested leave to see the oven where Plath had topped herself.
"It's still there," she said, "but I really mustn't invite you in." Apparently, I wasn't the only one stalking Plath's ghost. The poet's last home
had become a popular sight on the ghoul tour for many morbid young
artists and zealous liberationists.

A few weeks later I answered a call advertised on the bulletin board
of a counterculture café to demonstrate against Plath's widower, the
poet Ted Hughes. Hughes would be giving a reading at a plush London theater to celebrate his latest book publication. "Confront the
Murderer of Women's Poetry!" the sign exhorted.

On the night of Hughes's reading, about ten protesters gathered outside the theater. All of us were women, all scruffy, all wild-haired, all, it may be assumed, deep readers. We'd never met before, but we quickly determined that we were in agreement about the subject at hand. Hadn't Hughes landed Sylvia Plath with those babies (which, at the time, we could only picture as faceless, squalling obstacles to her writing)? Wasn't Hughes like every other selfish man in giving precedence to his poetry over hers? Hadn't he left her for another woman? We thought we understood why she killed herself. That night we agreed we felt like Amazon hunters tracking the words, the actual symbols of Plath's oppression back to their source.

I know of no equivalent today for the passion Plath's early death stirred among emerging feminists. Whether her devotees were moved by her poetry or her life, her writing was read as proof of martyrdom. In Plath's novel *The Bell Jar* and in her gorgeous, angry poetry, her narrators seemed trapped and tortured by the conventional expectations of a woman's life. If only . . . some of us mused. We dismissed the deep complications of the poet's life and substituted a happy solution . . . if only . . . she'd lived long enough to be liberated by the women's movement. In my own mind Sylvia Plath's life and work were richly and inextricably entwined. I wonder now how I could have been so sure on the subject. Perhaps I was still in rebellion against my high school English teacher Mr. McKay's New Critical rejection of "Antigone's Modern Relevance." Now, I'm convinced you may draw all the comparisons and conclusions you want, but if you can't distinguish between a writer's work and her life, no matter how close they seem, you end up limiting the literature and stunting the artist.

We gathered with our banners outside the hall where Ted Hughes was scheduled to read. I carried a "Women's Itinerant Hobo's Union" sign. Our plan was to interrupt him and demand penance and apologies. Meanwhile, the quieter, poetry-loving English audience streamed inside.

When Hughes was introduced we started a menacing hum. His defenders in the audience shushed us with fingers to their mouths. We laughed back, and as he began to read, we signaled to one another. Who would lead the attack? Which of us would be the first to accuse this man of murdering his wife? We cleared our throats and shifted our feet on the parquet floor, and when Hughes finished his first poem we absolutely refused to clap. One of our lot made a halfhearted attempt to boo. Perhaps because the room was full of his supporters, perhaps because none of us was really prepared to stand up and accuse Hughes to his face, perhaps because his poetry moved us against our will (and we came to see him in some slight way as the man Plath herself chose), the best we could do was leave. We pushed our way out in the middle of his reading, with all the noise we could manage, scraping our banners and placards along the backs of the seats. Out in the evening air we laughed hilariously at the success of our protest. We had seen him. This was just the first battle. I heard later that the group had other encounters with Hughes, but I never saw them or him again.

Absorbed by new impressions, I wasn't spending much time thinking about what I would say or how I might conduct myself at the Paris peace talks. I expected a brainstorm eventually, but as long as my ideas remained inchoate, I confess I felt a certain lack of urgency.

Many years later, I asked Amy where on earth I ever got the idea that I could just show up in Paris, on the diplomats' doorstep.

"You thought they'd want to talk to you," she said.

London

1971, October

Our plan was to settle in London for a few weeks with cousins of Sammy Friedlander, an old friend of my father's from his union days. I stayed in town while Amy went north to cash my traveler's checks. According to connoisseurs of the deed, bankers outside London were more trusting. In northern England, people reached out to help you, and young Americans never had to present their passports to cash a check. A smile, perhaps a tear of homesickness, an exchange about someone's aunt in Chicago went further there. The secret to this scam was not to be greedy. You could only double your money; if you reported more than a hundred dollars stolen, you could die of hunger, or boredom, waiting for American Express to process your claim.

In Amy's absence I stayed in London's East End among Sammy Friedlander's remarkable relatives. His cousin Pauline was the matriarch of an ice cream and sweets operation. The jewel in its crown was a profitable tourist kiosk at the Charing Cross embankment run by her daughter, Michelle. Pauline and her husband, Albert, were both longtime lefties. During World War II, Pauline had knit a hammer and sickle into a six-foot-long red scarf that Albert had worn wrapped around his neck through his entire hitch. Pauline's chauffeur, Arthur, was her current boyfriend, and to the casual eye all three had made the necessary accommodations. Young Michelle, who was in her late thirties, played out her love life on a grander scale, and it was more explicitly instructive. Michelle was passionately in love with a young cockney named Freddy on whom she showered gifts like bespoke suits and, once, a brand-new Bentley.

The kiosk at Charing Cross and its collateral merchandise were brilliantly successful in the early 1970s. Particularly in the high season tourists could hardly emerge from the tube or cross the bridge without finding their way to Michelle's kiosk, and once you were there, you'd be lucky to get off with ice cream in waffle cones with chocolate flakes for your whole family. Michelle sold cool drinks and sweets and maps and plastic "bobby" hats and mugs with the queen's face. Her soft sell was beauty and confidentiality incarnate. Every customer was "my love" or "my dear" or "my pet." She always wanted to know where a person was from and if this was their family and how old the children were and what they planned to do in London. She knew every alley and every shortcut, as well as where you could buy anything at the best price. And she employed her huge, happy laugh for the sake of the punters, no matter how miserable Freddy had made her that day. She often accused him of seeing other women, and he never saw any reason to deny the terrible truth.

I would sit by the hour at the Charing Cross embankment, eating the giant Cadbury bars Michelle pressed on me and watching her soothe and sweeten the vulgar hordes. She could have talked the queen into buying a mug with her own face, but she couldn't make Freddy love her. Amy and I worried about Michelle. We'd see her after a twelve-hour workday weeping with her head against her beloved pooch. But she'd say, "Look after yourselves," meaning *mind your own business,* but also, *you should be so lucky!* "Freddy does love me!" I believe he did. It's unlikely that anyone could have met the consuming force of Michelle's presence, and power, and kept himself intact. They played off one another like virtuosos. Freddy would never have been the lover he was if he'd surrendered.

·   ·   ·

Without any kind of warning I was starting to surrender—to a sort of diffuse sensuality. I'd never imagined that selling could be so sexy. Just by sitting hour after hour near that kiosk—at the center of London (which in 1971 still swung like the pendulum in Roger Miller's lyrics) while who-knew-how-many thousands slaked the edge of their desire with sweets—I began to fill some of the gaping holes in my social education. Michelle was effervescent and life-affirming, pink and blond and breasty. As an East Ender and a daughter of the left she held a strong sense of her place in the world. There'd been some missteps (she'd lived in Minneapolis for a while), but she'd come to terms, she said, and you knew from an accompanying sigh that her hard-won resolution had meant clambering over the wreckage of hopeless loves. In her presence I felt able, for the first time in ages, to let down my guard. Within the frame of her kiosk she looked like the irrepressible host of a children's program. I'd look up and see her benediction beaming out as I tore through what I considered the literary classics of love and rebellion, furiously copying lines into my notebook. I present them in order:

Pablo Neruda:

I have lived so much that some day
They will have to forget me forcibly
Rubbing me off the blackboard.
My heart was inexhaustible.

Blake:

The tigers of wrath are wiser than the horses of instruction.

Valerie Solanas, and the S.C.U.M. Manifesto:

Life in this society being, at best, an utter bore and no aspect of society being at all relevant to women, there remains to civic-minded, responsible, thrill-seeking females only to overthrow the government, eliminate the money system, institute complete automation and destroy the male sex.

Most often that autumn I submerged myself in the cool world of Don Juan, the wise sorcerer and teacher in Carlos Castaneda's *The Teaching of Don Juan: A Yaqui Way of Knowledge.* Don Juan was always "aware" of what he was doing, and I wanted desperately to profit from this instruction.

Before she had left for the north, Amy and I had several arguments regarding my lack of attention to details. For a month we'd been virtually living in each other's pockets. Just a few days after we'd arrived in London, we had a huge blowup on the street on our way to find the offices of London's embattled underground paper, *OZ.* Amy, always beautifully tidy, had raged that I didn't know how to fold a map. Besides that, she'd accused me of having a deliberately streaky neck. It embarrassed her.

OZ was a disappointment. It was embroiled in a controversial lawsuit over censorship, which made the editors and publishers national celebrities and unavailable. The office staff, dressed in high-style London hippie gear (ruffled blouses, macramé skirts, snakeskin boots), were busy running a defense fund and distinctly ambivalent about two very young reporters from the American underground press who must have looked drearily provincial in denim.

We're just paying a courtesy call, we said, and listened patiently as one young *OZ*-ite lectured us at length about ignorant Americans ignoring the greatest poet of the twentieth century. "Bob Dylan is the messiah. He's God!" he ranted. "And you take some kind of perverse pleasure in neglecting him!"

In the course of a half-hour conversation the ranter also let it be known that he lived on a houseboat near a palace where Henry VIII had decapitated his wives, and that incidentally, during intercourse, anything other than doggy-style was too boring, darling.

The men seemed different in England. I'd become used to American politicos who beat their breasts because they could not cry. It was sometimes hard to trust the "new man" like Mason Monroe when he blamed his mother for never letting him play with dolls, but I thought I understood them. Even the Chicago White Panthers seemed years ahead of their British cousins when it came to women's liberation.

Soon after we arrived in England, Amy and I had looked up the English White Panther branch. Neither of us had much interest in the party or its programs anymore, but we wanted to explore all possible entrées to the left overseas. We met Digby Crane, who at the time was head of all British White Panther ministries and its entire membership combined. Covered in buttons and obsessed with the ten-point program, Digby, in his enthusiasm, somehow made our own dalliance with the party seem even more like a short-run play or a long costume party.

He was trying to be "conscious," he declared (in terms of women's liberation), but he labored under the disadvantage of not having yet seen Chairman John Sinclair's manifesto on gender equality, "Free Our Sisters/Free Our Selves!" He was sorry we hadn't brought a copy from the States. Every day he waited for mail from Ann Arbor like the sole remaining settler of an abandoned colony.

Digby himself was a slight, sweet, pale fellow with dreadful teeth. Whenever Amy and I visited him, he would quiz us about how the party might react to this or that situation. Of course, by then we thought the party would react in the worst possible way to every situation. No matter what we said, Digby's delight in our presence seemed boundless. Only half joking, he insisted destiny had sent us. Destiny, or perhaps Chairman John himself, had read his mind and mail-ordered him a mate, two mates! (His gentle but gripping conviction brings John Fowles's novel *The Collector* to mind.) One night,

Digby confessed his dearest hope. Soon, he said, once the English "Guitar Army" found its feet, we would all start a party commune together. It would be Ann Arbor all over again, he said. Amy and I ran for the hills. After Digby I never encountered another active White Panther.

.   .   .

Amy and I realized we had to rely on each other more than ever. We had to at least be tolerant of each other's eccentricities. At first sight, she and I seemed a lot alike—we were both high-test enthusiasts. But there were big differences. Michelle noticed them immediately. "You're complementary," she'd said, kindly.

Amy was socially deft and scrubbed clean. I wasn't. I hadn't yet outgrown my earlier associations of nonconformity with the lack of personal hygiene. I knew people sometimes mistook my distraction for insolence and my inarticulation for truculence, but I didn't much care what people thought unless I was directly confronted, at which time I could be crushed by the slightest disapproval. Amy was more spontaneous. I was plagued by lifelong indecision—though I could be rash (I wanted that noted). Our friendship needed all the attention we could afford. We knew there was the chance, if we didn't shape up, that we'd find ourselves tearing each other's throat out—like those characters in *The Treasure of the Sierra Madre*—over a measly hundred bucks.

All along we'd known that an investigator would eventually interview me about the traveler's checks. Several weeks after Amy's return, I was invited to the London office of American Express, where Mr. Gerald Humphries evaluated the validity of my case. Mr. Humphries was a frail fiftyish man with pink eyelids and a pair of little hands with popping blue veins.

I'd practiced my story even to the weeping part. Most of it was true. I was eighteen, left without a dime on my very first trip outside America. I didn't have my traveler's checks anymore, and I didn't know who did. My only real lie was saying I was a college student.

Throughout our interview, Mr. Humphries had moved with the air of a man who'd heard it all before. If he guessed I was lying, he couldn't prove it. As he filled in the forms and checked the carbons, I wonder if he wasn't thinking, "What an amateur. Doesn't she know London is the home of the *Beggar's Opera*? Hasn't she read *Oliver Twist*?" Nevertheless, he'd resignedly ordered my checks to be replaced. Before parting, we shook, and his hand felt like a relief map with high jutting mountains and deep cutting rivers. Mr. Humphries's body seemed bloodless, just a prop, but those hands seemed capable of anything.

.   .   .

While we were staying at Michelle's I received an answer from Doris Lessing. The letter's been lost, but I will paraphrase it to the best of my recollection. I never forgot her salutation: "Dear Wholewheat," she wrote. The rest of the letter was brief but potent: Like you, I spend my time writing. I think you'll understand that if I were to meet with everyone who wanted to meet me, I'd never get any work done. Thank you for your nice words about my book *The Golden Notebook*. I wish you the best of luck. Yours sincerely, Doris Lessing.

It made absolutely no difference that she'd declined to meet me. At the heart of her note was the implied confirmation that I, too, was a writer, like her. I cannot overstate the strength of purpose with which I then felt imbued. Doris Lessing's letter was a concrete sign that I should spend even more time with my notebooks.

It was still only October. There would be plenty of time to get to Paris, visit the peace talks, and fly home before winter. It seemed a shame not to see Amsterdam while I had a little money, and such inspiration.

Amsterdam

1971, November

> My Father drives a truck
> On the L.I. Expressway
> Between junkyards
> I am an Aunt eating mushrooms in Holland
> Drinking soup with the truckers in morning
> Oh!
> I got the junkyard blues.
>
> B. GROATS

When we were still in London, I asked Amy to accompany me to the Paris peace talks. She agreed, and together we began to consider our graver responsibilities. When would we make our visit? Perhaps after Christmas. How should we think of ourselves? We were friends, but now we were also a delegation. Were we a youthful counterculture delegation, a youth-culture delegation, or simply a delegation of youth? We decided to iron out the finer points of diplomacy later that winter, when we would rendezvous in France. Amy, always drawn to the south, was going to Rome first.

Within a few weeks, I was living on a houseboat on a canal in Amsterdam, and my life was virtually unrecognizable. For one thing, I suddenly had sex appeal. I don't know where I got it. Maybe it fell with the drizzling winter rain. Or came with my newly hennaed hair and hippie threads (I'd ditched the farmer's overalls for a cat fur coat, embroidered Romanian blouse, and Indian voile skirt inset with sequins, tiny mirrors, and bells). Maybe it came with the boat. In the cafés and hash bars I'd visit at night I met lots of young men stuck at youth hostels or dirty dives or crashing on the floors of squats. Nothing made a girl more attractive than a boat of her own.

I was much more relaxed around men than I'd ever been. At some unmarked point, I must have realized that mankind was not going to change overnight and I wasn't born to be a human sacrifice. Once I'd abandoned my post as international queen of accountability, just talking to men became a lot easier. I met a man who imported citrus fruit and whose skin smelled of oranges; an Irish musician who played the mandolin and, mysteriously, never spoke above a whisper; an Italian intellectual who said he'd fallen in love with me at first sight and wanted to move onto the boat. But I was reluctant to share my sanctuary with anyone. It was a toss-up whether I enjoyed my improved sex life or my new privacy more. In fact, the two were indivisible.

I'd never lived alone before. In my teens the prospect seemed like exile. As a radical I'd thought privacy bred secrets, and secrets were always decadent and counterrevolutionary. In Amsterdam, I'd landed inside an incubator of luxurious mysteries, a sort of Aladdin's lamp of love. I was on a long lucky streak and only had to desire an encounter for one to occur. Every night I submerged myself in hashish and sex. I'd sleep through the afternoons while the stout little boat rocked like a cradle on the canal. Waking on my narrow bed, I'd be eye to eye with the ducks, ready for more hashish and sex.

The boat belonged to Jack Moore, a man I'd met casually through a mutual friend. Jack needed someone to keep watch over his boat while he was busy turning an old barn into a video studio in southern Holland. *Busy* probably comes nowhere near describing the pace Jack struck. He was an original—something of a mad and moody scientist. I always picture him rushing around with his arms full of Plexiglas and sometimes confuse him in my memory with the berserk genius Paul Williams played in the film *Phantom of the Paradise.* They were both long-haired blonds, explosive, and short. Jack was one of the founders of the underground newspaper *IT* in London, connected to *Suck,* in Amsterdam, and from what I could see, in the early vanguard of computer whiz and video razzle-dazzle. He always had grand schemes on all burners. When I first met him that winter in Arnheim, he was simultaneously designing what he claimed would be the first comprehensive international videotape library and developing a multimedia theater event to be performed at the Munich Olympics. His enthusiasm for the theater project moved me to write in my diary: "I have a good feeling about these Olympics. I think it will be like the greatest festival of festivals with more freaks than Woodstock and Altamont combined." (I don't know if his theater piece was ever performed. And it isn't for its counterculture "freaks" that the Munich Olympics is remembered, but rather for the murder of eleven Israeli athletes by a Palestinian group calling itself "Black September.")

Every day for a freezing week, I helped Jack carry Plexiglas from one side of the barn to the other. Finally, he sent me off to Amsterdam with the instructions that I enjoy myself and take care of the little red boat. I could pick up the key from Theodora, one of his neighbors.

Theodora, I discovered, was an anorexic aesthete, with a glassy stare and barely enough energy to open the door. She'd either had a rough night or a deeply disappointing life. In either case, she made it clear she wasn't in the mood for visitors—to her boat or to her city. Later, Jack explained that Theodora took her role as gatekeeper to Amsterdam's canals very seriously. She considered it her right as the hostess—not just of a social event, but of a nation—to inspect all visitors. To Theodora, the hippie invasion was undermining the character of her overtolerant town. She considered all hippies (with the exception of her friend Jack) to be rude, dirty, insensitive, and uncultured boors. Her dislike was palpable.

As I stood around, waiting for her to surrender the key to Jack's boat, I was impressed by her self-possession, that disinterested air of entitlement, the gust of fascism that blew through her boat. I felt obliged to confound her prejudices and, prattling like a debutante, complimented the decor—all that antique lace (all that ugly delft). Did she buy it at the flea market? She sneered and I barreled on. She couldn't possibly dislike me in general, I thought, when she saw how interesting I was in particular. Couldn't she tell I wasn't part of the herd? I was, for example, very well read. Currently, I was reading volume four of *The Diaries of Anaïs Nin*.

Theodora raised her hand for silence: "Isn't that a little fancy?" she sighed.

Now, I think, if Theodora hadn't pulled the plug, I'd have babbled myself into a hospital. Why I wanted this unsavory character's approbation I cannot tell you. Why does anyone want to be liked? She may have been remote and wan and arch (and she couldn't have been less like the red-cheeked, robust blonds featured in the tourist brochures), but she posed liked Amsterdam embodied. Maybe I was looking for a shortcut. In any case, she did everything but wave me away.

I've told this story a lot of times. Theodora had the talent to damn with faint praise, and perhaps, to be terribly amusing. But she was an awful bigot. Just how *fancy* was Anaïs Nin? Long ago, I thought

Theodora had criticized Nin's writing as too rich because her own taste ran to less romantic, starker literature. But over the years and, I'm sorry to say, some obsessing over Theodora, I've come to believe that beneath her words was a warning: a young woman dressed in army boots might find that such an extravagant book raised expectations above her station. In the end, for Theodora, Amsterdam would have been a better, cleaner place if hippies had stuck to books of moral improvement. Later, I asked Jack to explain how Theodora's death grip on order in the midst of raging eccentricity jibed with the famously tolerant Dutch nature. It's a big world, he said, or something like it. And actually, she's Scottish.

Before I left with the key, Theodora instructed me in houseboat etiquette: There was no toilet on board the little red boat, so I would have to arrange a healthful substitute. I was not to throw anything into the canals or harass the waterfowl. And, of course, I was never to smoke hash in bed—I might get too stoned and burn down the canal. Since hash for personal consumption was legal in Amsterdam, she recommended that I smoke in cafés and drink wine on the boat, quietly.

. . .

Travel writers over generations have remarked on the Dutch passion for orderliness and the silence and safety of the canals. The silence becomes menacing once you think of the thousands of Jewish people walking quietly alongside those canals to the internment centers of German-occupied Holland during World War II. Like every great city, Amsterdam plays both hero and villain. James Boswell complained of the city's "horrible fogs and excessive cold." To the staff at *Suck* magazine the atmosphere was just damp after sex. Some visitors found Amsterdam shallow and obsessed with trade. Others hailed its history of tolerance and fairness. The same Amsterdammers who delighted in flowers, in window boxes, in decent white curtains, controlled half of the Asian Pacific and left it reeling in the aftermath of its exploitation. For every image of wimpled maidens there are wet-lipped cavaliers; and for every pristine pitcher of milk, a still life of ripe mallards and split plums buzzing with flies. For Karel Čapek, the divergent streams of the Dutch character flowed together in Rembrandt's life—in his love of light and "search for darkness." In 1954, at the end of the colonial period, Albert Camus imagined Amsterdam's dual nature. It wasn't just thrift and trade that aroused the Dutch merchant soul, Camus wrote, it was the sea. The city's population might appear to be riding their bicycles through the city streets, but "Holland is a dream, Monsieur." In their minds those bicyclists were far away in "those islands where men die mad and happy."

Sounds like the Amsterdam I'd wandered into. It's not a stretch to imagine that the hippie subcolony might have provided the Dutch with the same kind of escape valve from the pressures of society that its former colonies had. There were few resources to be exploited (once in a while a hippie girl crossed over to the red-light district, and some profit must have been made from the trickle-down in the drug trade), but this time all the exoticism and license you desired could be found right outside your front door. Why else did they tolerate us? A Calvinist pledge to be civil whatever the price? A public scourging for their failures during the war? It was my experience that the Dutch didn't like us much but had decided to leave us alone to smoke and fuck to our heart's content. Some of us got the clap. Some of us got addicted. Some of us OD'd and died. We reveled through a decade of nights, and we wore ourselves out.

Hippie and bourgeois societies circled Amsterdam in concentric orbits. And though many among our hosts employed Theodora's intense gaze, many hippies, too stoned to notice or too selfish to care, thought themselves invisible to the Dutch. Those of us who chose to return the gaze came to recognize that Amsterdam was a voyeur's paradise.

.   .   .

The little red boat was docked on the edge of a neighborhood called the Nieuwmarkt. Its streets were lined with transient hotels, late-night hash clubs, student cafés, abandoned warehouses, and derelict gabled houses without electricity or plumbing from which hippies emerged night and day in full plumage. At all hours, bicyclists bent against the autumn winds. My neighborhood was dominated by De Waag, a medieval fortress built in 1488 as part of the city's gates. We called it the castle on the corner. Most of the neighborhood's Dutch occupants had moved away, and a multinational community of squatters had taken up residence in their old gabled homes. By the time I arrived the neighborhood was in the middle of a fight for survival. The city had plans to demolish several streets in order to build a subway, which, community activists argued, would ruin the character of the area and destroy historic homes that could be renovated.

Every night, huge klieg lights set up in construction sites lent the alleys and streets an alien glow, and bicycling on even the darkest nights became a theatrical experience. The massive corrugated iron fences surrounding the sites were canvases to the graffiti-prone residents of my neighborhood. Murals came and went. Words were the graffiti of choice, and from my boat I could see two huge spray-painted aphorisms. One fence painted in hot-pink English screamed: WORDS DON'T MEAN ANYTHING ANYMORE. The other, in smaller, neater, cursive Dutch script, read simply: Trepanation Waarom? In other words, "Why gouge a third eye?"

Why indeed? The rumor was that many pilgrims were doing just that in their search for wisdom and elevated consciousness. Almost everybody I knew claimed to know somebody who had been trepanned and was consequently perpetually high. The process was said to be no big deal—an X cut into your forehead just above and between your eyebrows. You let in a little air to open that third eye, and thereafter smoking hash was supposed to become redundant. That may have been all right for some, but I loved smoking hash. I liked the formality and the ritual of heating and crumbling the hashish into aromatic Dutch tobacco, of pasting together several cigarette papers like a perverse grammar school art project. I liked building the joint and licking it so that the fire would burn slowly. Most of all I liked the society. You were never alone with a joint in Amsterdam.

Working

1971, December

Many nights after some debauchery, I'd stop at Aggie's, my corner bar, and eat a stale yellow cookie with pink sugar icing fished from a tin containing hundreds. I fantasized that these "cakies" were leftover sea rations from the time Holland was an ocean power. At the bar, working men in wool caps, coming home from the late shift, drank shots of Geneva with coffee. Nobody ever spoke to me there, until Uncle Louie introduced himself.

Uncle Louie was a neighborhood institution. He was in his seventies when I met him, and famous for acting the clown among the hippies. He spoke most languages, smoked hash, and was always trying to cop a feel. "Don't give him an inch," I was warned, "if you value your privacy."

Uncle Louie's Dutch was made sloppier and more impenetrable by the absence of teeth. Everyone thought he was slightly mad, because he wouldn't accept the new housing the city offered, and because sometimes he wouldn't stop giggling. He could get terribly disturbed if you claimed you didn't understand his English—and sometimes his hysteria would collapse into weeping. His moods swung all over the map—though nothing embarrassed him. He'd wheedle your attention and then bore you to death. But, at the first sign of *your* impatience *he'd* act hurt and defensive, so if you weren't made of stone you'd have to coax him back to a good humor. After just a day's absence, he would shower me in a display of kisses and hugs worth a decade's separation. From our first meeting, Uncle Louie tried to take over my life: I should move in with him, he could find me a job, a husband! Had I ever seen the sunset in New Guinea? Those first few nights at Aggie's, I nodded off (having smoked hash all night) as he droned on. I was to come and visit him, he said. He had something he wanted to show me.

It didn't make sense that he'd become so attached to me so quickly. In any case he was unavoidable. Even when I skipped Aggie's, I'd run into someone, often a stranger, who'd say, "Uncle Louie's been asking about you." He's funny, I was told. He'll find a new friend eventually. But when he gets so fixated, you might as well surrender. He won't hurt you.

. . .

Uncle Louie lived on the second floor of a condemned building on Dijkstraat. The other floors contained the flats of squatters whom he'd invited to share his home. He'd been a sailor all his life, and that tiny airless apartment was filled with *chachkas* from around the world. I remember coconut halves with paintings inside, fraying straw donkeys, bolts of sun-faded batiks, a sombrero. Every surface was cluttered, and the only place to sit was beside Uncle Louie on an itchy horsehair sofa. Had I ever seen this? he asked, and rolled up his shirt to show me an anchor tattoo, a snake, then the blue numbers the Nazis had scored into his arm.

"Are you a Jewish girl?" he asked me.

Good question. About the same time I'd jettisoned New York, I'd stopped identifying myself as Jewish. Perhaps it was a defensive measure against the casual anti-Semitism I kept encountering among my European companions. Some held attitudes that were chilling. Although the Jewish people were rarely the subject of a conversation, it was common to hear individual representatives demeaned as money-lenders and shysters capable of dark, insidious plots. "That's ridiculous," I might remark in some dark club after a stranger's particularly bizarre observation—but only if I was feeling brave and awake enough. Other times I'd just wander away, wondering at the speaker's stupidity and my own apathy. I had become in a very short time a hippie of the don't-hassle stripe. I still felt the fires of rebellion heat up when I thought of the Vietnam War. I had a lovely memory of why I had come to Europe, but Paris seemed very far away. And its distance was a comfort to me. I was uncoiling, stretching out on the couch of luxury, a sybarite at last. I didn't feel the impulse to defend positions or engage in argument. I could justify everything but preferred not to. I had no real friends, but I wasn't lonely. I really did nothing, but it was all so exciting. I was, in George Bernard Shaw's words, "yielding and dreaming instead of resisting and doing," absorbed by the delicious state he calls "the sweetness of the fruit that is going rotten." I had some sense that I deserved to enjoy myself without care or thought, that somehow this time was owed to me like the R&R soldiers receive. Many of the

Irish, Italian, Dutch, British, French, and German youths with whom I shared that squatters' community also claimed to have sloughed off their pasts and their surnames (though few of us had lost our prejudices). In the psychedelic night world of Amsterdam, I was just Buckwheat Groats, cosmopolite, until Uncle Louie unearthed me.

He could tell I was Jewish, he said, because I looked exactly like Sada Levi, whom he'd adored at school. He'd never been much of a Jew himself, he admitted. He'd been bar mitzvahed but disappointed his parents by quitting school and joining the merchant marines.

"Here they are." He pulled over a photo album to show me his parents, plump and smiling for eternity. "The Nazis killed them."

I was utterly miserable. It was so hot, and the kitsch cluttered in Uncle Louie's little room made me claustrophobic. His was one of the few buildings in the Nieuwmarkt where the plumbing worked, and he'd cranked up the steam high enough to drive a locomotive. The couch itched. Uncle Louie had spread the album on my lap, and he kept leaning over to pet my hands, as if he were consoling me. I felt like a prisoner, a really ignorant prisoner.

Here was a picture of Sada Levi. Didn't I see the likeness?

I saw a girl around my age with dark wavy hair who looked a lot happier than I was.

"The Nazis killed her. Did you know," Uncle Louie asked, "that most of the Jews who lived in the Netherlands were murdered by the Nazis?" (This number was close to 113,000 of the 140,000 Jews in the Netherlands in 1940.)

"No."

"Did you know they rounded us up here, around De Waag, before we were sent to the camps?"

"No."

I remember he looked at me as if I were from Mars. Here, a generation later, a young Jewish woman who looked like the revered Sada Levi knew fuck-all about the most catastrophic events of his life. The same canal side streets where people had strolled unsuspectingly to roundups were the shortcuts I took. There was nothing I could do except know it now. Uncle Louie was determined to make me know it.

"These are what I want to show you." He turned to a group of snapshots of his younger self. In all of them he is clowning. In several he stands with his arms around friends. In others he's alone, waving his sailor's cap. In several blurry close-ups he tilts his face at the camera.

But in every picture there is a screen between Uncle Louie and the photographer. "It's a barbed wire fence," he said.

His Dutch buddies, the men he sailed with and drank with, had stopped by De Waag to say hello. One of them had had a camera. "In jail again, Louie?" they'd joked.

"I could have run," he said. "But I thought I could protect my parents. You understand?"

·   ·   ·

By that time I was out of money and living on candy bars. And though Uncle Louie's offer to lend me money and feed me and find me a husband was tempting, I suspected he needed more attention than a hundred young women could provide. I'd never felt motivated by guilt before. I know some historians suggest that the whole New Left emerged in reaction to guilt and privilege, but I wasn't conscious of any such thing. It wasn't until I'd met Uncle Louie that I knew how it felt to fall weak with guilt—and afraid. If I didn't find the money to get to Paris, I'd be trapped forever among the souvenirs and photos and ships in bottles.

I tried panhandling but found rejection too hard to take; and I couldn't pretend to be grateful for the pittance I received. Next, I tried offering tarot card readings in front of the Amsterdam American Express, but the competition there was stiff. As I observed in my journal:

> You can buy anything outside American Express. Cons and
> hustlers and hippies in army coats, pass out cards to announce
> their merchandise: rugs, charter flights, cars, tours, coats, hair-
> cuts, and then there are the whispered advertisements: Hash,
> kif, uppers, downers, trips. Somebody shouts: "Where'd that
> cat and that chick go, I was looking for that van they had."
> One regular has a sign on his chest with 6 cars and descriptions
> listed on it. Down the block a calliope plays constantly. A
> grizzled gypsy man dances a two-step with a hat in his hand.
> Tourists run the gauntlet to get their mail. For us American
> Express is the height of bourgeois culture, for them, its the
> worst dump in Amsterdam.

In the end I was lucky. I met Sergio, an Italian intellectual who swore undying love while he presented a business proposition. I could make enough to get to Paris, he promised. In fact, my earnings would only be limited by my imagination. Before we could begin, though, he wanted to confess he was married and still loved his wife. Sadly, she'd left him a few nights before, and he needed another partner in a hurry.

For some time, Sergio and his wife, Marie, had been performing live sex acts at the Monte Carlo Club in the red-light district. The money was very good, he said; you made a hundred guilders per night, and without your glasses you couldn't even see the audience.

I had often bicycled through the red-light district, and I was always curious about the prostitutes who displayed themselves in the shop windows there. Each one posed against a different backdrop—offering different commercial lures. One had a white tablecloth on her bed; another, red velvet drapes opened just far enough to see an old wing chair with tassels hanging over its arms. Ever since Oakland I'd thought that prostitution was pretty much a possibility for anyone. Some of these women were in hock to pimps and dealers. Some considered themselves independent businesswomen. I wasn't going to judge them. Now I'd be working down the street from them at the Monte Carlo Club.

.   .   .

"Take a look. Fucky-fucky, ladies and gentlemen, things you wouldn't do at home!" The barker took a minute from his spiel to show me where to park my bike.

The stage door led into the private club, where a low stage ran the length of one wall. This was where the special acts were performed: orgies, whips and chains, enemas, animals, Sergio explained. I thought he was teasing. "Enemas?"

"Sì," he said. "You do it yourself or a lady can assist."

We were to perform upstairs on the much more wholesome public stage, where the audience was composed of tourists, mainly American, Middle Eastern, and Japanese men, who liked to watch couples. For their delectation there were two of every briefly considered cliché: a he-man and a sexy woman, a pair of students, a couple of Dutch peasants, two cowboys, a Balinese duet. Sergio and I were the hippie act.

The performance would be fairly straightforward, but it was helpful to know a few tricks in advance, Sergio said. First, we were expected to walk onstage nude, except for a prop or two. Hippies wore love beads; Dutch peasants, wooden shoes; and so on. You lie down, the man lies on top, and you pretend to fuck. The audience always has to believe that he is erect, even if he isn't. Under those conditions, Sergio admitted, he couldn't stay hard. So my primary job was to block his dick with my hand or some other part of my body, until it looked like he'd entered me. We were then to act out wildly improbable orgasms and exit quickly. Each act was to take exactly twenty minutes, and we were to perform twelve times a night.

The dressing room was a Tower of Babel. As my fellow actresses donned the hats or collars or shoes they would wear onstage, they joked caustically in several languages about their hopeless partners or the ridiculous audience. Many of the women working there were junkies. Management conveniently offered its employees the opportunity to be paid in heroin or cocaine; or they could get cash and exchange any amount for customized drugs right on the premises.

"It's not a bad job," the cowgirl told me as she primped naked in front of the mirror. "The money's good. Who's your partner? Oh, Sergio. You're lucky, Sergio's very nice."

Some of their partners beat them or took their money. But to the cowgirl, all that dope made all that suffering tolerable. Her boyfriend was a brute, but at least she wasn't turning tricks. "As long as I get my smack, this place is invisible," she said, and offered me a sniff of coke and heroin combined, for my own "stage fright."

I demurred, not because I was particularly opposed to those drugs, but I didn't want to lose focus and miss my cue. And in all honesty, that cowgirl was no great advertisement. She'd slathered heavy makeup over several neck bruises and a fading black eye. There had to be a better atmosphere, I thought, for my first taste of heroin. If I was going to fall into oblivion, I wanted to be someplace I could wear my glasses.

To the music of Isaac Hayes singing "Shaft," Sergio and I strode onstage, naked, and pretended to make love. The only place I diverted from the program was at the very end, when—with respect for the Asian people in the audience—I took a bow. That irritated Sergio, who reminded me of his instructions to "exit quickly."

I had less enthusiasm during our second performance. "It could have gone better," I agreed afterward. But Sergio seemed inconsolable. He called me incompetent and untrainable. I wasn't doing the *one* thing he'd asked. "They should never see me without an erection!" he complained. "If I don't have an erection, they feel cheated. They paid for my erection! They must believe in my erection!" Sergio was turning into Balanchine, and his choreography starting to feel too much like work. By the five-minute call for our third show, he and I were hardly talking. Waiting in the wings for our music cue, I whispered, "You're overreacting!"

He hissed, "This isn't about fun. It's about money!"

I said I wasn't staying another second, and Sergio grabbed my arm. For a moment we both shared the same thought: if he'd pulled me on-stage and raped me, the audience would only have clapped.

"Not a guilder," Sergio wagged his finger in my face. He let go, and I ran to my bike. "Take a look! Fucky-fucky, ladies and gentlemen!" The barker's command followed me down the canal.

·   ·   ·

A few days later, Jack showed up at the boat. In exchange for taking a few bundles of *Suck* magazine to his friend Jim Haynes in Paris, he'd pay my train fare. So, saying good-bye to the little red boat and good-bye to Uncle Louie and good-bye to Amsterdam, I blithely set forth for France.

Dress neatly, Jack had suggested. You don't want to encourage nosy customs officials. By that time I didn't really have any neat clothes with which to camouflage myself. I might have made more of an effort, but Jack had neglected to tell me that *Suck* was banned in France. I'd hardly have believed it. Who'd bother to ban *Suck*? It was an irrepressibly goofy magazine that proclaimed sexual liberation the salvation of civilization. As a veteran of underground papers I agreed it had panache and enthusiasm for its subject. (And, at least in its intention, it was different from *Screw* or *Penthouse* or *Hustler,* which reduced women to only the meaty objects of smirky humor.) *Suck*'s graphics were exciting, lots of sunburst psychedelia. Its big problem was re-dundancy, and good luck if you were looking for an article to read. It's impossible to measure just how much *Suck* influenced the social climate. I do know, from personal experience, that it was considered a dangerous threat, because when representatives of the French state—the France of French letters and French postcards!—tore open my bags at the Belgian border, they called my bundles of *Suck* obscene "contra-band" and detained me overnight on charges of being a pornographer.

Mrs. Warder had prophesied just such a dire fate. "Pornographer!" she'd shrieked back in second grade, before beating the crap out of me. I'd become the criminal Mrs. Warder had imagined, the *vildechaya* Mrs. Klein had predicted. It remained to be seen whether I'd become the writer I hoped to be.

Paris

1972, January

Was I a nice girl, or was I a prostitute? Did I like to do these things myself? Who had given me the papers? Where was I taking them? The French customs officer grilled me for hours with a copy of *Suck* opened to its centerfold: a black-and-white photo of twin succubi ravishing the cartoon of an erect cock. This insolent juxtaposition so staggered my interrogator that he polled the station for every man's opinion. His colleagues crowded behind him, shouting out their own questions: What would my family think? Did I know I could be arrested and kept in prison?

The police looked like actors. Their extravagant costumes included peaked hats and medals on their breasts. The railroad station was a set in a New Wave film. I couldn't take it seriously. No, I couldn't remember the name of the man who gave me the contraband. No, I didn't understand much French. (Still, I recognized a few insults.)

This was the third time in my life that a comic strip had caused me grave aggravation. The first time, at the Goddard media conference when I'd tried to accuse Gilbert Shelton of sexist representation of women, I'd been drowned out by that couple fucking in the back of the room. The second time in Ann Arbor, when I'd stood by as Violet had argued with Red the Biker about his cartoons, I'd lost my standing in the commune. I could talk a good game but in social practice, Violet had said, I was useless. This third time, I stood in the heat of the interrogation lamp while the cops waved this lurid rendering of a putz about to pop. The absurd conditions of my arrest demanded an absurd response. The lights were hot, the chaos of an incomprehensible language frustrating. The best I could do was retreat into a cartoon myself, and the cops seemed equally one-dimensional. The spirit of a Resistance fighter possessed me—not the robust young men and earnest women of the Paris struggle—no—I was Snoopy, the hero of the "Peanuts" comic strip, beret akimbo, jaunty scarf flying. I was a dog who walked: rueful, sophisticated, keeping secrets, soaring above the corrupt human race, and it was my duty to keep Jack's name mum.

In the end, I gave the officer a false name for my boss—"Monsieur Walter Mitty"—and a false address for my drop-off site. He confiscated both bundles of magazines, called me a whore, and went home (I imagined) to add *Suck* to his collection.

It was one in the morning. The waiting room was locked; I had five hours ahead before the morning train and, aside from my thin coat, no protection from the January weather. Across the station a sick bum, with even less, huddled under some newspapers. My journal entry for that night begins: "Burnt and busted."

My departure from Amsterdam had been less than auspicious. I had moved from the red boat the week before and been crashing in a cold, crowded squat. The night before leaving, I'd drunk too much wine and smoked too much hashish, then fallen asleep in a borrowed blanket. Somehow I had managed to roll into the room's one electric bar heater and slept on while the blanket had smoked, until someone fortunate enough to wake up had smothered the spreading fire. I wasn't hurt, but I was shaken, and there were no more extra blankets. It was miserably cold, and I couldn't sleep and there wasn't a working bathroom for a block in any direction. So, I smoked more hash and started for Paris smelling of singed hair and fabric.

More and more my life seemed to possess the made-up quality of an adventure serial. I'd become used to living intensely, and every new experience had to be more and more extreme to make an impression. "A poet must reject normality," I wrote in my journal that night. "Being 'normal' disgusts me. It is just another idealogy—The result of corporate advertising. Normality is as cultivated as Maoism. It is just another style. Normality is perversion."

I was an outlaw with bells on my skirt and a dirty neck. Better to spend my life stoned than live *their* hypocritical, lie-stained, boring little lives. Being detained by the French police was only what a wandering poet should come to expect.

It is interesting that in trying so hard to be original, I was on the verge of becoming just one more dippy romantic, swept away by sentimental clichés. When the subject arose, I told people I had a gypsy mother. In Canada? they asked. Earlier, I'd adopted existentialism as my ethos. But it wasn't the kind of philosophy that made a person happy. I didn't want doctrines. I wanted, finally, to enjoy all this freedom. I wanted to surrender myself to the romance of art and poverty. But I was needled by one undischarged responsibility. I still hadn't decided what to do or say to the Vietnamese. Whenever I tried to focus on the subject my mind clouded over. I didn't want to think about the war. And I didn't want to *feel* it either. The war and who I was in opposition to it had become like a jingle in the distant corners of my mind. It was a tune I couldn't shake but couldn't really remember. It was like the theme to *The Andy Griffith Show,* or *My Three Sons,* music heard repeatedly and filed away, the sound track of my life. It had occurred to me sometime earlier that ending the war would demand some desperate act. I pictured myself holding both the U.S. and the Vietnamese teams in the negotiating room and freeing them only in exchange for an immediate ceasefire. There'd have to be a lot of derring-do involved to suit my current tastes. Movements to block, costumes to design. I wanted to wear pantaloons and a ruff, pearl drop earrings and over-the-knee leather boots, carry a long sword and jump on tabletops. *"This action can only work,"* I wrote, *"If I am emotionally unengaged."*

That night, with no money and no food, I felt, despite my discomfort, emotionally pure, careless and thoughtless, down and out, a little crazy, and awfully literary. Huddling in that deserted train station would become another story in the distant future. The alternatives had been reduced to suburbia and the death culture, or coughing my guts out alongside other sick bums in the deserted train stations of France.

· · ·

By the time I arrived in Paris, I had my own raging fever, and by the time Jack's friend had rushed me to the American Hospital, I was in a state of complete collapse. I also had an infected abscess on my side for which I had been treating myself with large quantities of hashish and for which the examining doctor immediately ordered surgery.

It's not uncommon to awake weeping after anesthesia. After my surgery, all alone, in a white gown, in a room with gleaming surfaces— I was inconsolable. Outside, the Paris I had never really seen was an enigma of dog barks and traffic horns. Through the door, I heard the murmurs of indistinguishable French words. Everything was disorienting, immaculate; and I'd been deeply drugged. The Marquis de Sade himself would have had a hard time cultivating vice in those conditions.

The pain in my side, I wrote in my notebook, was *diabolical*. I'd never felt pain like that before; and it provoked unwelcome memories of my mother's last days, her screams for morphine until my father, in a murderous rage at her doctors, had demanded they provide the drugs she needed. "We don't want her to get addicted," the doctor had argued.

The week passed, and I remained in a stupefying fog. My room-mate, Mrs. Morello from Queens, was as stoned as I. "Where are my gardenias?" she'd groan, in a New Yorkese that the nurses couldn't understand. She used a pidgin to speak to them. "I wanna make a wee-wee," she'd say, or "Aqua!"

Mrs. Morello was sixty-five and suffering from a complaint located, in her words, "down there." I was horribly fascinated and described her agony in my diary: "Today, they pinned her cunt together after sticking a bag inside and measuring for urine. Mrs. Morello's daughter is very good to her, and comes every night. Since I never have visitors, she brought me flowers."

The morning nurse was as pretty and sympathetic as a character in a TV doctor drama. Her name translated into English was "Monica Swallow."

"Wouldn't you like to call your parents?" she asked every day.

I said I'd think about it. Of course, I had already thought about it, obsessively. And I wanted the impossible. I wanted my father *to have been there* when I came out of surgery. (There was no way he could have known what I wanted. I never phoned. And I only ever wrote that I was fine, and having a wonderful time.) I suppose I wanted a magic father who could have sensed my suffering, appeared at my mental command, and departed likewise—really more of a genie than a father. In the absence of either, I was angry and stubborn. The doctor had assured me I'd had an unusual eruption of boils brought on by my nervous disposition and infected through poor hygiene. It wasn't cancer. He was a young man, a distant acquaintance of Jack's, and so sympathetic I was sure he was hiding the truth. He told me that if I calmed down, the boils would probably never return. If I washed more carefully I could avoid infection. If I phoned my parents I could recuperate peacefully in my own home. I interpreted everything the doctor said as a systematic effort to undermine my independence. I saw him as a lying functionary whose only prescription for a rebellious young woman was submission. I wouldn't speak to the doctor, and I refused to call my father. Going back to Massapequa seemed far more frightening than staying in Paris without money or friends.

There was a boy from Scarsdale down the hall, Terry, who'd been in a motorcycle crash. He was pissing blood and on more drugs than Mrs. Morello and I combined. I met him the day his mother was supposed to arrive.

"What's that ring?" Terry asked me.

He was mesmerized by the story I told of almost going to Cuba. "That's made from a downed plane? Wow! It's like wearing an ear around your neck!"

I tried to explain that my ring was altogether different. It was jewelry made out of the weapons of destruction. Something beautiful made out of waste. A token of esteem, not a "souvenir." "What's the difference between it and a lampshade made of human skin?" he asked. "The Nazis thought Jews were waste."

Terry was obviously too whacked out to engage in a rational discussion. Later, when Monica Swallow changed my dressing I showed her the ring. She asked, "Do you ever imagine the man who was flying the plane?"

I didn't say so, but the truth was, I hardly stopped thinking about him. Sometimes, the ring felt hot on my hand and its number—3200— glowed in the dark. I wanted to give the ring away to the next person who admired it. But I couldn't because it was my reward. At the peace talks the Vietnamese would understand that I wore their token, though it was hard.

I had a relapse and was stuck in bed again. In my journal I vigilantly documented Mrs. Morello's decline:

> Nappy time and I'm resisting. Mrs. Morello is groaning more than ever. Her waxy skin looks pulled tight everywhere except for her face and legs which are oddly pleated. Her daughter came this morning and polished her nails. Afterwards, the room stunk of nail polish remover and Glade. I didn't want to cry tonight, but after Monica Swallow told me there was a restaurant in Paris that sends everything it makes to North Vietnam I started to sob. Mrs. Morello groaned at me. She said I was keeping her awake.

· · ·

As I felt less and less drowsy I tried to imagine the Paris outside my window. Monica Swallow described the cafés along the boulevards and the book stalls alongside the Seine. She herself had been involved in the demonstrations of *soixante-huit* but rarely visited the Latin Quarter anymore because it had changed so much and so quickly. In her estimation, the Left Bank had become an "armed camp" where police, carrying guns like soldiers, patrolled every corner. Monica Swallow told me I was fortunate. Paris was enjoying beautiful weather—an early spring. The trees were blossoming in the Bois de Boulogne. I began feeling more and more argumentative, more and more hungry. In the middle of the night, a flock of nurses moved Mrs. Morello to the hospice ward. The next day Terry's mother flew him back to Scarsdale.

My journal shows that over those last few solitary days in the hospital, I didn't lend much thought to my future. Instead, I fretted over whether or not to read *Hanoi* by Mary McCarthy and recorded this argument with myself:

> McCarthy is a liberal's liberal. Flipping through the pages every other word is moral this or moral that. Genet says, "the beauty of a moral act depends upon the beauty of its expression." I want to read this because its a book and I'm out of books. I want to read it because its about Vietnam but I don't want to think about Vietnam because Vietnam gives me a head ache. Everything gives me a headache. I've decided to stick to poetry because moralizing and judging make my head hurt more than anything.

I decided to read the book and afterward recorded a positive review. One passage in which McCarthy describes a woman she saw in the Hanoi War Crimes Museum even inspired me to plan a poem. "They told us, lowering their voices, that she had been haunting the museum ever since she had lost her twenty-year-old son early in the year," McCarthy reported. I don't remember starting that poem, but even just reading McCarthy's book set me back on track. The answer to what I would do next was stay in Paris. Paris was where the peace talks went on and on.

La Dolce Vita

1972, February

Released! In a taxi on my way to Jim Haynes's flat. Nowhere else to go and I was down to my last few coins. The only address I had in Paris was that of Jack's partner.

Jim Haynes had a reputation for gallantly collecting strays like me. Born in Louisiana, he'd been an expatriate for sixteen years and at thirty already called himself "Europe's oldest hippie." He was a friend to the world, and proved it by opening his apartment and his life to thousands of fellow travelers. From my perspective—recuperating on a mattress in his loft—Jim's flat was where the beau monde, the demi-monde, and the hipoisie met up in a sort of counterculture think tank. From my perch I would look down into the kitchen where several mornings a week an extravagant *coiffeuse* held court and styled the hair of beautiful people. Gossip drifted up: "While we were there Joan Buck called. She did my chart. I read some cards for her." Aristos and the children of movie stars stopped by or phoned at all hours; playwrights and actors and poets and art critics drank and smoked and argued and kept me awake. During the day, the flat overflowed with loud, bright, often naked people; at night you could hear the multilayered moans and whispers of lovers fucking on every surface but mine.

Jim was a devoted utopian and an irrepressible mediaphile. In the early sixties, he had owned a bookstore where American Beat writers performed their work to a new generation of readers. He'd started fringe theaters in Scotland and London and founded underground papers in England and Amsterdam. He had a little press that published the work of young poets and new music scores and radical pamphlets. All these projects were funded by his own small income as a professor at the Sorbonne or through contributions from his vast circle of friends (sometimes a millionaire like John Lennon or Mick Jagger would whip off a check) without interrupting what appeared to be one of the most fulfilled sex lives in counterculture Europe.

The project that interested me most at the time was Jim's production, along with his friend Gary Davis, of "World Passports." Davis had renounced his U.S. citizenship in protest against the nationalism at the heart of every modern political crisis. "World government" provided a deliriously utopian alternative. In its ideal form, as I understood it, all countries would participate equally in a sort of Camelotic Round Table (functioning without the need or desire for even the most benign King Arthur). No messiahs were wanted—just a commitment to making the world's resources available to every individual equally. Under world government, the injustices of wealth and poverty would be redressed, without the petty intrigues and nasty grievances of tribalism. Peace and freedom and poetry would reign. I found these ideas irresistible, and they went a long way toward refreshing my own drooping utopianism.

Jim's flat doubled as the World Passport movement's embassy. Many of his visitors were stateless travelers, some of whom would sit in corners and smoke by the hour. Occasionally, I'd have an interesting conversation with an Eastern European or Latin American refugee who'd confuse my mattress with the ambassador's (he has the water bed downstairs, I'd explain).

The only other house regulars as entrenched as I were two Italian anarchists who called themselves Sacco and Vanzetti. They were camped out in Jim's tiny kitchen area on their way to Brazil to follow the revolution. In the quiet moments between the samba music they played repeatedly, I'd hear them practicing their English lessons: *to-morrow, to-marry, to-mato.*

Once his friends heard that he was taking care of an invalid, visiting me soon became part of the Jim Haynes experience. At first I enjoyed the attention. It didn't bother me when sightseers trooped into the loft for some charitable commiseration on their way to the Louvre or to the Café Deux Maggots. Mine seemed a small enough part to act for food and shelter and the time to recuperate. Perhaps I even fooled myself, playing "Camille," until one encounter shook me up.

That day, a beautiful Iranian model had come upstairs with her equally beautiful but impatient brother. They both sat on my bed and we made small talk. At one point, the beautiful brother pulled the collar of my pajamas out, peeked down at my breasts, and made a face. I was slow to react, but his sister slapped his hand and apologized. What had that face meant? That my breasts hadn't met with his approval?

Were they too small, too large? I'd just turned nineteen—how bad could they have been? He stood up, and turning from me, yawned and stretched. I wanted to kick him over the banister for making me feel like a freak in a sideshow, but his sister stood in the way.

How long could I deny it? I *was* a sideshow freak. Maybe I'd have launched myself over the banister if I hadn't felt in some sense at home on the midway. Everyone seemed a little out of control, a little lost and stoned. Only Jim seemed to hover above the fray. I know there were plenty of people who found him vulgar and dominating, his promiscuity over the top. Even as his friends enjoyed his hospitality, they gossiped about the way he basked in the reflected light of celebrities, about his affection for young, Ivory Soap–clean coeds, the bizarre habit he had of trying to matchmake everyone in a room; and they often laughed about his "seminal" message of peace and sexual freedom. To me he seemed at once complex, forceful, and old. I didn't really know who he was but whatever else, when I was ill, he *took me in*. I see myself as he may have seen me back then, short-tempered, dirty-haired, red-eyed, silent: his very own madwoman crouching in the loft.

The decadent style of Jim's friends, the money they desired or threw about, their mix of politics, the occult, and high society confused me. Everything clashed, roles blurred. Debutantes flirted with refugees. I couldn't keep up. Even the poets and playwrights and critics rarely discussed *art*. They drank Jim's wine and borrowed cigarettes and ogled one another. Malice seeped through the cracks in every conversation. Rumors would sheer off me to target more responsive players. Even now, I have a hard time separating whatever else may be true from the benevolent protector Jim seemed to me to be.

· · ·

Linda, Jim's assistant, was closer to my age than most of my visitors. After reading some of my poetry, she offered to introduce me to Germaine Greer, one of my idols. Linda, like Stanley Kowalski, had "go." And like her boss she refused to believe in the impossible. She was deft, unself-conscious, and apparently unaffected by the kinks and procrastinations that tortured me. Most days my brain was a fog of fantasy and fatigue. In the past, frustration had rendered me inarticulate in public; now, I could hardly speak to myself. I had started to doubt the kind of writer I was. I no longer wanted to show off my political poems. I couldn't explain that I didn't have any work I considered worth showing Germaine Greer. Linda only thought she was helping. She asked why I didn't respect her opinion. I wasn't able to say. Didn't I want her help? I groped for the words. You have some talent, she said, but you're boring. I didn't protest.

I've occasionally wondered how Linda's can-do spirit survived fate's roller coaster. I heard she became a movie producer. Linda's Paris roommate, René Ricard, has been easier to track. A habitué of New York, Paris, and London's art and intellectual circles, he has never been out of the gossip columns long. The first day we met, René lectured me on the vulgarity of museum postcard reproductions (an aeroletter was more tasteful). In 1996, Ricard sold the rights to his name and writings for forty thousand dollars to the producers of the movie *Basquiat,* in which an actor plays him in various published reports as a "bitchy hanger-on," and a "gifted, exasperatingly self-defeating poet-critic."

René Ricard never came up to Jim's loft to visit me. He was a fan of sparkling conversation. I had squandered my sparkle, and it would be a while before I could speak with ease. I worked up a few lines that I thought offered the appearance of conversation. When anyone asked what was wrong with me, I could mumble how I'd been wounded in a knife fight or had thrown myself over a balcony. I whispered that I was an underground guerrilla fighter, exiled from my country and forced to flee Nixon's spies. I'd clear my throat and fall back to silence. I couldn't say I'd suffered a mental collapse. I didn't know I had. I couldn't admit that boils had broken out all over my body. There was something about the word *boil* that seemed to wreck the atmosphere. The word *abscess* wasn't any prettier, but carbuncle meant both nasty sore and dark red jewel. Whatever I said, I knew there were holes in me that weren't healing, literal pockets that needed to be cleaned. Who wanted to see them?

For the Love of Howard

1972, March

When Jim decided I was well enough, he asked me along to a party. I hadn't been outside since the day I left the hospital the month before, and I still wasn't feeling very festive. The only thing I wanted to do was lie on my mattress in the loft and eavesdrop on the multitudes below. My host, however, had a plan to encourage me to get well and move on.

I have no pictures of myself from this period. No know-it-all portraits to lecture me in the future. Instead, my notebooks sketch a girl crouching in the loft and dodging the light, who washes her hair because her host insists; who is skinny for the first time in her life; who has stopped taking pain pills and is trying to unfog her brain. The Amsterdam sybarite seems long ago and far away. Instead, the voice in these notebooks is that of the brooding artiste, the sickie in Paris who has rejected her own work, and for whom the great on-the-road experiment has turned nasty. She is lost, out of touch, annoyed, and annoying. The things that meant so much are remote and meaningless. Reading the journals that she keeps compulsively, you can track her change into just another paralyzed American. The activist as mute as the sybarite except in the occasional remark: "I used to think something was expected of me."

I want to console the girl in the journals, but more than that, I want to wake her up. Of course I can't do either. Instead, I have to read in excruciating detail about a breakdown, a crisis of faith so full of clichés it embarrasses me. I find myself wishing I'd thrown those journals out long ago. I am tempted to censor them, and of course I do, even as I choose what to tell you about them. There are more doodles than words on these pages. When the writer does write, she excoriates herself. She says she's stupid, ugly, hopeless, weak. The words are as horrible now as they are unintentionally comic. (Could I have possibly been that bad? Did it make me feel better to say so?) When she's not blaming herself for her misery, she blames her family or her friends or the state. She feels she has been unfairly forced into a corner by the U.S. government.

The system is responsible for her troubles. She is its victim. This part is perhaps the most painful to read because, as victimized as she believes herself to be, she cannot represent her torture except to curse and splash around in bathos. When it comes down to it, despite her passion, her wit, she can't explain herself. (Here I have to read things I have tried to forget, and say what I have long known.) In the end she's just like everybody else. She thinks she's a failure. She made the choice but hasn't the strength of her convictions. She wants to be different, but can't tolerate the loneliness. Nothing and no one is reliable.

> The people. What do they want? They make everything worse. I used to feel the suffering of the poor, the oppressed and the wounded. My own pain should make me feel even more for them but it doesn't. It makes me want them to care for me. I feel sorry for myself. I don't want to think of them. I want them to think of me.

She was finally admitting what she'd been trying to deny: she was on a collision course with the revolution as she'd come to know it. Sickening of ideology, she'd become just sick. In another age, this kind of testimony would have sentenced her to the guillotine or to a firing squad. Why, given the circumstances, didn't she just go home? Her notebooks provide the evidence: she was amazingly stubborn. Here, under a violently etched doodle of four baby chicks squawking around a suburban dining room table, she explains: "Going home means this is all only an adventure. Staying proves it is my choice."

. . .

I agreed to go to the party, and in the van en route complained that the city lights made my eyes tear. I felt dizzy and sick and begged to go back to Jim's. Either Sacco or Vanzetti suggested I stop whining and take notes. I still have them: "Across a lawn, through an ornamental garden, past a fountain, to Lotte's unfurnished, candlelit ballroom. Everyone knows and greets Jim."

I felt we'd stepped into the hippie version of *La Dolce Vita*. Lotte's house was enormous and full of echoes. Scattered groups of beautiful people in slinky clothes migrated from secret circle to secret circle trailing clouds of patchouli or opium. A sitar sang from a distant corner.

I watched Jim spring like an animal from a cage into a group of quiet

Anglophones. "What's your story?" he demanded."Where would you be if you weren't here?"

"That's easy," a young Tunisian scientist answered. "I'd be locked in my laboratory looking for the fountain of youth." An English actor who wanted to be a director declared he'd be "fucking a French actress." Reva, an American student speaking on behalf of her two boyfriends, said, "Why, we wouldn't want to be anywhere else."

"Hello! I'm unhappy and bored," our hostess, Lotte, announced from the top of a circular staircase. "You look unhappy, too!" Descending, she offered me a drink from the bottle in her arms.

Lotte lived alone in a mansion with a deluxe king-size circular water bed and nine other beds in six rooms upstairs. She invited me along on a guided tour of the beds, all now crowded with guests, and in a monologue inveighed against the misery wealth brings. She had come to Paris to be a model but hadn't worked much lately. She didn't have to. There was a man, a great and powerful businessman, who had inherited her from the cad before him, who had met her through the tyrant before him. All rich. Every bed was a notch dedicated to a lover. Out the window they went when it was over. No regrets! All those beds. Did I want one? Take any one you like, she said, but take it away. She used to have guests to stay, hippie crashers even, but no more, they always abused her hospitality. Sometimes her boyfriend stayed over, not the great and powerful businessman. She always flew to meet *him* in some neutral territory, like Burma. The truth was, usually she rattled around all alone. Her latest lover was the English actor-director. Did I know where he was? "Trevor!"

We found Trevor on Lotte's circular water bed combing the long hair of a sleeping nymph. "My daughter," Lotte said.

I can't say why, but within minutes Trevor and I fell into a drunken argument that I faithfully recorded. "Jim says you're sick. You're not so sick. You're plastic," he said. "If you were that sick you'd kill yourself."

"Assassination, not suicide," I answered.

Trevor shouted, "Bullshit! Political theater!"

Lotte interrupted, "I really have to go to sleep now. It's such fun to tell people to leave."

. . .

Sacco and Vanzetti and I, Jim, Reva and her friends, Howard and Jay, who planned to stay the night, all trooped home together. Jim said he didn't have the heart to move the two stateless refugees who'd fallen asleep on his water bed. Instead, invoking his rights as host, he and Reva settled between the blankets of my bed. He invited me to join them and when, I declined, suggested that I hug Reva's friend Howard to relieve whatever tension I was feeling. It seemed like a harmless suggestion—something to please the grown-ups.

Since there was no room for Howard or me to sleep in Jim's flat, we spent the night in Sacco and Vanzetti's van. On our way outside we passed the two Italians making love to Jay in their kitchen camp.

Howard and I talked through the night. He wanted to be a poet or a painter; and to me, his college-y innocence seemed rather exotic. Too tired to sleep, I fell into my old habit of exaggeration and lies. The more Howard tried to *understand* me, the more outrageous I tried to appear. I said I never made love with men, except for money; I was a thief, a drug smuggler, a pornographer, a well-kept fifty years old! This ring I wore was a little something I'd forged from the shell of a B-52 the last time I was in Hanoi. This bandage was the result of a knife fight.

Howard wouldn't buy any of it. "You're a strange girl, but I like you," he said. "I don't know why you have to say you have a gypsy grandmother."

Howard loved baseball and Picasso and scotch and crepes. He was on track for a diploma, then a corporate job in Syracuse, then a family, then retirement and fishing as much as he could fit in, then death. He had the face of an underage Confederate soldier. It was hard not to like him. And that was my problem. It wasn't easy for me to just like some-one or something or some idea. I had to become their lover, their cham-pion, their acolyte, join their party, fight their fights, wear their tokens. So, liking Howard was a terrifying prospect. I believed that if I let myself go, the next thing I knew I'd be living in the suburbs and driving a station wagon. It would be wretched for him as well. Al-though he resisted my lies, they titillated him. He said he thought an artist required some madness in his life. Would I be his? I'd be a ter-rible influence, I promised him. I might want to be good but I'd always be afraid of the consequences. Is that another lie? he wanted to know. No, I'd never be able to shake the impulse to shatter his complacency, as long as I liked him. Oh, he said, maybe he had to experience mad-ness in order to be a better artist. Maybe my craziness would bring him closer to the source of art. Men! I resented that this had to be my job.

Why couldn't he undo what he'd done himself? He invited me over to see his paintings and read his poetry.

The next night in Howard's garret (he really had a garret), near Notre Dame, we both got very drunk. I'd already told him so many lies I couldn't remember half of them. He didn't care about the lies, he said. I was in trouble and needed someone to look after me. He wanted to do that.

Later, as Howard slept, I thought, what harm could this possibly do? He was sweet and kind, maybe it was time for me to slow down. But what was his problem? Couldn't he see I was a mess? I don't know what he imagined. Surely not the descent into catastrophe that I anticipated. He looked like a cherub drooling on his pillow. What would happen once the impulse to resist, which I'd nurtured, was gone? I hadn't really been in love yet, and if love meant simpering, I wasn't ready. I could stay and try to be good, or leave and really do something positive for Howard. The real thrill was slipping out in the middle of the night.

I prowled around the cathedral, hoping he'd come out and look for me. I fantasized about our deeply dramatic reunion, but that didn't happen. I sat through the dawn mass, and afterward bought a rosary and stole two holy medals. That was the last of me. By nightfall I was suffering a relapse and raving with fever again. No visitors, I begged Jim.

Never Say No

1972, April

I slept through a day and a night in fits and starts, then awoke to Jim padding upstairs as a voice below commanded, "Let me see the sick girl!"

"How many sleeping pills did you take?" Jim asked. All I could think was that I was weak and it was his loft. He could display me in a glass box if he wanted. If I made a scene I risked eviction. All I wanted to do was sleep.

"How do you feel?" Jim asked. "Up to a visit? Want to run a comb through your hair?" He plumped the pillows under my head. "Wouldn't you like to pull yourself together for Dick Gregory?"

"Pull yourself together for Dick Gregory." It sounded like a campaign slogan. Was I supposed to get up and salute? Dick Gregory, Winston Churchill, Harry Winston, the Duke of Earl, everybody came to Jim's. At another time and place I would have felt honored by a visit from Dick Gregory. The man had abandoned his career as a satirist to become a full-time human rights activist. As a celebrity he'd attracted a great deal of attention, and in the past few years had engaged in several well-publicized fasts against U.S. government policy and the Vietnam War. At another time and place I might have carried him around on my shoulders, but that day, as Jim later reminded me, all I said was, "Let me sleep."

Gregory charged upstairs in a nimbus of energy and folded his lanky body into a full lotus. Pretend sleep was no match for this kind of awakening. The visit commenced. (When my temperature went down I copied as much as I could remember of our conversation into my journal. Some of the following is verbatim, some is paraphrased, the rest is the result of my fevered imagination—then and now.)

"Are you getting better?" he asked, sitting on the sweaty sheets.

I couldn't say. He looked so thin, an Orthodox icon with that gaunt face. Perhaps it was only the drugs that added the disc of light I saw behind his head, I can't be sure. I asked if he was fasting again.

No, but he'd become a vegetarian. He ate only organic food and suggested I do the same. "I'm sending over some fruits and vegetables for this young lady," he yelled downstairs.

"That's just fine," Jim said.

He took my hand. "Leslie, do your parents know you're here? Because I think they'd like to know. I want you to think about going home, and later going to college. Do you hear me?" He touched my ring. "I've seen those before."

"It's made from the body of a B-52 shot down over North Vietnam. Do you want it?"

"I wouldn't wear it," he said, "but that's a decision everybody has to make for themselves. Don't ever let anybody answer for you. OK? Take care of yourself now. And don't eat meat."

He was looking directly into my eyes and holding my hand, and frankly it was even money whether I'd weep, faint, or throw up in his arms. Although I felt my face was jumping with tics and my eyes were rolling in their sockets, none of this was apparent to my visitor, who described me as a weary, but attentive, young woman.

Gregory's heartfelt advice was the sort any decent adult might offer a troubled kid. I was listening for a message beneath the words, coded to me. (If I'd heard "jump," I think you'd have found my brains on the pavement.) But in the fever music between my ears the word I heard was: "HUMAN

HUMAN

HUMAN."

I'd come a long way from Woodstock. In the preceding months I'd felt uneasy in the presence of anyone but hippies like myself—who'd made a big show of rejecting everything *normal* and *comfortable*. In Paris, my world had shrunk down to the size of a mattress in the loft of a man I'd just met (and though he was kind, he too had started looking at his watch). The World Passport movement had stirred my utopian impulses again, but in this last relapse I was defeated.

You say to yourself: They think I'm the freak. But, they can't hate me more than I hate them. I blamed the war makers, who I believed had divided the world into those who could live with it, and those who could not. I'd come to despise the people I'd once hoped to enlighten. So, in many ways the war was killing me too, and I knew it. I'd absorbed my war, as all veterans do. But now I'd lost my bearings and I was desperate. As I sorted through Gregory's words, I didn't know what I wanted to hear—an exhortation, or maybe a lullabye. Instead, something much more businesslike buzzed in the words beneath his words: "Congratulations [I heard], you've launched yourself. You caught a tailwind, then you started to tumble. Now you'll find out if you can fly."

Listening to Gregory, I knew I wasn't a world-saving heroine or a writing prodigy. I was just smart enough to know that the future probably held a more common destiny, and I wanted that postponed. I had always wanted to be different, but I didn't want to stay in bed forever, like the R. Crumb character who refuses to emerge from his bathtub, or be doomed to stay in my bath forever like Jean-Paul Marat. I might not be strong enough to resist "the establishment," but I wouldn't work for them, and I wouldn't extinguish the light for them. I might be unpleasant, inconvenient, tiresome, filthy, but I wouldn't go away. That was the substance of my subterranean discourse with Dick Gregory. As we held hands, my ring glittered in the light of the aura around his head. How much of this was real? Perhaps the better question is: how do you locate the moment when you know you want to rejoin the human race?

I come out of the humanist tradition. Maybe I'm among the last of my kind, dwindling away like the Shakers: not-always-so-rational-humanists opposed to fundamental absolutes, opposed to one god, opposed to the idea that more possessions make better lives. I come from the old immigrant socialist traditions of brotherhood and sisterhood and equality now and peace and justice and solidarity forever. I think the wealthy should spend money on the poor, the powerful should protect the weak, science should be practiced in the public interest, and everyone should respect the rights of the psychologically unstable. I think there should be more family farms, and more and better art. I think literature is a humanizing discourse. I think people should talk to each other and eat more meals together, be kind to strangers, and dance together more. There should be more festival days. People should sleep more and work less. I know I have a tendency to refer to the world wars, but as a child of the midcentury, it's my birthright. I think of all those sophisticated people in all those advanced nations who watched in disbelief during both world wars as cruelty filled the void. Vietnam was my war and it was wrong. However the future sees us, I am here to say, we tried to answer emptiness with meaning.

. . .

I know Dick Gregory's gift basket of fruit and vegetables arrived. I remember devouring oranges and melons with Sacco and Vanzetti. I know that for days after, I couldn't stop thinking about Mrs. Doyle's son, Patrick, who had loved Florence Grizzetti. I knew Patrick Doyle hadn't flown any B-52s. B-52s were flown by an elite corps, and Patrick Doyle was just a kid who used to hang out in the pizza joints along Hempstead Turnpike, and who'd been blown up in the jungle before he turned around twice. But what if he *had* flown a B-52? What if Patrick Doyle had been one of those top-gun airmen who never saw the civilian villages they vaporized thirty thousand feet below, or the land they rendered uninhabitable for generations? Those were the genies in my ring. It was so easy to confuse poor old Mrs. Doyle with that woman haunting the war memorial museum in Mary McCarthy's *Hanoi.*

I had loved my ring. It was a symbol, not just of the destruction of an American plane and the resilience of the Vietnamese people, but of my own wildness. I would never be like anyone else as long as I wore it. I would never stay in one place. I would never fall in love. I would never go home.

My temperature eventually came down. Jim was a gracious host, but he wasn't sad to have his loft bed back in time for some spring equinox orgies.

Amy and I had kept writing to each other, and as planned she arrived in late March. Within a few days we had invited ourselves over to the North Vietnamese embassy to discuss the issues of American antiwar youth. On the day appointed, Amy and I wore all our political buttons for the first time in months. We had directions, of course, but neither of us had spent much time on the Paris Métro, and instead of going to the place de la Concorde, we ended up near the flea market in Porte de Clingancourt, a long ride in the other direction. We were already two hours late when we knocked on the embassy door.

No one from the delegation was available; the consul and all important embassy aides had moved on to other meetings with more punctual participants. But a hospitable Vietnamese steward served us tea, and his young assistant kept us company. In that elegant high-ceilinged room, sitting at a long, perfectly burnished wood table, both Amy and I felt overwhelmed. We were reduced to small talk.

Amy mentioned that she liked the music playing in the background.

"It's Vietnamese," our host informed us.

"The tea is delicious," I said. "What kind is it?"

"Vietnamese," I was told.

We were ushered in and out within fifteen minutes. As the embassy door closed—and with it our last opportunity to convey messages of peace, dissertations on world government, or even greetings of the season—I blurted, "Where do you think I can buy that tea and that music?"

"Vietnam," his last word.

On the Métro back, Amy noticed, "You're not wearing your ring."

"I lost it." I'd taken it off in the embassy to wash my hands, and it had rolled into the sink. There was a moment, as I watched it swirl in the basin, when I could have saved it. I felt an ambivalence, not unlike the confusion of sorrow and relief you feel when someone who's in dreadful pain finally dies. As my ring plunged into the Paris sewer, sliding through shit and garbage, I imagined it coming to rest on the head of a giant albino alligator. I saw it rolling past the Phantom's organ, past Jean Valjean in flight, past vampires and ghouls and mutant winos, past all the lamenting spirits of the underground into the ghost dens of Resistance fighters, where with any luck, it would be scavenged by a fugitive, and recycled again.

.   .   .

Young women, please attend, the peroration is about to begin. I have no graphs, no flip charts, no statistics to show you the rise and fall of the Age of Aquarius. I have no celebrity portraits, no magazine illustrations, no ray-o-grams to illustrate the public view of the woman whose story you have read. There are no photographs of her from this time, except perhaps those taken by CIA agents hiding in the bushes— and those you will never see. There are no brain scans or lie detector tests to show you the way her mind works. I think you know her slightly.

Returning on the Métro, she and her friend stopped again at the Paris flea market. There, she fingered old silk kimonos and lace handkerchiefs, paged through used books, and wolfed down a box of nougat candies, one of which broke a back tooth and caused no end of pain. In the hour after she deliberately lost her ring in the washroom of the Vietnamese embassy, the young woman had come to understand, not consciously but remotely and reactively and joltingly, that the ring she thought was a harbor was an anchor.

That day in Paris, in the hustle and bustle of the flea market, surrounded by ovenware and chipped porcelain, fruit and candy, used clothes and tools (on one table an assortment of screws to be sought under sofas for hours), the symphony of voices, held, amid a welter of sensation, a wealth of stories. Here, the anxious flower vendor; there, the haughty almond merchant; across the aisle, an ecstatic butcher. She stops to wonder: Can stories that have been told millions of times still be worth telling? Can actions repeated a million times still be worth doing? Must everyone alive and dead tell their stories at the same time? It is a dizzying, mind-blowing notion. Quick, grab a pen! She wants to be a writer, she wants to be original, she wants to be human in the finest sense, she wants, she wants . . . She doesn't need a ring or a hole in the head to remind her where she stands, or what she believes. It's just spring but in her the sultry season is starting. In a pile of rags, she finds an old torn lace handkerchief. Once, every thread of it had been pulled taut and all the broken threads cast aside. She cannot hold it without seeing the lacemaker, a hundred years past, already on her bench at eight years old, marrying in a blaze of pride at seventeen, going blind at fifty. The presence of one thread recalls the absence of another. If you go on in this way it can drive you mad. This story was the story of one thread who resisted, insisted, and kept notes.

My friends, history is made from the common thread and the crooked thread and that is the truth.

Epilogue

"Resist much, obey little."

WALT WHITMAN

In the fairy tale "Prince Darling," the Fairy of Truth gives a spoiled prince a ring to help cure the defects in his character. The fairy warns him that every time he does a bad deed the ring will prick his finger, and she swears that if he continues his wicked ways she'll become his enemy. The prince tries to be good, but the ring hurts every time he backslides, so he finally tosses it away and abandons himself to evil. Bad as he is, the prince falls in love and as a result he has to go on a long, perilous journey and overcome nearly impossible difficulties to find the Fairy of Truth again and recover his character. Perhaps his hardest task is to remember why he is suffering.

By the time I was seventeen in 1970, I'd lived almost half my life in a country at war. Our national identity was as a great military power. My heroes were the people who recognized how that mask obscured our better nature, but it was like trying to stop a nose-diving jet. That we had some success makes it all that much sweeter, and all that more important to remember.

I've come to think of the peace movement against the war in Vietnam as the ring that encircled the hand of the state, and like the prince's ring, we pricked it at every bad deed. Because we were young, because we were wild, because it was crazy, or it was dreadful or because it was so brief and now it is gone, perhaps it is hard to remember our youthful character, how we protested and why our country suffered. But I continue to hope that the hundreds of thousands of people who opposed, even briefly, the assembly line of conformity, who stood up to the machinery of government and declared that the war in Vietnam was wrong, will say so to their grandchildren. If the Fairy of Truth has anything to do with it, their grandchildren will heap praises upon them.

Acknowledgments

Thanks for their help with research: John Hanrahan, Dr. Palumbo, The State Historical Society of Wisconsin, Harris Fairbanks, Jonathan Hufstader, "The Black Shadow," Edward P. Morgan, Judy Clavir Albert, Zena Nason, Robert Freedman, Gabriel Gomes, Lauren Brody, Erica Brody, and Woody Amdahl. For interviews, shrewd observations, and advice: Stew Albert, Jonah Raskin, Lisa Gottlieb, Sylvia Brown, Michele Linfante, Elena Engel, Kristina Boden, Greg Lehmann, Bill Lehmann, Richard Brody, Robert Brody, Jane Cohen Brody, Ann Brody, Steve Brody, Mary Galluci, Jerry Phillips, Sam Pickering, and Ann Charters. For their help early on, both literary and legal: Bart Schneider, Pat Towers, Jan Z. Grover, Sharon Friedman, Pearl Kilbride, David Unowsky, Suzy Staubach, Wally Lamb, Elizabeth Wray, and Masha Amdahl. Thanks again to my dear crew of readers: Janis Franklin, Regina White, Margaret Todd Maitland, and John Richardson. For their service above and beyond: Joan Joffe and Nevil Parker. And finally, to my one and only Gary Amdahl.